HOUSES

some forthcoming titles

THE HISTORIC ENVIRONMENT
David Baker

CHURCHES IN THE LANDSCAPE
Peter Burman

PREHISTORIC
AND ROMAN AGRICULTURE
Peter Reynolds

SETTLEMENT IN ENGLAND
Christopher Taylor

published titles

VIKING AGE SCULPTURE
Richard N. Bailey

GLASS
Ruth Hurst Vose

MATHEMATICS
IN ARCHAEOLOGY
Clive Orton

THE ARCHAEOLOGY OF
SOUTH WEST BRITAIN
Susan M. Pearce

THE ARCHAEOLOGY OF
THE WELSH MARCHES
S. C. Stanford

Series editors: Eric Wood and Cherry Lavell

COLLINS ARCHAEOLOGY

HOUSES

R. W. BRUNSKILL

COLLINS
14 St James's Place, London
1982

William Collins Sons & Co Ltd
London · Glasgow · Sydney · Auckland
Toronto · Johannesburg

British Library Cataloguing in Publication Data

Brunskill, R.W.
Houses. – (Collins archaeology)
1. Architecture, Domestic – Great Britain
– History
I. Title
728′.0941 GT285

ISBN 0-00-216243-1

Distributed in the United States, Canada and Mexico by
Humanities Press Inc.
First published 1982

Photoset in Bembo
Made and Printed in Great Britain by
William Collins Sons & Co Ltd Glasgow

CONTENTS

LIST OF PLATES

Key to photograph credits:

GDB:	G. D. Bold
JB:	J. Brotherhood
RWB:	R. W. Brunskill
PJME:	P. J. M. Eyres
RF:	R. Foster
JMcC:	J. McCann
WGM:	W. G. Muter
NMR:	National Monuments Record
RCAHMW:	Royal Commission on the Ancient and Historical Monuments in Wales
GW:	Wheeler
RW:	R. Williams

LIST OF FIGURES

NOTE ON THE FIGURES

The figures form a major part of the book and a note on the intentions behind their preparation might be helpful. There are five sets:

1. *Development of simple house plans*
This is a theoretical diagram showing the variations in position of door, staircase and principal hearth or fireplace likely to be found in a small house of rectangular plan shape. It shows examples of variations coming from use of different door and fireplace positions, given a constant doorway location.

2. *Summary diagrams of rural and urban house plans*
These attempt to show on one sheet each the main plan-types which are elaborated in other diagrams. Rural house plans are divided between Large Houses, Small Houses and Cottages, and Laithe Houses and Almshouses have been added. While the plans within each size-type are arranged roughly in chronological order there are many overlaps and some parallel developments, and no typological sequence is presented. Urban house plans have been divided between earlier houses (generally with open halls), later houses (generally multi-storey) and urban cottages. Again, no typological sequence is put forward. In all the diagrams the positions of doorway, fireplace or hearth and, where appropriate, staircase are indicated, but purely diagrammatically. These are summary diagrams only and not intended to deal with variations within each plan-type.

3. *Diagrams of individual plan-types*
These are in more detail but are still intended to show plan-*types* and not plans of actual buildings. Generally a ground-floor plan, a cross-section and an isometric sketch are included together with examples of common variations. The plans etc. are drawn approximately to scale but not to a uniform scale. Conventional indication of building materials is given but usually the same plan-type could be used with any walling or roofing material. In some of the earlier plan-types both for town and country there was no certain position for the staircase, which may be omitted or conventionally indicated in the diagram. The time scales are intended to show the range of dates during which the plan-type was commonly in use; no attempt has been made to distinguish between advanced and backward regions or

between superior and inferior versions of the one plan-type. The diagrammatic distribution maps, where included, are intended to give only the very broadest indication of where a plan-type might be found, as known from current information. Where no map is given then generally the plan-type may be found in any part of the country.

4. *Diagrams of methods of construction*
These show only a selection of the constructional systems and materials used in domestic building.

5. *Diagrams of development of various plans over a long period*
These are idealized, not based on specific examples but on combinations of examples.

PREFACE

This book is about houses as subjects for archaeological study and seen mainly through their plans. It is about the houses of ordinary people in town and countryside: the houses of important and wealthy people may be studied by historical methods, but the humble dwellings of ordinary folk are best understood initially through archaeological study. It is about the results of archaeological investigation rather than about archaeological techniques – though it is hoped that some readers will be inspired to learn and practise such techniques independently or in association with the steadily increasing number of study groups working in different parts of the country. It concentrates on house plans rather than materials and methods of construction; for however vital may be the peg-holes and straight joints in elucidating the complex history of quite unpretentious structures, ultimately the most detailed investigation is intended to discern the relatively simple arrangement of spaces on plan and in section which the designers intended at each phase.

Although my training is architectural rather than archaeological, I have ignored matters of proportion and decorative detail. This is not because the buildings lack architectural merit – indeed it is the beauty which stems from simple but consistent proportions and sparse but well-controlled ornament which makes their study so agreeable – but rather because we must assume that these houses were intended to be utilitarian first and decorative only secondarily.

The main purpose of the book is to draw together the basic information on standard house plans which were used or intended by unnamed designers at various times in the past. The rapidly growing body of literature on vernacular architecture is producing many published house plans, and the archives, especially of the National Monuments Record, are beginning to swell with large numbers of such plans; but most of the archaeological or architectural reports are based on single buildings, covering in greater or lesser detail the sequences of development on a single building site, and it is not always easy to see to what extent the example studied is typical or unique. Many village or district surveys, which study all the houses in a locality, are now being published; but here again the focus is necessarily on the detail rather than on the overall picture. The handful of published regional or national surveys by definition take the broader view, but even here there is sometimes a tendency to detail the exception and the variations which have been discovered rather than concentrate on standard plans.

Although I have concentrated on house plans I have included a basic introduction to materials and methods of construction. Most plans may be found clothed in timber, stone, clay or brick according to period or location, and so constructional matters have been omitted as far as possible from the main text and illustrations.

In order to keep the treatment as clear as possible the classification of plans and sections has in the main been prepared and illustrated as if all houses were built from scratch and never altered. This, of course, is rarely the case even in the most modern domestic property, and if it were much of the archaeological detective work which generates so much enthusiasm for the subject would be eliminated. Examples have been included, therefore, of some of the more common sequences of development, recognizing always that the story is taken back only as far as the earliest substantial surviving structure in the sequence, and that excavation might well reveal even earlier stages. Few essays in *total* archaeological investigation of small houses and their sites have yet been made.

Although ideally a book such as this should deal with the geographical entity of the British Isles in fact Ireland and Scotland have been omitted because of lack of opportunity for field work in the one and the relatively backward though rapidly improving state of the study of the subject in the other. The book therefore is about houses in England and Wales. Historical (i.e. pre-1974) county names have been used throughout.

The period covered in the book extends mainly from the early fourteenth century to the late nineteenth century. However some of the plans illustrated were used rather earlier and a note about some more recent domestic plans has been included.

The study of small houses is now out of its infancy but certainly has much development ahead. It may be considered premature for even such a broad view as this to be taken. Nevertheless it is hoped that the general reader will welcome this essay as an introduction to the interpretation of many houses, if by no means all, and as an introduction to that detailed archaeological study of selected examples which proves so fascinating.

A summary such as this is bound to depend very considerably on the published works listed in the bibliography and especially on those by M. W. Barley, P. Eden, R. Machin, E. Mercer, P. Smith, J. T. Smith and R. B. Wood-Jones, to whom grateful acknowledgement is made. Very considerable benefit has also been gained from discussions with members of the Vernacular Architecture Group, both on the occasion of papers read at its Winter Meetings and by way of discussions on site or in the bar at the Spring Meetings in the field. The preparation of the book has also been helped by the comments of Eric Wood and Cherry Lavell and by their tolerance of delays in trying to fit its preparation into a busy academic and professional schedule.

CHAPTER ONE

The Study of Houses

The process of design and construction of houses nowadays is straightforward and well understood. The architect or other designer takes instructions from his client, be he private individual, local authority, housing association, or speculative housing developer, agrees a brief and then presents proposals which take into account the client's requirements, the opportunities and limitations presented by the site, the suitability and feasibility of materials and methods of construction, the requirements of a hundred and one regulatory bodies, the factor of cost, and, usually rather surreptitiously, matters of aesthetics. All the necessary compromises having been made and the proposals agreed the house is erected. It is then occupied by an individual or family practising a particular life-style within a particular social and economic setting.

Since we are all familiar with the socio-economic circumstances of our own time we see in each newly-erected house confirmation of what we already know. The vulgarly opulent mansion of the tycoon confirms what we know or suspect about him just as the plain anonymity of the council house inhabited by his office cleaner confirms what we know of her life-style and position on the social scale. The enthusiasm with which members of the public buy magazines full of plans of houses which they could not afford, and in which they would not be comfortable, or visit show-houses on housing estates to which they have no intention of moving shows that the comparison of artefacts (in the form of houses) and needs or aspirations (which may be formalized in clients' briefs), is a constant delight.

Many people are equally fascinated by old houses. They flock in their thousands to visit the stately homes of this country and overseas, they attend in surprisingly substantial numbers the excursions of archaeological and historical societies which include visits to houses not normally accessible, and their tours of the Cotswolds or Cumbria are planned as much to see the villages and farmhouses as to see the mountains and hedgerows. Their interest may sometimes be purely architectural; but one suspects that more often than not the visitor is concerned to observe a way of life, still perhaps perpetuated as a shadow of itself in certain stately homes or some remote farmhouses, or to be sensed from the bricks and mortar, the timber frame and thatch of houses erected by past generations.

Any examination of an old house begins to put into reverse the process of construction and design: given the artefact one may, in theory at least, deduce the circumstances in which it was created. Anyone making a systematic observation of a building such as a house would record the plan and section of the building on its site, note the materials used and the way in which they had been put together, establish what appear to be levels of extravagance or economy, and, comparing the house with others, ascertain which features appear to be conservative or even archaic, which are derivative and which are innovatory. From such study the factors which had been considered by the original designer may begin to come to light, the brief or set of requirements given to the designer may, in the right circumstances, be deduced, and, one hopes, the way of life which determined that brief may be ascertained and understood.

The systematic study of old houses has been developing over the past hundred years or so, and with increasing intensity over the past twenty or thirty. It has attracted the attention of many scholars and each one has brought the techniques of study developed in his own field to the overall task. Social and economic historians have balanced evidence of phases of house construction with other data the better to understand accumulation and dispersal of capital, for instance. Geographers have examined the distribution of houses at various periods in the past as essential pieces of data in their studies of areas and grouping. Sociologists have begun to relate developments in house planning to the changing patterns of family life. Students of folk life can see in certain aspects of house construction and detailing further evidence of the web of mystery and superstition which quite recently enveloped life in the countryside. Archaeologists see in surviving houses pieces of evidence which are essential to the understanding of the pattern of house design and construction, of the sequence which culminates in above-ground elements but which must be pursued in excavation.

While each approach to the study of houses brings with it a particular method of study there are really two main groups of methods: those which are *of* the buildings themselves and those which are *about* the buildings. Legal documents, diaries and travellers' descriptions, longbeards' memories, folk tales and superstitions are all pieces of historical evidence about houses in general; plans, sections, elevations and photographs are pieces of evidence stemming from specific houses. It is with this study of buildings that we are concerned and in this we follow the recommendations of Sir Cyril Fox and Lord Raglan, authors of *Monmouthshire Houses*, a pioneering and still very influential study.[1] Fox and Raglan believed that by using archaeological methods they could hope to find out how each style of house design and construction developed in their survey area, when the various styles developed and what gaps remained in the picture as it emerged to be filled by further archaeological investigation or by other studies. The success of *Monmouthshire Houses* and its continuing influence testifies to the value of their recommendations.

It is not my intention to explain in any detail the procedures to be followed in making surveys of houses: there are plenty of handbooks in existence or preparation which do this;[2] but it is important to note that there are various stages or levels of recording which are selected according to the objectives in any study of houses and according to the resources available. If a quick and acceptably superficial impression of the general characteristics of houses in an area is required, then a survey based on a photograph and set of notes on each house, prepared, perhaps, with the aid of a checklist, may be all that is needed and all that can be afforded. If a rather more comprehensive record of a smaller number of selected examples is required then sketch plans or small-scale measured drawings supplemented by notes and sets of photographs would be prepared. Where a full record is to be made of a house about to be destroyed, re-erected, or substantially altered then a painstaking survey will be necessary, every stone and peghole being recorded on large-scale drawings and every nail and window catch being measured, photographed and catalogued. Many houses have, of course, been recorded at the first level; village surveys are now being published which have been made at the second level; understandably very few full archaeological surveys have yet been made at the third level.

It is the custom for archaeologists to classify their findings. If the artefacts which have been discovered are grouped and recorded into a set of types, and then the types arranged into a series, the haphazard collection of objects with which the study begins may be converted into a logical sequence – as an end in itself or as preparation for a further set of studies. As more and more has been discovered about more and more, precise classifications of design, constructional methods and architectural details have been made.

The major part of the present work consists of a classification of smaller houses and cottages according to plan-types.[3] The first stage in the classification was the division into town houses and houses of the countryside on the grounds that social, economic and legal differences led, until quite recently, to different lines of development. The next stage was to eliminate, both in town and country, the houses of the very rich. These, the Great Houses, were taken to be those of royalty, great magnates of church and state, major landowners, rich and powerful merchants and industrialists and so on. People of such standing would generally expect to be able to command houses of unique design from professional designers and erected in those circumstances which produced the sort of documentary evidence which would allow each building to be studied primarily by historical methods. By the same token some of the smaller and more recent house-types which may be expected to carry similar documentary evidence have also been omitted.

The remaining houses are of the type which is now generally called vernacular. When found in the countryside they have next been divided into the Large Houses of people of considerable local importance, the Small Houses of ordinary farmers and people of like quality who had some stake in the land, and the Cottages of the lower ranks. When found in the towns they have been divided into the earlier and later groups of plans adopted by the minor merchants, shopkeepers, and members of the urban middle class generally, and the cottage plans adopted by those who worked for others. Finally the classification has been directed towards distinguishing plans or room arrangements which appear to have sufficient common characteristics to be called types.

Each plan-type has been described and illustrated, with such variations as can occur within the type being separately noted. Where possible some indication has been given of the dates at which the plan was in common use and those parts of the country where examples can be found. The term 'plan' is also taken to mean 'section', since changes in the number of storeys, development of roof-spaces, provision of staircases to give access to upper storeys and cellars are as significant as other matters in the development of plans in the full sense of the word. The plan-type is taken to be the basic arrangement of customary dimensions, it being always accepted that members of one social class did differ at any given time in the resources which they could devote to buildings and the degree of individuality which they felt disposed to give to a plan-type which they shared with their neighbours; the plan might be the same, the size generally similar, but the individuality came in some little extravagance in decoration. The date-range has to take into account that even in a pretty rigid society some houses were forward-looking in design while others were backward, and that some districts tended to accept the influence of nearby sources of innovation while others heard about plan developments reluctantly and late. The distribution maps are very generalized and inevitably must in some cases reflect the rather haphazard progress of regional studies. The illustrations are of types and not specific buildings. While the various parts are drawn in correct proportion one to another the houses are not drawn to a common scale.

As the plans are widely used and examples are very numerous it might be misleading to quote specific houses as if they were cathedrals or abbeys to represent various classes. At the end of the book, however, there is a selection of some examples which are open to the public.

The classification of plan-types is supported by notes on the building materials and methods of construction. This is deliberately regarded as supporting material: it is considered axiomatic that the plan reflects the client's brief, that the building materials were chosen according to circumstances of economy, custom or fashion, suitability for the purpose, but that they were chosen to clad and support a set of spaces which themselves reflected the intended uses. Many good studies of traditional structures and building materials have been made and are in preparation.

As some token of the fact that many houses have come down to us in the form of the latest in a series of modifications, and that many house sites are very ancient – normally much older in human occupation than the houses which stand upon them – a chapter has been included which explains briefly some of the common transformations whereby one plan-type has become another on the same site. It is this sort of modification which can best be studied by archaeological methods.

DEVELOPMENT OF SIMPLE HOUSE PLANS

A Position of main door
1. in end wall
2. in front wall near one corner
3. near centre of front wall

B Position of staircase
1. at one end against fireplace
2. in rear wall
3. in the middle of the plan: a. transversely b. longitudinally c. as a dog-leg stair
4. at one end away from fireplace

C Position of source of heat
1. an open hearth near middle of plan
2. a fireplace on one end wall
3. a fireplace in middle of plan
4. a fireplace in rear wall
5. a fireplace in front wall

D to G show plan variations given a constant position for the main door but with variations in the position of the staircase and fireplace. H = hall or living room/kitchen; P = parlour

D Door near corner, fireplace in end wall
1. with staircase associated with fireplace
2. with staircase in rear wall
3. with staircase near middle of plan
4. with staircase in end wall far from fireplace

E Door in corner, fireplace near middle of plan
1. with staircase associated with fireplace
2. with staircase in rear wall
3. with staircase near middle of plan
4. with staircase in end wall

F Door in corner, fireplace in rear wall
1. with staircase associated with fireplace
2. with staircase in rear wall
3. with staircase near middle of plan
4. with staircase in end wall

G Door in corner, fireplace in front wall
1. with staircase associated with fireplace
2. with staircase in rear wall
3. with staircase near middle of plan
4. with staircase in end wall

H Cross-section
1. one storey
2. one and a half storey
3. two storey

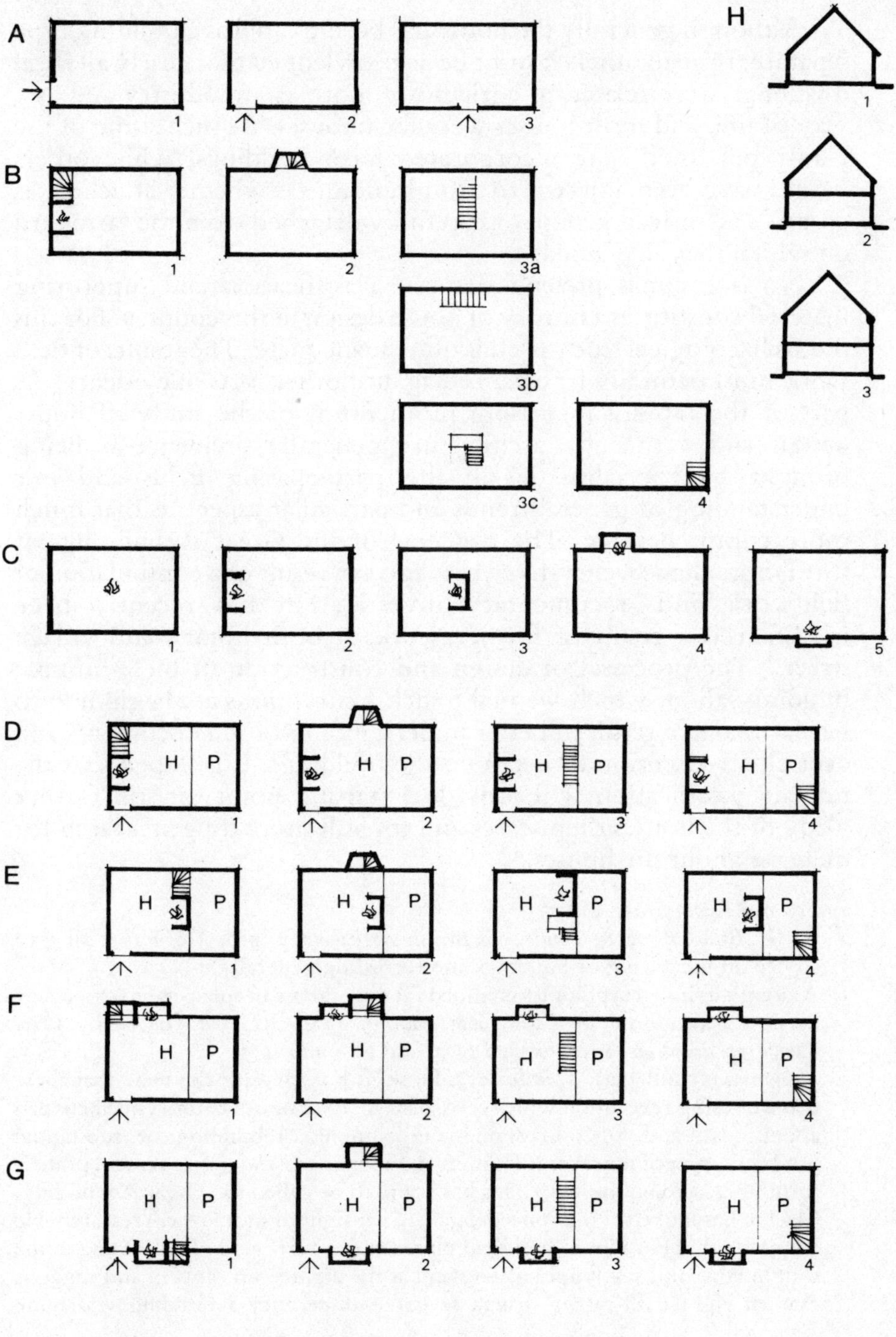
A
B
C
D
E
F
G
H
H
P

Although generally the house has been treated as a building type separate from all others it must be acknowledged that nearly all rural dwellings were related to agriculture, both as an industry and as a way of life, and most houses were farmhouses. As such some of the plan-types listed here incorporated farm buildings, while others would have been adjacent to farm buildings – whether attached, as part of a farmstead group, or carefullly detached from the farmyard on which they depended.

No one could pretend that the classification and supporting material constitutes a history of house design in this country. For this the archaeological study itself is quite inadequate. The results of field work must naturally be balanced against other sorts of evidence. As part of the rapidly increasing momentum of the study of house design and vernacular architecture generally, evidence is being brought by specialists in all the participating fields and our understanding of general trends and particular aspects is that much more comprehensive. The concepts of the Great Rebuilding set forth more than twenty-five years ago as a result of a combination of fieldwork and documentary investigation has recently been modified as a result of further work in both library and village street.[4] The processes of design and construction of these humble buildings about which we make such assumptions are beginning to be clarified as a result of better understanding of the documents and ever closer attention to detail on the buildings. It is hoped that the present classification will provide a starting point for still further study of the houses themselves and for still more diligent search for material about the houses.[5]

1. *Fox and Raglan 1951–4.*
2. *R. W. Brunskill 1978*; *Council for British Archaeology 1980*; *Major 1975* all give advice on measuring of buildings and recording generally.
3. Among published typologies intended for general use or for specific regional or local use are those in *Eden 1969*; *Machin 1978*; *RCHM (England), West Cambridgeshire 1968* and *Stamford 1977*; and *P. Smith 1975*.
4. *Hoskins 1953* and *1965*; *Machin 1977*. Hoskins put forward the view that there was a housing revolution which took place in the English countryside between about 1570 and 1640 involving the complete rebuilding or substantial modernization of the fabric of houses and an increase and improvement of their furnishings and equipment. This has come to be called the Great Rebuilding. Machin has looked at the concept again in the light of more recent research. He has noted that Hoskins himself had placed the great period of rebuilding in the four northernmost counties of England as the eighteenth century and suggests that an eighteenth-rather than a seventeenth-century rebuilding was quite

widespread. But Machin questions the thesis of a Great Rebuilding at some specific period and suggests that we should look rather at the successive rebuildings of vernacular houses from the late sixteenth to the early eighteenth century and their eventual replacement, later in the eighteenth century, by copy book designs, acknowledging all along regional variations in timing.

5. For aspects of planning theory see P. Dickens in *D. L. Clarke (ed.) Spatial Archaeology*, *1977*, 33–45.

CHAPTER TWO

Rural Houses

The evolution of rural house plans

House plans should reflect the way of life of the people for whom they are intended; but the plans of houses built for members of the rural population of England and Wales do much more than reflect a single set of domestic functions. For the functions vary not only according to the wealth and social status of the inhabitants; they also vary according to time, and are modified by a generally improving standard of living at each social level. The functions vary according to the occupation of each family: virtually all rural inhabitants were tied to the land in some way, most being full-time farmers, but many, from priests to blacksmiths, combined farming with some other occupation. The functions vary according to fashion or rather the changing conventions of domestic behaviour: what was considered essential to a high standard of living at one time being considered less important at another. The functions to be housed varied, then, in many ways; but since they were essentially quite simple functions it is to be expected that certain standard solutions to the functional problems were devised and widely adopted.

Even if function were the principal determinant of house plans (and not everyone would accept this) it was certainly not the sole determinant; siting, security, structure and available materials were also important, and the humbler the dwelling the more significant might such factors be against the otherwise ideal method of housing certain domestic activities.

Siting might seem less immediately important in the countryside than in the towns, for whether built as isolated dwellings, in hamlet groups, or in villages one would expect the rural house site to allow ample freedom to the designer. In the less crowded days of the past the countryside was relatively empty and building land in total must have seemed more than adequate; but study of villages and hamlets would suggest that *available* building land was no more plentiful then than now. Building sites were precise in extent and their use was limited by law and custom; the late eighteenth- and early nineteenth-century Small Houses and Cottages of the villages were often contorted in shape because adequate sites were not in fact available in crowded communities; the squatters' cottages of that same period were confined to the restricted sites which custom or boldness allowed on open waste land, or were squeezed into odd pockets and corners between plots whose legal owners could prevent encroachment. Even where some freedom in siting was enjoyed by the housebuilder there were fashions in siting and especially in orientation to be observed. At one time the fashion might be for houses to face the street or village green, at another time a position at right angles might be desired; at one time houses were built to face the sun, later it was more customary to face the view, prospect taking precedence over aspect; at certain times, places and social levels, houses were mixed in with farm buildings, at others they were deliberately, almost self-consciously set apart.[1]

Security was an important factor in house planning in certain times and places and for certain social levels. For the small farmer or cottager with little to lose the security of the individual dwelling might not be a major factor in planning, whereas, for his contemporary lord, security might be all-important. For master and dependent, the communal security of living in villages rather than scattered in isolated settlements might dictate the house site and so, indirectly, the house plan. During the period from which most smaller houses survive the countryside was at peace, and threatened only occasionally by disturbances or civil war. For the ordinary householder no more precautions than shutters or bars at ground-floor windows might be necessary: the defensible high-walled farmyards of some European countries are rarely to be found in England and Wales. There were, however, periods of general unrest, especially during the Middle Ages, when any landowner or the occupier of an isolated house might need a refuge in which he could protect his family and goods. There were also localized areas of insecurity, especially on the Scottish border and sometimes in the south west of England, in which quite humble proprietors required defensible dwellings, and, at times, in such areas, the tenant had even less occasion than elsewhere to build anything other than a house which could be as swiftly re-erected as it was destroyed.

Structural limitations and available building materials affected architectural form but do not appear to have affected house planning to any great extent. Obviously a housebuilder could have a particular arrangement of rooms only to the extent that technology and

---

RURAL HOUSES: SUMMARY OF MAIN PLAN-TYPES

A: *Large houses*

1. Ground-floor hall, aisled hall
2. First-floor hall and bastle house
3. Tower house
4. Single-ended hall
5. Double-ended hall
6. Multi-storey house
7. Compact house with projecting wings
8. Double-pile house

B: *Small houses*

9. Wealden house and other open-hall houses
10. Small House with lateral chimney
11. Longhouse
12. Cross-passage Small House
13. Lobby-entrance house and house with back-to-back fireplaces
14. House with central service rooms
15. Internal cross-passage house
16. Two-unit house
17. T-shaped and L-shaped houses
18. House with an extra bay
19. Continuous outshut house
20. Double-pile house

C: *Cottages*

21. One-unit cottage
22. One-and-a-half-unit cottage
23. Single-storey and croglofft cottages
24. Double-pile single-fronted cottages
25. Other multi-storey cottages

D: *Special purpose houses*

26. Laithe houses
27. Almshouses

A LARGE HOUSES

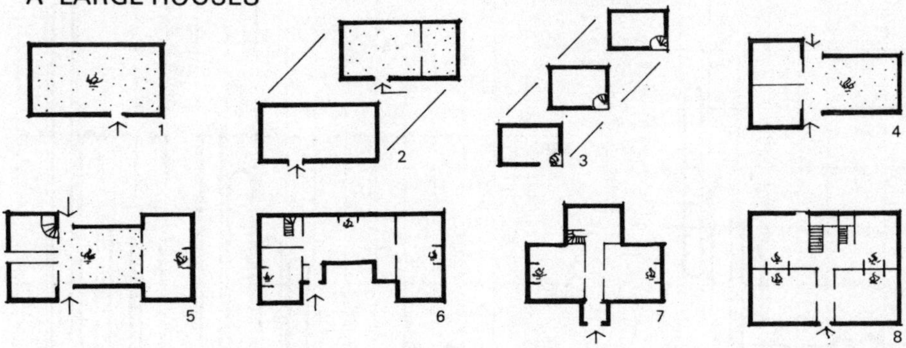

B SMALL HOUSES

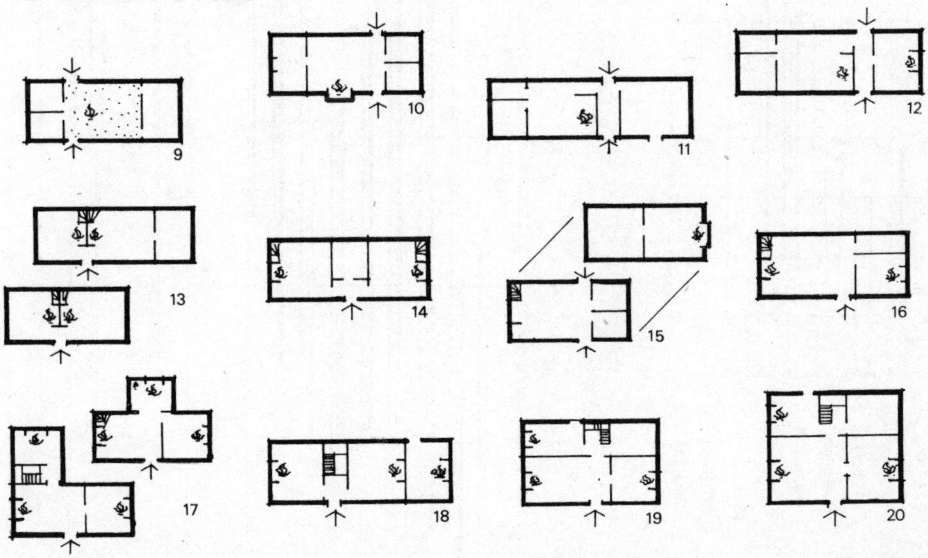

C COTTAGES

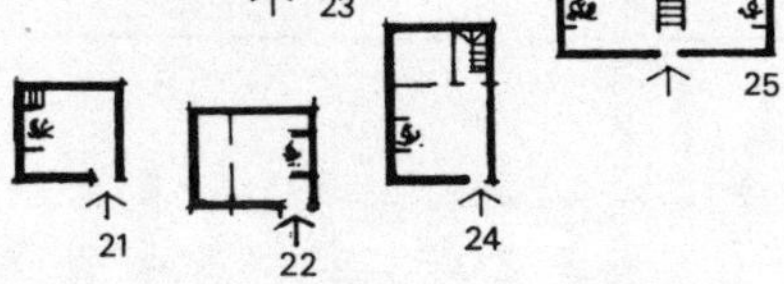

D SPECIAL PURPOSE HOUSES

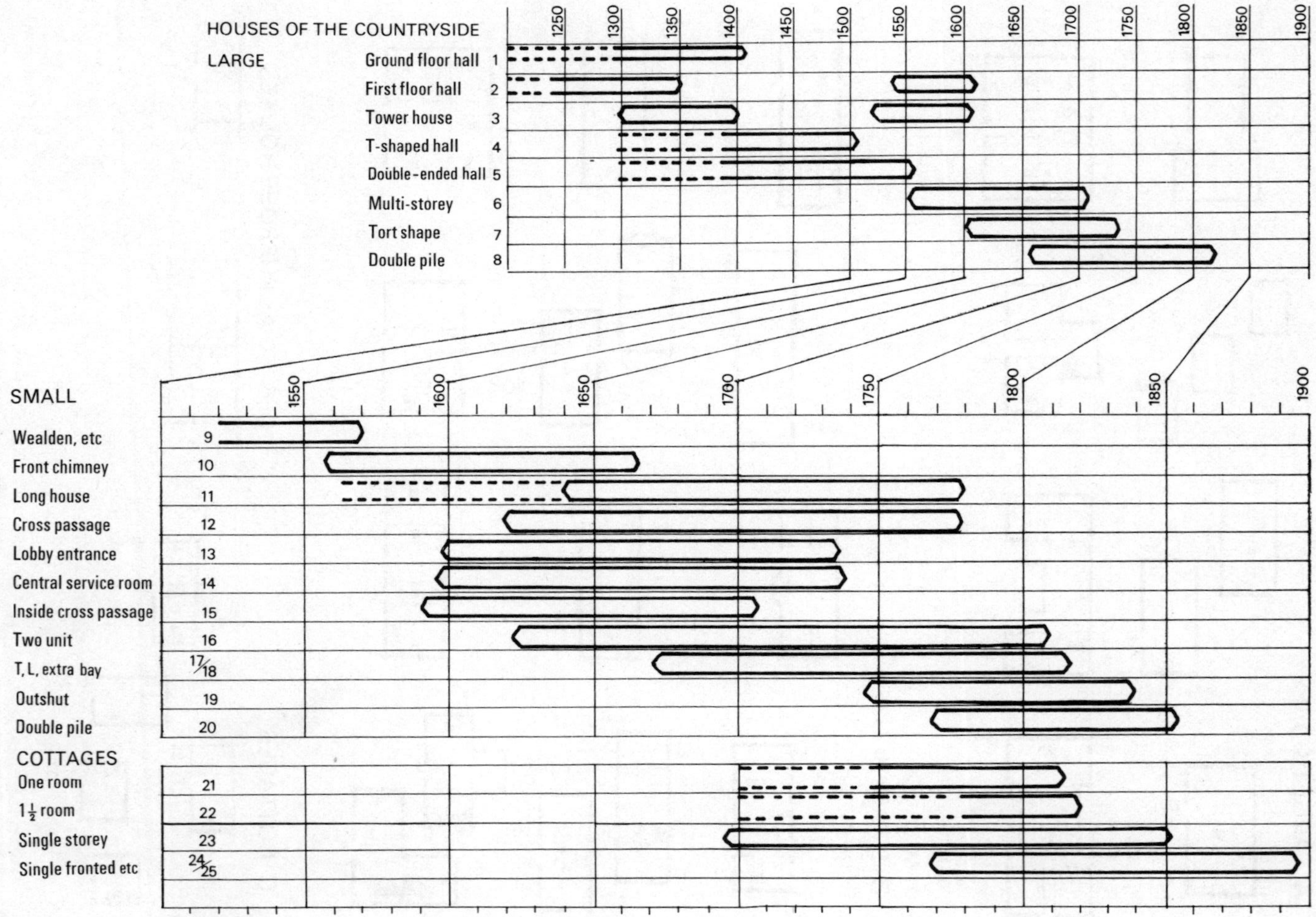
HOUSES OF THE COUNTRYSIDE
LARGE
Ground floor hall 1
First floor hall 2
Tower house 3
T-shaped hall 4
Double-ended hall 5
Multi-storey 6
Tort shape 7
Double pile 8
1250
1300
1350
1400
1450
1500
1550
1600
1650
1700
1750
1800
1850
1900
SMALL
Wealden, etc 9
Front chimney 10
Long house 11
Cross passage 12
Lobby entrance 13
Central service room 14
Inside cross passage 15
Two unit 16
T, L, extra bay 17/18
Outshut 19
Double pile 20
1550
1600
1650
1700
1750
1800
1850
1900
COTTAGES
One room 21
1½ room 22
Single storey 23
Single fronted etc 24/25

materials would allow, but it is hard to believe from the plans of surviving houses that materials inhibited design: the same plans may be seen in timber frame and stone and brick and under thatch, slate or tiled roofs. For the very largest houses, the limitations on span may have encouraged the use of, say, the aisled hall, while for the very smallest houses the stage of primitive or temporary building might have been extended until cheap manufactured materials became available to supplement poor quality local materials of natural origin.

Fashion is perhaps the second most important determinant of house plans. For those at the highest levels of society the choice of a plan seems increasingly to have been for reasons of fashion rather than function; for those at lower levels the desire to imitate their social superiors was evidently very strong and may be seen as getting stronger all the time. Over and over again one can see plan arrangement as well as architectural detail working its way through all social levels. The influence of fashion is easy enough to understand once pattern books and, eventually, cheap journals and magazines were freely circulating; it is less easy to accept during those periods in which the dissemination of ideas committed to paper was difficult and expensive. Yet in the absence of elaborate drawings the model for each housebuilder would most conveniently be an existing building modified as necessary, the traditional plans being improved, or altered, following experiments made by those at higher social levels who had both the incentive and the means to make innovations.

What applies to the ground plan of a building applies also to its cross-section: the number of storeys, the roof construction and materials, the method of access from floor to floor. Limited sites encouraged building upwards, security suggested height as refuge, fashion determined that an imposing elevation should be several storeys high. The open hall of the medieval Large House reappeared as the principal living-room of the Wealden house and could be seen again as the basis of the croglofft cottage in Wales; the tall rooms of the eighteenth-century mansion required a staircase of two flights as did the mid-nineteenth-century farmhouse and the remarkably tall rooms of the late nineteenth-century cottage. Plan and section go together and it is important to ensure that the archaeologist's affection for the ground plan is extended with the aid of the more architectural device of the cross-section.

LARGE RURAL HOUSES

1. *Ground-floor hall*

The ground-floor hall was the nucleus of most pioneering rural house plans at every social level from medieval Great Houses to eighteenth-century Cottages; at every level except the lowest a substantial proportion of the ground-floor halls had one side or both sides aisled.

The essential characteristics of a ground-floor hall were its rectangular shape and its undivided section, the room rising open and unobstructed to the ridge or apex of the roof. In the basic hall the roof was carried by the walls or by piers or posts set in the walls so that the whole floor area was unobstructed, but in the aisled hall the roof loads were carried by way of trusses on to a series of stone piers or timber posts which ran along the length of the hall, dividing the floor space into a central nave and flanking narrower aisles. In the basic hall the rafters were carried by the walls, perhaps with the aid of trusses and purlins; in the aisled hall the great arcade plates or braced beams ran from post to post while carrying rafters on their journey

---

1. GROUND-FLOOR HALL, AISLED HALL

a. Plan of an aisled hall of four bays on the ground floor, showing two rows of aisle posts (1) with an open hearth heating the main part of the plan (2), a space at one end (3) sometimes partitioned off the main room, and the entrance (4) near the middle of one wall.

b. Cross-section showing the trusses based on aisle posts (1) and the roof sweeping down to cover the aisles and carried on the low outer walls (5).

c. Isometric sketch of a timber-framed aisled hall; in this instance the roof has a half-hip and gablet (6) at each end but sweeps over the aisles on the side walls (7).

d. Plan of an aisled hall with stone piers serving in place of aisle posts.

e. Sketch of a stone-walled and gabled aisled hall.

f. Plan of a small single-aisled house of four bays with a cross-passage (8) hearth near the cross-passage (9) and inner room (10).

g. Plan showing such a house hidden within a later set of stone or brick walls.

h. Sketch showing the incorporation of a single-aisled hall in later walls.

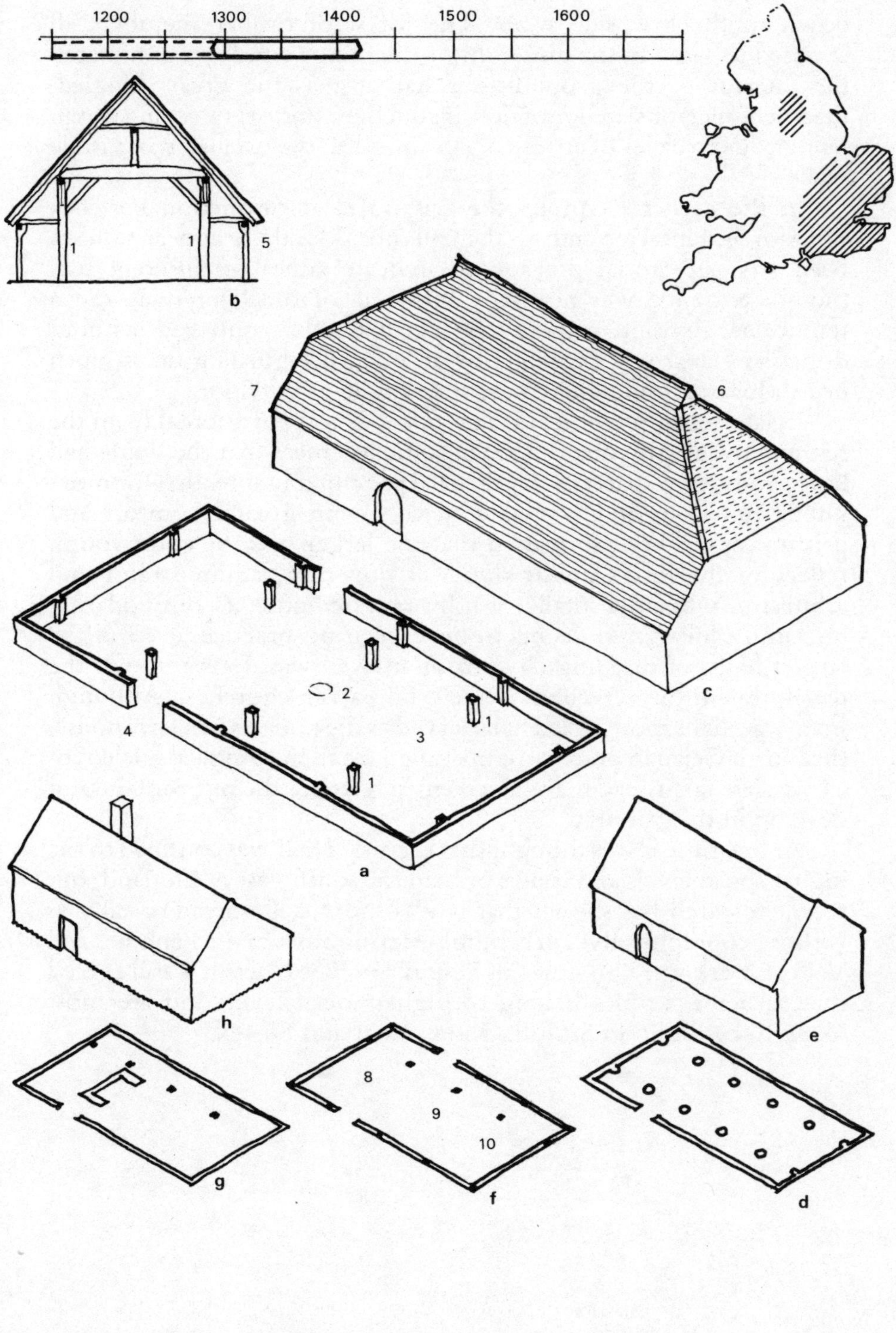
1200
1300
1400
1500
1600
1
1
5
b
7
6
c
2
4
3
1
1
a
h
e
8
9
10
g
f
d

down to the low side walls. The forest of timber members all exposed to view in the dim light of the fire or windows dominated the interior of the ground-floor hall just as the great shingled, thatched, tiled or slated roof dominated the exterior, sweeping down from ridge to eaves of an aisled hall almost to the exclusion of visible walls.

In the earlier examples there is no clear distinction between superior and inferior ends to the hall, nor does there appear to have been any substantial division to indicate zones of different use, though entrance was normally into one of the long sides and a temporary division into two spaces could be contrived without difficulty. Heat was provided by an open fire burning on an open hearth located somewhere near the middle of the floor.

In later examples it seems that one end was partitioned from the rest and eventually one can see in some instances that the single hall has become two spaces: a larger space presumably intended for more public functions and a smaller space giving greater comfort and privacy. It has been suggested that the larger was the court room, reflecting the lord's public duties as governor, administrator and arbitrator, while the smaller was his private house, accommodating his family life. There seems to have been no practice, even in the largest halls, of dividing nave from aisles as was done through the development of screened chapels in parish churches. Although many, perhaps most, aisled halls served as the nucleus of a farmhouse, the North German practice of making the hall the physical nucleus of a complete farmstead maintained entirely under the one roof did not develop in this country.

At one time it was thought that the aisled hall was confined to the higher social levels and found only in the south-east of England, but recent research has shown that it was more widespread socially as well as geographically: fairly humble farmhouses in the Pennines and Vale of York were built to this design.[2] Nevertheless it is still agreed that earlier examples belong to higher social levels and are most likely to be found in Suffolk, Essex, Kent and Sussex.

2. *First-floor hall*

As the name implies the characteristic feature of this group of houses was a room open to the roof and raised substantially above ground level. Normally the hall occupied most of the first floor of an elongated building, a smaller room (which might be ceiled) occupying the rest. Entrance was by an external staircase up to the hall, the smaller room being entered through the hall, and there was usually no intercommunication between the hall and the space beneath. The ground floor, which was sometimes divided and sometimes had two rooms corresponding with those above, often had a stone vault to carry the upper floor. The hall usually had a side-wall fireplace but the ground floor was often without a fixed heating source, though the larger room sometimes had a side-wall fireplace smaller than that serving the hall above. It is likely that the larger first-floor room served as a public room or court space and the smaller as a private or domestic space; the ground floor may have been devoted to storage (though of what is not clear) but alternatively the floor may have provided domestic accommodation for a separate and inferior household.

The first-floor hall was generally a mark of high status: most castles from the early thirteenth century to the middle of the fourteenth century had at least one; much domestic accommodation in monasteries may be seen as a series of first-floor halls, with the church as an aisled ground-floor hall and the chapter house as a ground-floor private room. Comparatively few secular examples of first-floor halls survive and these are nearly all of stone; it is impossible to speculate on how many timber first-floor halls may once have existed and since been destroyed.

First-floor halls are sometimes called 'King John's Houses', and a proportion of those surviving date from the second half of the twelfth century; but such halls were built throughout the thirteenth and well into the fourteenth century, especially in Wales and Marcher counties.

2a. *Bastle house*

There is another sort of first-floor hall, much later in date and rather smaller in size than the others but of which many examples survive complete or in part. This is the bastle house, the defensive dwelling of the most substantial farmers of the Scottish border, erected mainly during the period of border raiding during the sixteenth and the beginning of the seventeenth century. The bastle house consisted of a first-floor hall, with a smaller room at one end which was usually ceiled and sometimes had a garret room over. Both hall and smaller room were raised over a ground floor which was equipped for the accommodation of cattle and, probably, horses. Access to the first floor was by a retractable ladder which has been replaced in surviving examples by an external stone staircase; access to the ground floor was through a stout door protected by a drawbar; there was often no apparent means of intercommunication between the two floors. The intermediate floor was sometimes vaulted in stone but more commonly a timber floor made of boards, joists and beams in the conventional manner was provided. Walls were of stone, usually

---

2. FIRST-FLOOR HALL AND BASTLE HOUSE

a. Ground-floor plan showing larger room (1) and smaller room (2) which, in this case, are entered through separate doors (3 and 4). The larger room has a fireplace (5).
b. First-floor plan showing larger room (6) which is the first-floor hall and, opening off it, the smaller room (7) or solar. The larger room has a fireplace (8) in the side wall and is approached by a door (9) from an external staircase. In this example there is no intercommunication between ground and first floors.
c. Cross-section showing ground-floor room (10) and first-floor hall (11) carried here on a set of vaults (12).
d. Sketch showing first-floor hall, approached by its external staircase.
e. Plan showing barrel-vaulted undercroft beneath a first-floor hall; here there are three interconnecting rooms with entry into one (13) and a mural staircase (14) rising to the first floor.
f. Ground floor of a bastle house with direct entry into the cow-house (15) which occupies the whole of this floor.
g. First floor of a bastle house with the door (16) reached by an external staircase or ladder, leading into the first-floor hall (17) off which opens the ceiled inner room (18).

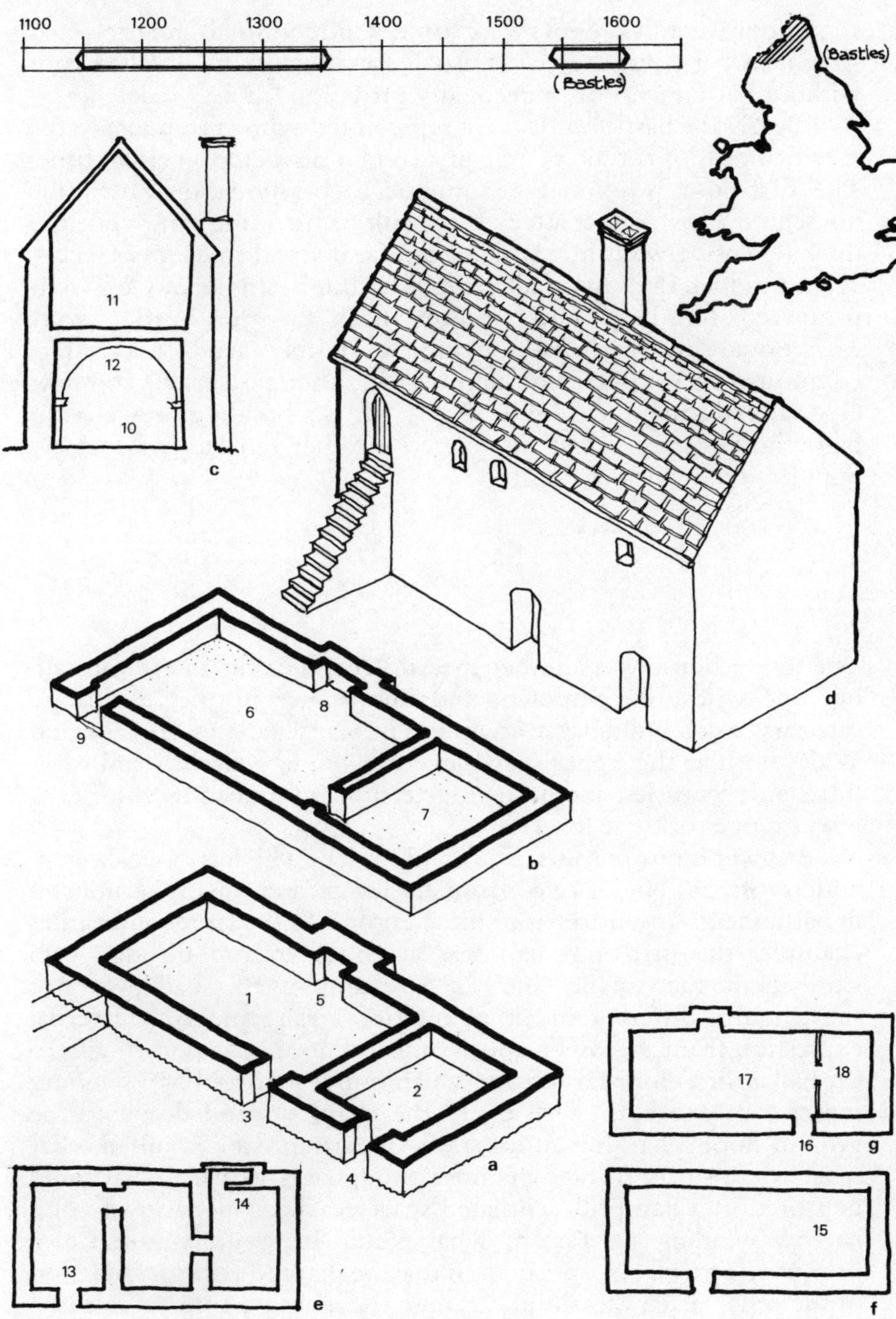

1100
1200
1300
1400
1500
1600
(Bastles)
(Bastles)
11
12
10
c
d
6
8
9
7
b
1
5
3
2
4
a
17
18
16
g
13
14
e
15
f

about four feet thick, doors were stout, windows small and protected with iron bars, but there was usually a conventional pitched roof without battlements or, indeed, any provision for active defence.

Clearly the bastle house form represented a direct response to the specific needs of certain people in a certain district at a certain time. The first-floor position for domestic accommodation raised the household above direct attack by assault or battering ram while the thick defensive walls meant that both family and stock were secure against sudden raids by small bands who might smoke out less well-protected families. The circumstances on the border were exceptional but perhaps not unique: family feuds and inter-communal rivalry were not unknown in other parts of the country, especially during the Middle Ages, and so buildings resembling bastle houses may yet be discovered in other remote and sparsely populated parts of the country.[3]

3. *Tower house*

The tower house was another special version of the first-floor hall, but one whose development and importance justifies a separate category. Such buildings were found in many parts of England and Wales both at the upper social levels in the late twelfth and early thirteenth centuries, and in the fourteenth and sixteenth centuries at lower ranges of these levels.[4]

A tower house consists of a first-floor hall which is raised over an undercroft, has one or two chambers above, and usually terminates in battlements around a flat or pitched roof. In the larger and earlier examples the first-floor hall was extended to run through two storeys; in the smaller and later examples the hall was not substantially different in either interior arrangement or external expression from the other upper rooms. Entrance was normally to the hall at first-floor level from which mural staircases or a winding staircase in one corner led up to the chambers and down to the ground-floor cellar. It is customary to regard the stone vaulted cellar space as a prison or storage chamber, though it is not clear what could be stored in a damp ill-ventilated space reached only by way of a narrow winding staircase or what would be securely stored in a prison cell apart from a prisoner. It may be that the principal function of the cellar space was simply to raise the hall to a comfortable and relatively secure position; comfort could have been obtained if the upper rooms had been raised on posts or piers but security required as solid and fireproof a base as possible. In the larger examples the ground-floor level could have been occupied by a separate household, as beneath first-floor halls, but surviving examples suggest that this was uncommon. Apart from a few brick buildings, all the surviving tower houses were built of stone, wall thicknesses varying from about four feet to as much as ten feet, and many had a stone vault beneath the hall, protecting the main part of the house from attack by fire.

In some of the largest examples there is a transverse wall dividing each floor into two long and rather narrow spaces. These walls may have been military in purpose, ensuring that a breach in one part of the wall did not automatically give access to the whole tower, but equally they may have had a domestic basis, dividing the hall floor into a larger and smaller room for more public and more private use and dividing the chamber floors into similar accommodation for other households. Again, many of the larger tower houses had rooms hollowed out of the thick walls of the upper levels, preserving the stout appearance of the whole tower but leaving only the bottom storey as of truly defensive wall thickness.

In some of the smaller examples, the so-called 'pele towers', the entrance was at ground level, a stout door and a wrought iron 'yett' protecting the entrance against sudden attack by battering ram or fire. A narrow winding staircase rose up through the various floors linking entrance with hall, chambers, and roof walk. In English examples the staircase was usually tucked into a corner of the building; the projecting staircase turret of Scottish examples which eventually led to the L and Z-shaped tower-house plans was rarely found south of the border.

Although in their abandoned and often ruined state tower houses now stand isolated, they were usually built as part of a complex of walls, courtyards and subsidiary buildings and served as the fireproof defensive refuge, amid more flimsy expendable buildings, within the curtain walls of a castle or the barmkin walls of a border strength.

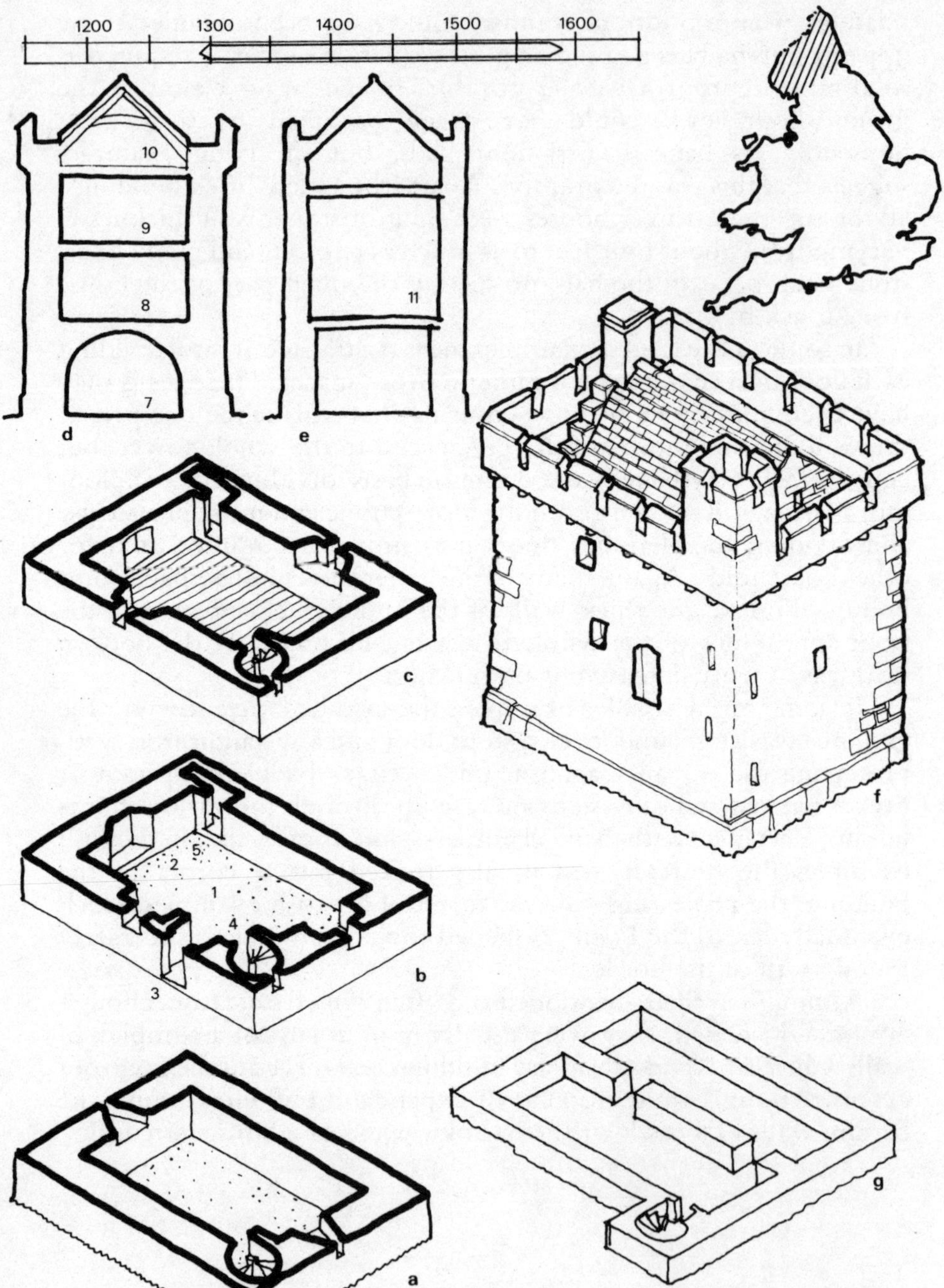
1200
1300
1400
1500
1600
10
9
8
7
d
11
e
c
5
2
1
4
b
3
f
g
a

3. TOWER HOUSES

a. Ground floor or undercroft, shown here as reached only by a winding staircase from above, unheated and lit only by narrow slits.
b. First floor containing hall (1) heated by an end-wall fireplace (2), with an external door (3) reached by a ladder or external staircase. A winding staircase partly built into a corner (4) connects the various floors. There is a garderobe (5) in the opposite corner.
c. Second floor containing, in this instance, a single-heated chamber with its own garderobe.
d. Cross-section showing a stone vaulted undercroft (7) with hall (8), chamber floor (9) and garrets (10) which have timber floors between.
e. Alternative cross-section showing timber floors throughout and a hall (11) which rises through two floors.
f. Sketch showing a gabled roof hidden behind battlements.
g. Plan to show a longitudinal wall dividing each floor into two flanking apartments and with a fairly spacious winding staircase housed in a projecting wing.

---

4. *Single-ended hall*

Sometimes known as the T-shaped hall or the end-hall house, the single-ended hall plan consists of a one-storey open hall with a two-storey domestic block attached at one end. The hall may be aisled or without aisles; it was usually designed to have an open hearth but may have a fireplace along the rear side wall. The domestic block consists usually of a small first-floor hall or solar, open to the roof and raised over one or more subsidiary rooms. The upper room may have had a fireplace but often had no fixed form of heating; the lower rooms did not usually have any heating provision at all. Access to the domestic block was often by an external staircase; at least in the earlier examples there might be no intercommunication between upper and lower rooms or between upper rooms and the hall.

The single-ended hall may be seen as representing the combination of the public duties and private activities of a minor lord: the large assemblies of local courts, major social activities etc. taking place in the ground-floor hall while ordinary domestic life was enjoyed in the first-floor hall, the ground-floor subsidiary rooms serving upper or lower hill as required. Indeed we have the two traditions of first-floor hall and ground-floor hall coming together in one house. Insofar as the entrance position became established at the junction of the two parts of the house, we have an instance of the convenient location also expressing the double nature of such a house plan.

Usually the multi-storey wing was roofed at right angles to the single-storey main block, just as the wing usually projected from the walls of the hall; but this was not essential as one could have a T-shaped roof over a rectangular plan and even, in the smaller examples, a rectangular roof over a T-shaped plan.

Most T-shaped halls were built either of timber frame or stone and, at least on the evidence of surviving examples, it could not be said that use of the one material preceded use of the other. However a stone wing and a timber hall may have been a not uncommon arrangement. This would have been reasonable both structurally and functionally: the stone used for the multi-storey structure where height and stability were important and span of roof or floor beams less significant, and the timber used for the hall where desire for width and uninterrupted height dominated the planning. It would also have been a reasonable arrangement where occasional need for

---

4. SINGLE-ENDED HALL

a. Plan showing hall (1) with open hearth (2), screens passage (3) stretching between opposite doors; buttery (4), pantry (5) and kitchen passage (6), a winding staircase (7) leads to the first floor of the cross-wing.
b. Upper-floor plan showing the upper part of the hall (8) and first-floor hall or solar in the cross-wing (9).
c. Cross-section looking towards the cross-wing and showing the spere truss (10).
d. Sketch which shows the different eaves lines of the hall and the two-storey cross-wing. A saddle louvre is shown over the hall.
e. Plan showing a common method of improving a single-ended hall in the sixteenth century by the insertion of fireplaces and an intermediate floor. The cross-passage is blocked by an inserted fireplace and staircase (13) while the lower part of the cross-wing (12) has become a habitable room with its own fireplace.
f. Sketch showing the chimney stacks serving the new fireplaces and dormer windows lighting the chambers formed in the upper part of the hall.
g. Sketch showing how the roof formation reveals that a rectangular plan is really that of a single-ended hall.

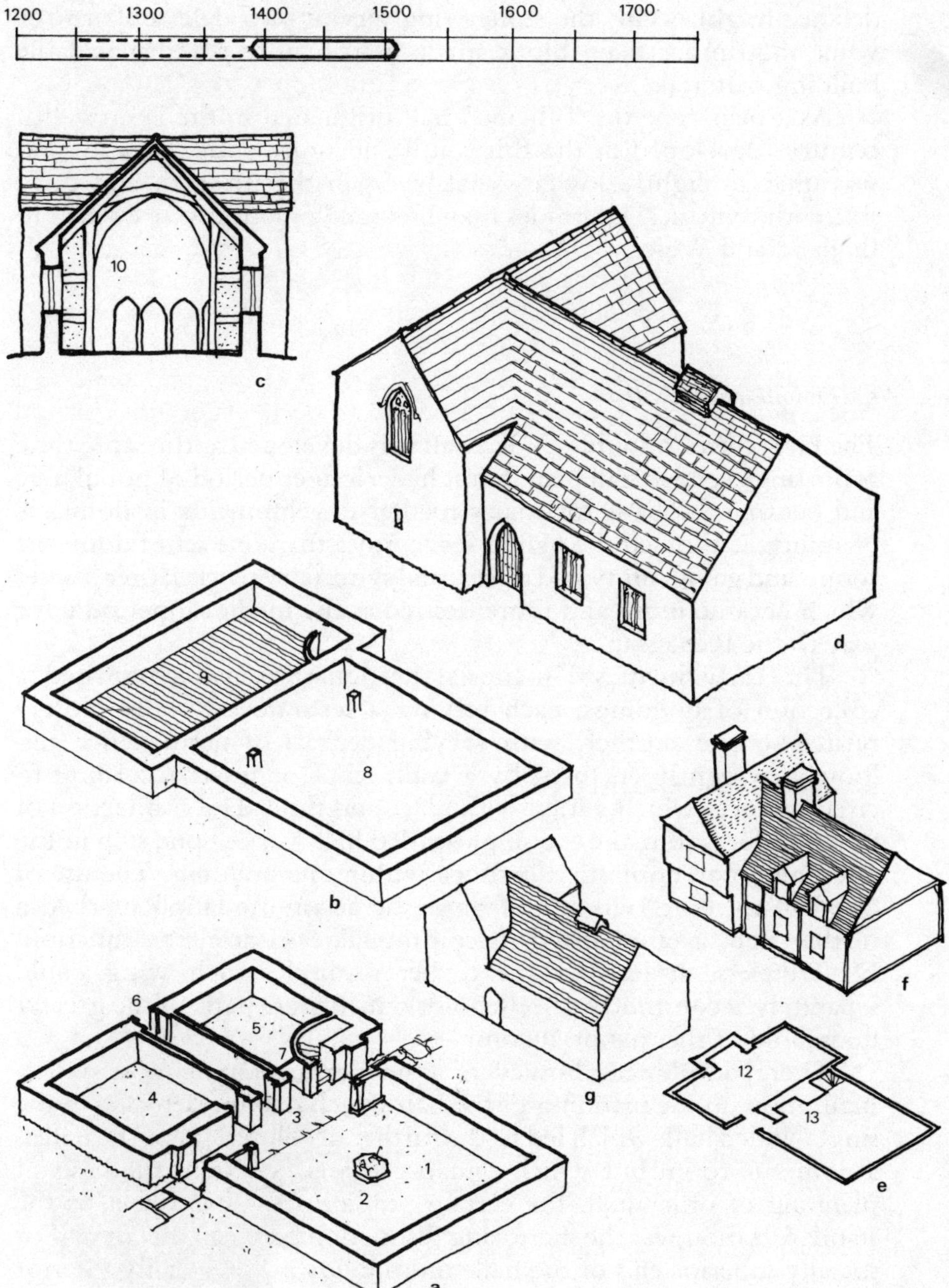

1200
1300
1400
1500
1600
1700
c
10
d
9
8
b
f
g
12
13
e
6
5
7
4
3
1
2
a

defence might occur, the stone wing serving as a defensible tower while the timber main block made use of more readily available building materials.

As a plan-type the T-shaped hall originated in the late twelfth century, developed in the thirteenth and fourteenth centuries and was used at slightly lower social levels in the fifteenth and early sixteenth centuries. Examples may be found practically anywhere in England and Wales.

5. *Double-ended hall*

The H-shaped or double-ended hall was developed at the same time as the single-ended hall plan, but it had a longer period of popularity and became the basis for many further developments in domestic planning. It allowed the hall to serve more than one set of domestic rooms and gave a unity and a potential symmetry to the larger houses which became more and more desired as the medieval period gave way to the Renaissance.

The early medieval manorial headquarters had comprised a collection of buildings, each serving a separate use, only loosely related to one another, with varying degrees of permanence and loosely or tightly enclosed by a wall, fence or moat according to circumstances which varied with place and time. The connection of two buildings to make the single-ended hall marked one step in the assembly of all domestic functions within one building. The use of one hall to serve two sets of domestic accommodation marked a further step: it emphasized its communal, non-domestic function. Nevertheless, at least in the earlier examples each wing could separately accommodate households which were parts of the greater household of the manorial complex.

There developed, however, a standardization, almost a formalization, in the planning of the hall which may be detected in the single-ended hall, which led to the further development of the hall as a domestic room but which remains to a large extent the basis of planning of other halls for certain public uses. One aspect of the standardization was the increasing distinction between the 'upper' or socially superior end of the hall, and the 'lower' or socially inferior end, between parts above and below the salt.

At the lower end there was a concentration of circulation space.

Entrance to the whole building was at the junction between the lower end of the hall and one of the cross-wings; opposed doors led into a cross-passage which was taken from the lower end of the hall and defined by the short partitions of the spere truss and the free-standing screen in between. Across the passage, doors led into the lower portion of the cross-wing, and here accommodation became standardized as buttery and pantry (for liquor and dry goods respectively) with a corridor in between leading to an outside kitchen. There was also in many examples a winding staircase which led from the passage to the room on the upper floor of the wing. Thus the circulation space at the lower end of the hall contained front and back doors, the doors to buttery, pantry, kitchen and staircase, and the two openings which led into the main part of the hall; it served as an inner porch, protecting the hall from the worst of the draughts, as an ante-room when the hall was used as a court room and as a servery space when the hall was used for those banquets which many can picture and some try to recapture.

At the upper end of the hall developments took longer. The socially superior status was marked by the provision of a dais, a platform raised slightly above the general floor level, and those sitting on the dais were protected by a coved canopy of timber or plaster from the worst of the smutty downdraughts which resulted from the use of a central open hearth. In later examples their status was further marked by a bay window, sometimes of complex plan and elaborate decoration, which gave light and distinction to the upper end of the hall. Doors were provided at each end of the dais to give access to the cross-wing at the upper end of the house, and sometimes there were short screens which gave further protection to the occupants of the dais from any draughts which might come through the doors. With a public entrance and assembly space at one end, an unobstructed main area capable of being furnished in various ways, and a raised platform at the other end, panelled, protected and with its own doors to private retiring rooms, one can well see how the medieval hall became the court room, council chamber and even parliament hall of subsequent centuries and, indeed, how strong is this tradition which prevents the British parliament from adopting the amphitheatre pattern of Continental assemblies.

The earlier halls had a central open hearth with smoke rising to the rafters and emerging through uneven tiles or slates, being absorbed in thatch, or passing fitfully through a draughty louvre. Some such halls still survive. The central position meant that heat was evenly distributed throughout the room. Later halls and improved earlier halls had a fireplace usually placed on the rear side wall where its heat was still quite well radiated; only in a few small and northern halls was the fireplace made to back on to the cross-passage.

Later developments affected the main entrance and the dais, for it became the practice to give architectural acknowledgement to the importance of these two ends of the hall. The dais had its bay window becoming ever more pretentious, the most magnificent example being probably that at Hampton Court Palace, but then changing to become a link with the cross-wing rather than a separate projection. The entrance door was given more emphasis and was made more effective as a protection to the hall by the provision of a porch, usually of two or three storeys. Previously the front and back

---

5. DOUBLE-ENDED HALL

a. Ground-floor plan showing hall (1) with side-wall fireplace (2), entrance by way of cross-passage or screens passage (3), off which leads the kitchen passage (6) running between the buttery (4) and pantry (5), and a staircase (7) leading to the upper floor of this wing. At the opposite end of the hall is the dais (8) with flanking doors leading to a heated parlour (9) which has its own staircase to a solar above.
b. Cross-section looking towards the dais and its canopy (10).
c. Sketch to show the single-storey hall and cross-wings.
d. Ground-floor plan of a semi-fortified hall: the open hall (11) has a fireplace (12) which backs on to the cross-passage (13) off which opens a kitchen (14) now brought into the house. There will be a chamber above but in this example the two-storey portion does not project as a wing. At the opposite end of the hall is a service room (15) with solar and chamber above; all this projecting wing is strengthened so as to act as a place of refuge or defence.
e. Sketch showing the defensible wing, the hall chimney and the massive kitchen chimney breast.
f. A late example of a double-ended hall showing on the ground floor the hall (16) which might have a gallery joining the upper floors of the two wings or might already have an inserted floor. The hall is heated by a fireplace (17) which backs on to a cross-passage (18) off which opens a kitchen (19) and service room (20). At the 'upper' end of the hall there are parlour, staircase, and chambers above. The porch at the front end of the cross-passage is built into the adjacent wing.
g. Sketch showing the appearance of such a house.
h. The dais end of a hall was often marked externally by use of a bay window.

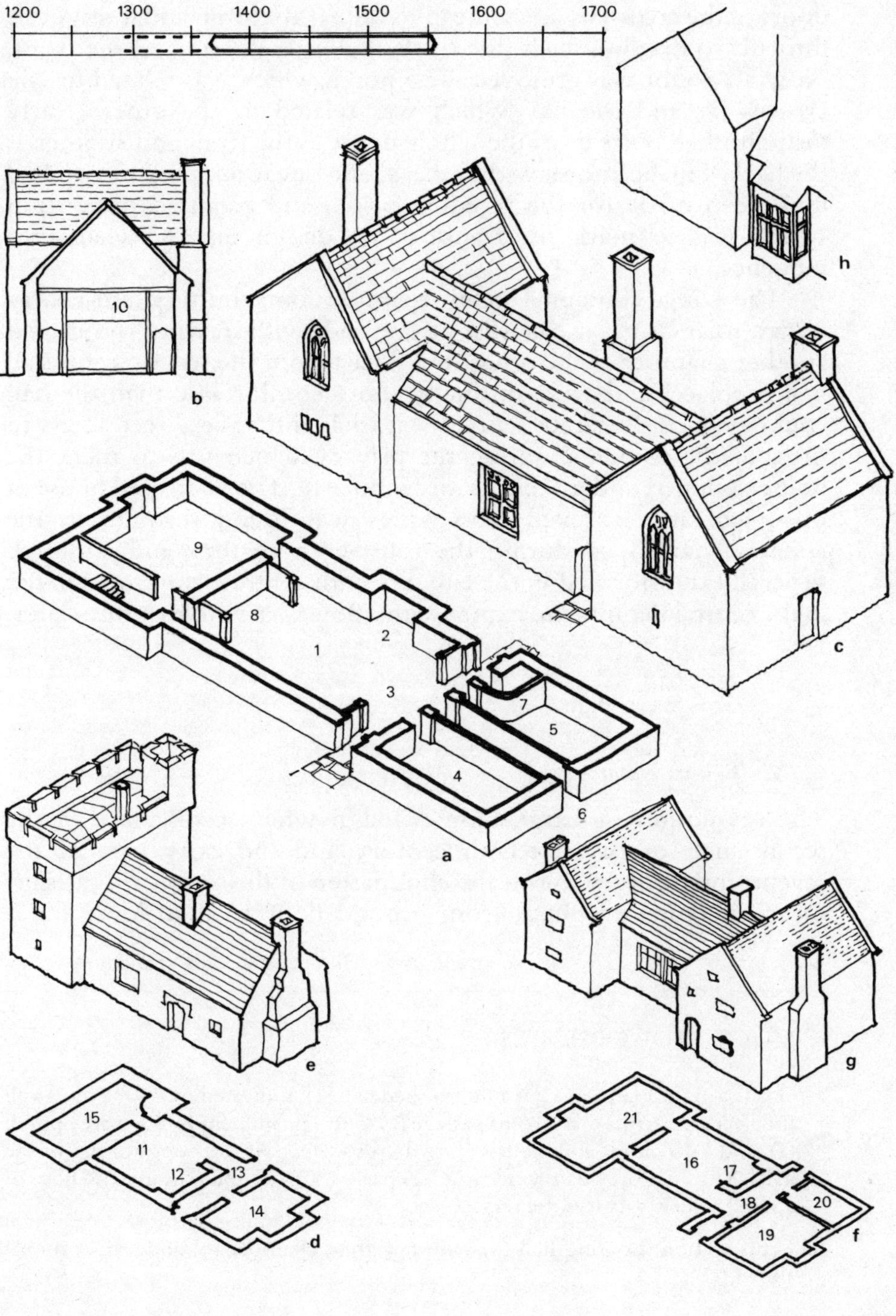

1200
1300
1400
1500
1600
1700
10
b
h
9
8
1
2
3
7
5
4
6
c
a
e
g
15
11
12
13
14
d
21
16
17
18
20
19
f

doors to the cross-passage were given equal attention and it might be difficult to decide which side of the hall was considered the front. Now all doubt was removed. The porch which was related to one cross-wing and the bay which was related to the other clearly distinguished one side of the whole house as the front and another as the back. Furthermore, within that front elevation, preparation had now been made for the receding planes and balanced disposition which was to mark the transition to design under Renaissance influence.

The wings contained small separate rooms: buttery and pantry with a solar or great chamber at one end, withdrawing rooms and another chamber at the other end. Apart from the service rooms all had fireplaces and were distinctly more comfortable than the hall could ever be. Separate staircases at each end gave direct access to most of the rooms, ensuring the privacy which was to mark the house designed under Renaissance influence. The H-shaped house of open hall and storeyed cross-wings was found throughout the country, developed during the fourteenth century and although generally transformed in the late sixteenth century continued in use in the central Pennines to expire with a flourish a whole century later.

6. *Multi-storey house*

The revolution in Large House design which took place in the second half of the sixteenth century and the early part of the seventeenth century meant the elimination of the open hall, the shift of architectural emphasis from ground floor to first floor, and a

---

6. MULTI-STOREY HOUSE

a. Ground-floor plan showing a diminished hall (1), unheated or with a rear-wall fireplace, remnants of a screens passage (2) with a prominent multi-storey porch (3), and kitchen (4) and pantry (5) in a cross-wing. At the opposite end of the hall is a multi-storey bay window (6). A parlour (7) occupies the ground floor of a wing which balances the service wing.

b. Cross-section showing hall (8) with tall great chamber (9) and garret rooms above (10).

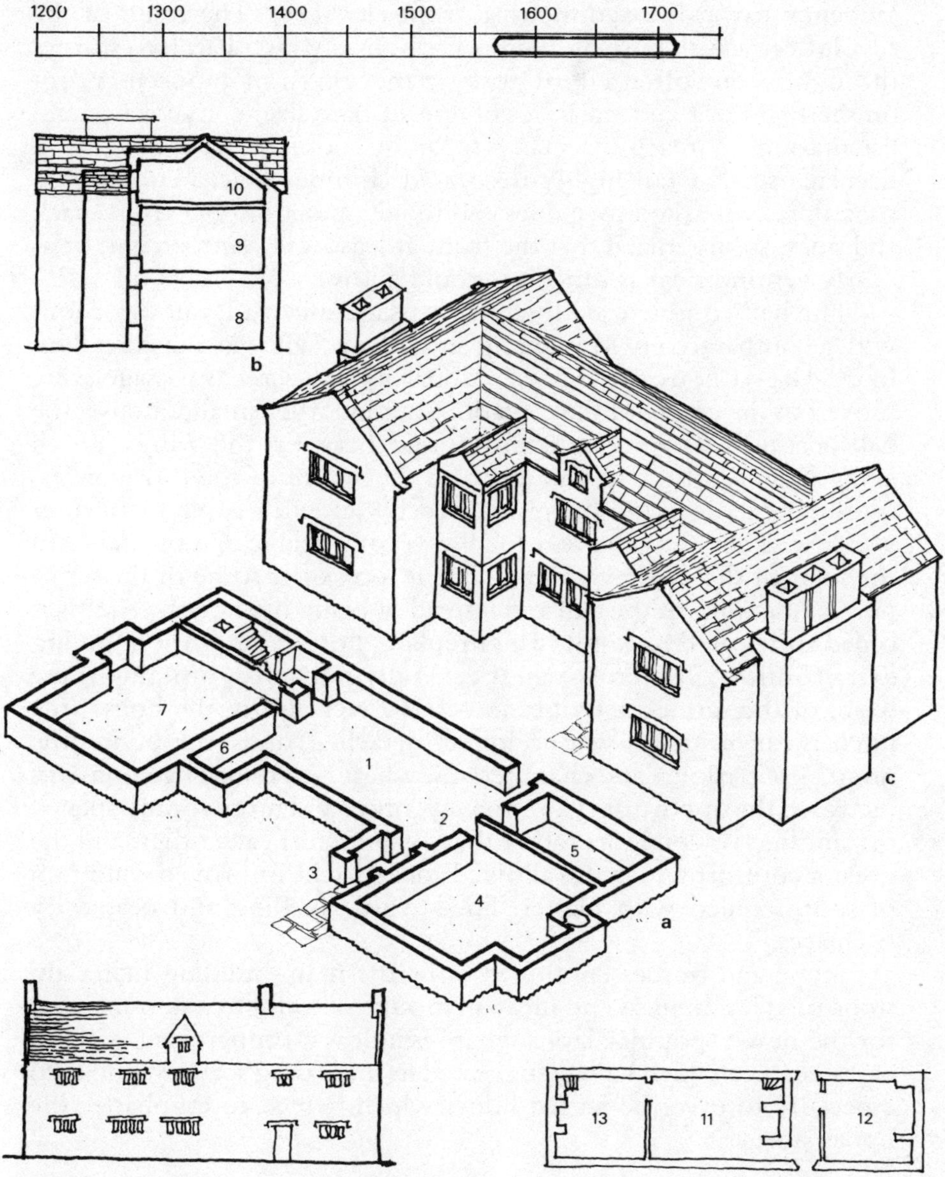

c. Sketch to show the broadly symmetrical arrangement of facets receding to the wall of the hall and great chamber.

d. A common alternative with several storeys of rooms arranged in a line.

e. Sketch to show the two storeys and garret storey often used.

tendency towards a symmetrical front elevation. The result of the revolution was the use of designs for houses which had two storeys throughout and often a third storey in the wings; an important room on the first floor and staircases of appropriate size, convenience and ostentation to reach it; many separate rooms served each by a fireplace so that tall highly-decorated chimney stacks enlivened a roof already marked by gables and finials; and a distinct front, back and sides, so organized that the front at least was symmetrical, or as nearly symmetrical as function would allow.

The hall complete with screens passage survived, but as a room with a comparatively low ceiling and usually without a distinct dais. In the largest houses, the porch, doorway and screens passage were moved to the centre of the elevation, but in rather smaller houses the hall occupied its conventional position between the wings, porch being balanced by bay window and the centre of the more or less symmetrical elevation being marked by an extra gable or dormer window. The room above the hall was comparable in importance to the solar of the medieval house, but it took over some of the semi-public functions of the hall and instead of being open to the roof was ceiled and heated by a side-wall fireplace, both modifications giving extra comfort. The cross-wings generally remained, bringing some more of the service activities into the lower end of the house (the kitchen, for instance, was no longer detached) and multiplying the number of parlours and chambers elsewhere. All these developments increased the opportunity for privacy; more and more rooms opened off landings or corridors rather than opening off each other, and the greater comfort which this allowed added to the improved condition of rooms ceiled with plaster, lined with panelling and heated by fireplaces.

Stone and timber continued to be the main building materials: stone used less in mass and more in moulded mullions and transomes for the newly-popular large square windows; timber used with an extravagance which hardly suggested its increasing scarcity, and used especially to give the jettied floors which helped to emphasize the upper storeys.

7. *Compact house with projecting wings*

A house plan which is represented by comparatively few examples, but is important in the stages of development to the standard Renaissance plan, is that in which a compact central block, several storeys high, had a number of projections from each face, making a more or less balanced collection of elements, and a set of more or less symmetrical elevations. This sort of house was forward-looking in being symmetrical (often about both axes) and having the lines of symmetry architecturally emphasized, but it was backward-looking in that the symmetry was usually marred by such elements as windows which were introduced for functional or traditional reasons (even though their position might be architecturally inconvenient) and in that the roof line was punctuated by gables, dormers, turrets and chimneys in a lively and not always well-ordered profusion. Internally such a house was forward-looking in the importance of staircase and upper rooms but backward-looking in that elements of hall and parlour sometimes remained.

One version of the plan had hall and parlour or withdrawing room in the central block with a kitchen wing at the rear, a projecting multi-storey porch at the front, and possibly staircase turrets at each side. Another, larger, version had two principal and two service rooms on the ground floor, chambers above, and either a front porch and rear staircase turret or front and rear porches and staircase projections on each side. There were several experiments, but the most significant examples had a centralized entrance/lobby/staircase system which allowed all the rooms on each floor to be separately entered. It has been observed that the combination of a multi-storey porch at the front, staircase and kitchen at the rear and hall or other circulation space in the centre together with bold projection of fireplaces and chimney breasts from the end walls 'produced the characteristic cruciform plan of the mid-seventeenth-century gentry house' in Wales, but also in England.[5]

One further point about this plan deserves note: while the medieval house often had no front, both sides being of comparable importance, and the multi-storey houses had a front on which all attention was lavished, giving a back and sides which were ignored architecturally, these houses often had four fronts, each elevation receiving attention from the designer and each establishing its own symmetry.

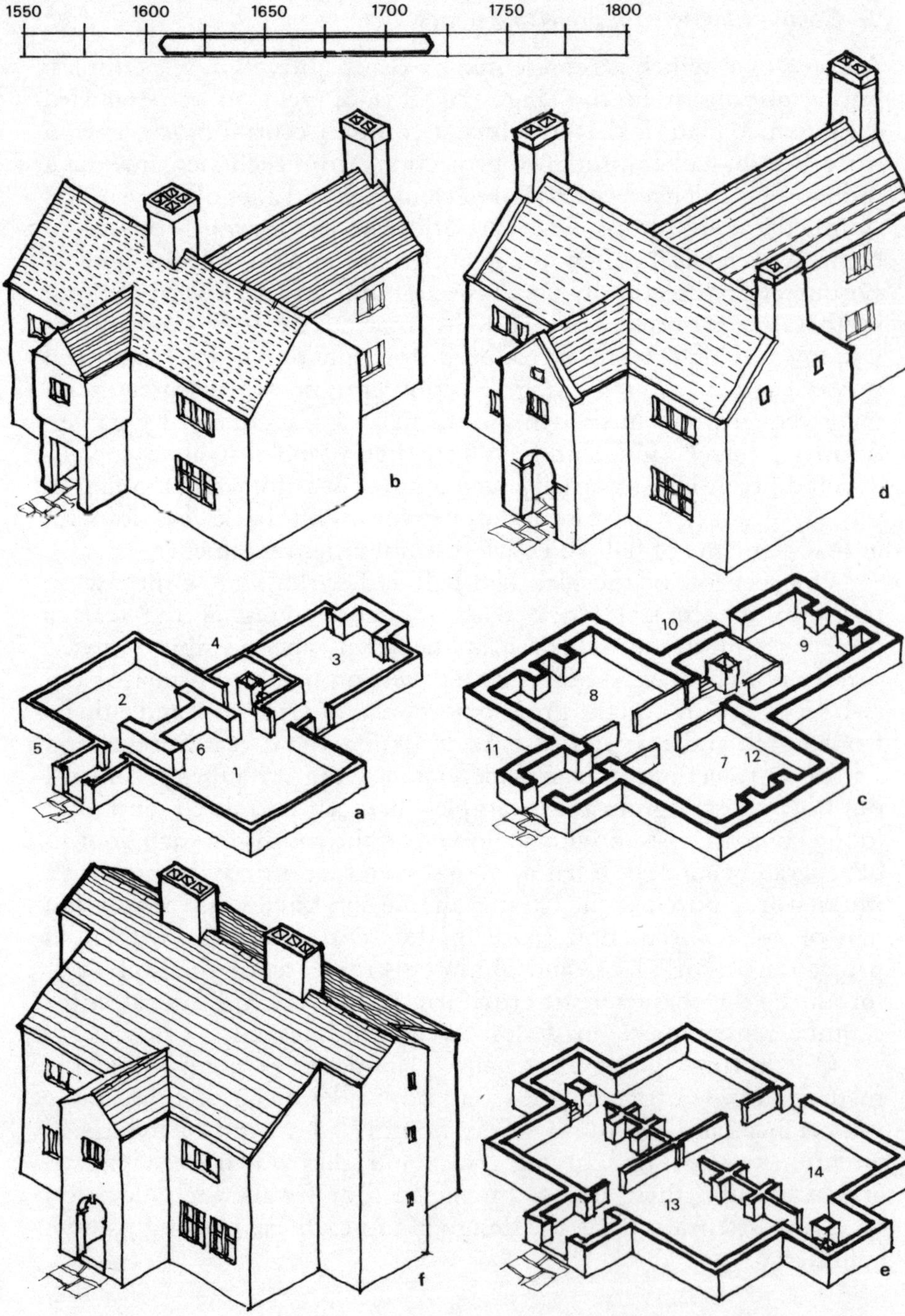
1550
1600
1650
1700
1750
1800
b
d
4
3
2
5
6
1
a
10
9
8
11
7
12
c
13
14
f
e

7. COMPACT HOUSE WITH PROJECTING WINGS

a. Ground-floor plan showing hall (1), parlour (2) and kitchen (3). A staircase (4) gives easy access to the chambers and garret floor. The multi-storey porch (5) marks the approximate centre of the front elevation. The fireplaces (6) are back-to-back and their flues combine in a single tall chimney stack.
b. Sketch to show the main block and projecting wings which produce a cross-shaped plan.
c. Alternative ground-floor plan which also has hall (7), parlour (8), kitchen (9), staircase (10) and porch (11). In this case the main fireplaces (12) are on the gable walls and so the compact block of flues is missing.
d. Sketch to show the distribution of chimney stacks as well as the cross-shaped plan.
e. Ground-floor plan of a house with internal chimneys and projecting staircase wings. Entrance through the porch is direct into the hall (13) off which a staircase rises to the chambers on one side of the house. In this example the house is two rooms deep as well as two rooms wide.
f. Sketch to show that a stubby cross-shape emerges from use of porch and staircase wing.

---

8. *Double-pile house*

The medieval houses had tended to symmetry about the long axis; once inside the hall there was symmetry about an imaginary line leading from the centre of the screens passage to the centre of the dais; for on looking at the entrance or garden fronts there was a generally asymmetrical disposition of rooms and windows. The short axis was paramount in the Renaissance house even though there might be subsidiary symmetries about the long axis on the end elevations. The medieval houses were conceived as one room in depth: the hall spanned from front to back walls, the wings, though placed at right angles, were composed of rooms of full depth; the Renaissance house, however, was conceived as a compact, centralized, cubiform block, two rooms in depth, and for this the contemporary term 'double-pile' is appropriate.

The normal arrangement of the double-pile Large House gave a central entrance lobby leading to a double-flight fully exposed staircase at the rear; the two principal living-rooms were at the front, one on each side of the entrance lobby, the two principal service rooms were at the rear, one on each side of the staircase; the principal bedrooms were on the first floor, subsidiary bedrooms were above, partly in the roof space, subsidiary service rooms were below the entrance level and partly underground. There were variations in the position of the main staircase, which was sometimes at the side between living and service rooms. The fireplaces were usually on the side walls but might be placed back-to-back on spine walls and were sometimes clustered together in a massive stack in the middle. There were roofing problems in houses of such a deep plan, solved by having either two parallel roofs with a vulnerable gutter in between; a hipped or gabled roof at the front and two short stretches of roof at the rear; a hipped roof at the front leading to a central flat roof with a cupola, balustrade and 'widow's walk'; or a deep overall roof of shallow pitch making use of good quality slate. The aim really was to diminish the importance of the roof in a composition which was as

---

8. DOUBLE-PILE HOUSE

a. Ground-floor plan which shows a central entrance door leading to a lobby (1) off which open the living-room (2) and parlour (3), kitchen (4) and dairy or pantry (5) with main staircase (6) and service stairs (7).
b. First-floor plan showing the bedrooms (8), many with fireplaces.
c. Cross-section showing ground- and first-floor rooms and the garret storey; in this example the double-pile plan is roofed by means of two parallel roofs and a valley gutter between (9). Sometimes there is a cellar beneath the front rooms (10).
d. Sketch to show the arrangement of roofs and gable chimneys.
e. An alternative ground-floor plan with fireplaces back-to-back rather than in the gable walls.
f. Another version of the plan with all fireplaces grouped together in the centre of the building and the staircase in one corner.
g. Sketch showing how a simple roof of shallow pitch covers the whole depth of the plan.
h. An alternative roofing system giving a clean eaves at the front but two gables at the rear. This method of roofing is suitable for steeply-pitched roofs and also for a plan with internal chimneys as in plan e.
i. Another roofing system used with low-pitch roofing material and for plan f.
j. Sketch showing the rear of a house which approximates the double-pile plan but has two wings a few feet apart rather than a continuous run of rooms.

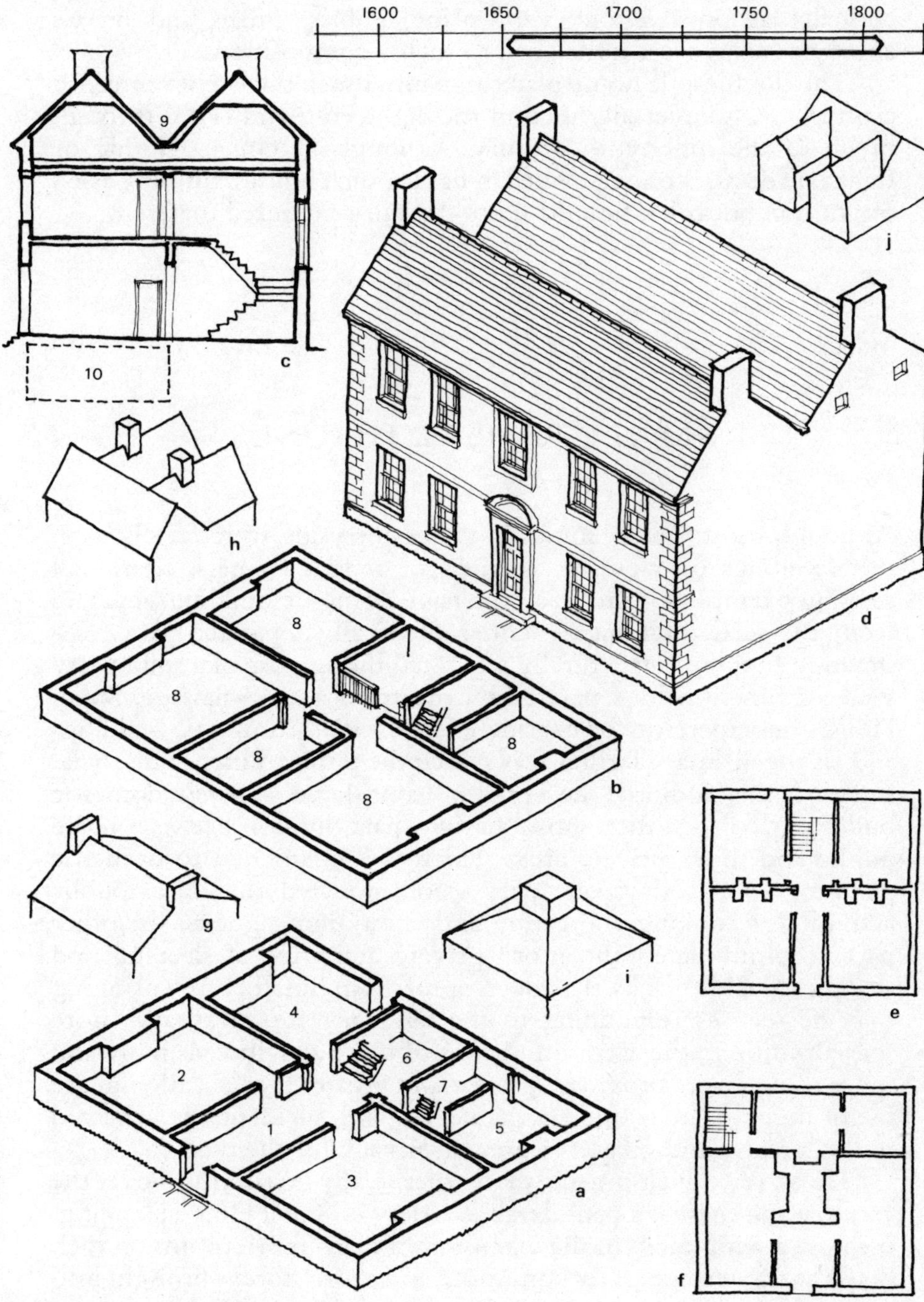
1600
1650
1700
1750
1800
9
10
c
j
d
h
8
8
8
8
8
b
e
g
i
4
2
6
7
1
5
3
a
f

compact as possible on every plane; gables, finials and ornate chimney stacks were quite alien to such a composition.

The double-pile house plan came into use in the late seventeenth century, was universally used in the eighteenth and lasted through much of the nineteenth century – though in Greek, Gothic or Italianate dress. Stone remained in use for such houses, timber passed out of use, but brick became quite the most favoured material.

SMALL RURAL HOUSES

Although most Small Houses in the countryside were farmhouses, the dwellings of working yeomen or tenant farmers, nearly all existing examples of this size-type have domestic buildings separate from the farm buildings – either physically separated as a free-standing building, structurally separated though use of a solid party wall, or functionally separated by means of a cross-passage. Small Houses may therefore be considered as *essentially* domestic buildings and, as the ordinary farmer was spared the public duties of his social superior, the landlord, they may be considered as *purely* domestic buildings. As such they show the two-part division between more public and more private areas which is fundamental to domestic planning even today; one part accommodated the more public activities of cooking and eating and entertaining guests; the other part accommodated the more private activities of sleeping and storing valuable goods. The developments in Small House planning may be seen as responding to the tendency for more and more specialization in the accommodation of these activities: as more and more rooms were provided, greater and greater specialization in the use of the separate rooms was achieved, and, incidentally, achieved with a greater and greater degree of privacy for the users.

However, development was neither steady nor uniform over the country and there is a considerable variety in Small House planning. It shows itself mainly in the extension of plan (more rooms on each floor) and extension of section (more and more storeys brought into use) and in the varying relationships between entrance door, means

1 *Preston Cottage, Alderley Edge, Cheshire.*
This house appears to have had a hall and cross-wing with a further wing added in 1628. A dormer window lights the chamber formed through the insertion of a floor in the hall. The chimney stack position indicated conversion to a lobby-entrance plan. Construction is of timber frame, but brick has replaced the daubed panels and there is a brick cladding to the weather side. The roof covering is of stone flags but this probably replaces thatch. (RWB)

2 *Farmstead near Lowick, Lancs. (now Cumbria).*
A small farmstead contained within a single range of buildings. The farmhouse is of continuous outshut plan; attached is a barn (whose tall doors are protected by a canopy) incorporating a stable with loft over. A further extension contains a cartshed and loft. (RWB)

3 *Manor House, Boothby Pagnell, Lincs.*
A well preserved example of a first-floor hall, this building was erected about 1200, though later architectural details may be seen. (NMR)

4 *Priory Place, Little Dunmow, Essex.*
An example of a double-ended or H-shaped hall house, this building illustrates well the relationship between hall and cross-wings. The rear elevation is shown in order to indicate the extension of the hall as an aisle or outshut. The massive chimney stack marks the position of the inserted fireplaces. Decay reveals the later cladding in lath and plaster of the original timber-framed structure. (NMR)

5 *Bodwrdda, Aberdaron, Caernarvonshire.*
This multi-storey Large House was built in 1621. The use of brick at that time in a remote location in North Wales is very unusual. (RCAHMW)

6 *House at Allt Mawr, Breconshire.*
A compact house with projecting wings, this building was erected probably in the early seventeenth century. Although small in size it ranks as a Large House in its locality. (RW)

7 *The Leys, Willoughby Waterless, Leics.*
This double-pile Large House was built in 1740. The roof is steeply pitched around the perimeter of the plan but rises to a central flat. Door and window frames have been replaced. (RF)

8 *House at Scriven, Yorks. W.R.*
A lobby-entrance house of three units, this Small House has in fact developed from a timber-framed single-aisled hall to the plan and mixture of masonry and brickwork which we now see. (NMR)

of access between storeys, and nature and location of principal heat source.

As we have seen, possible variations of plan depend to a large extent on the relative positions of these three items, but this is particularly so for the Small Houses of the countryside whose plans originated as simple rectangles and developed as variations within the rectangle and extensions from the rectangle.

There were three feasible positions for the main door: in the end or gable wall, at the corner of the main side wall and at or near the centre of the main wall. All have been used in the plans which follow. There were four possible positions for the staircase: alongside the main fireplace, at the rear of the main living space, near the centre of that space, and from an inner room which opened off the main living space. Again, the use of all these positions will be noted, though, as staircases became more generous in dimensions and easier in rise the position alongside the fireplace fell out of favour. The nature of the principal heat source varied from open hearth through smoke bay or inglenook to fixed fireplace and the position tended to vary in each stage of development.

The earliest Small Houses (such as the fourteenth-century Wealden houses of Kent and Sussex) were heated by an open hearth in a hall or living-room which was open to the roof. The fire of wood or peat was loosely located on a paved hearth and smoke rose to be absorbed into a thatched roof or evacuated through slates or tiles or, occasionally, through a louvre. The small size of the living space of a Small House meant that a central position was less convenient than in the lord's great hall and the absence of a separate kitchen meant that control of the fire for cooking purposes as well as room heating was very important. The open hearth, therefore, tended to migrate towards a fireback wall built for the purpose with smoke confined either within the partitioned section of roof which has been called a smoke bay or into the funnel-shaped timber and wattle chimney which has been called a smoke hood or hooded chimney. The smoke bay was inefficient and quickly superseded by what we would regard as a conventional brick or stone fireplace, flue and chimney stack; the smoke hood was rather more satisfactory in operation and as it helped to create an inglenook, 'room within a room', the peat fire against a fireback wall and beneath a smoke hood remained popular until the late eighteenth century in many parts of the country, before being superseded by fireplaces designed for burning coal.

Although rooms became increasingly specialized in their uses there were very long periods in which rooms served several purposes, either in sequence or simultaneously. This may be noted in the case of the parlour which was bedroom, dining-room, storeroom and workroom. In the more advanced areas the use of a first-floor chamber as a bedroom began at a very early period but in the more conservative regions first-floor sleeping was reserved for servants, children and poultry, the bed of the master and mistress of the house being in the ground-floor parlour. Since this was the main function of the parlour a heat source was not considered necessary and, for a long time no fireplace was provided. In most farmhouses regular dining around the long table and more formal entertaining around the circular table were both activities confined to the living-room, but in the more pretentious households the parlour came into use as a dining-room, though for a long time such a heated parlour was also in occasional use as a bedroom. In the smaller and earlier of the houses the parlour acted as the storeroom for grain, fleeces or other valuable products of the farm and also for the food for the household, but even in such houses it became common practice to partition an area from the parlour end of the house to serve as a pantry or dairy. Finally one should not ignore the use of the parlour as a workroom for spinning or weaving; the self-sufficient farming household needed space for storage and use of the simple machinery required, and, during the boom years for hand crafts at the end of the eighteenth century and the early part of the nineteenth, virtually every available space was conscripted to house the loom. Here, again, the heated parlour would suit some activities and the unheated parlour would be more suitable for others.

The plans which follow show variations according to time (and the improving standards demanded) and to place within the general levels of status accepted by the Small House dweller.

9. *Wealden and other open-hall houses*

As the name suggests, open-hall Small Houses are those in which the main room consists of a hall at ground level and open to the roof. The Wealden house is a specific version of this plan.

In its basic form the open-hall house has two-storey portions at each end of the hall; entrance is by way of a cross-passage or a cross-entry (i.e. a cross-passage induced by opposed doors but not precisely defined by parallel partitions) into one end of the hall, with service rooms beneath a chamber at the entrance end of the hall and a parlour beneath another chamber at the opposite end. The open-hall house resembles the double-ended hall among the Large Houses but the two-storey portions are usually contained within the simple rectangular plan and do not project as wings, while the whole house is, of course, on a much smaller scale. The oldest examples of the open-hall plan retain a central open hearth but the majority of surviving examples display improved heating provision by way of a smoke bay locating the hearth at the service end of the hall, an inglenook backing on to the cross-passage, or a fireplace inserted into the passage or backing on to it.

This house plan is probably very old, was probably widespread in use and probably lasted for a long time. The vast majority of buildings originally erected according to this layout have been altered especially by the insertion of an intermediate floor within the hall, but some few still remain without substantial alteration and may be dated as medieval in the south of England, late medieval or sixteenth century in the West Midlands and the eastern counties of Wales, but probably of late sixteenth- or seventeenth-century date in the North.

The so-called Wealden houses form a large and easily recognizable group within the general body of open-hall Small Houses. A Wealden house is one in which a central hall is open to the roof and flanked by two-storey bays but in such a way that the upper part of the bays is jettied out to project at the front, to one side, or even to front, sides and rear. On the ground floor the plan is rectangular, at first-floor level it tends to an H shape, but at the roof it reverts to a rectangle as the hipped or gablet roof covers the jettied plan, mastering the central part with the aid of deep eaves, the outer wall-plate being carried on brackets in the most characteristic examples.

Entry was into a miniature screens-passage or into a simple cross-entry space, taken off the open hall, and doors led into the service rooms at one side. From the hall two further doors led into one or two parlours at what one might consider the dais end of the hall. The first-floor chambers, though enhanced by their jettied floors, were reached by a pair of separate mean and unobtrusive staircases. The hall was heated by an open hearth, the smoke escaping by a saddle-type louvre or vents in the gables at each end of the hipped roof.

Wealden houses are often very well built, ample timbers of heavy section being used, and they were often decorated both on roof trusses and external timberwork. The type emerged fully-developed towards the end of the fourteenth century and flourished until towards the end of the sixteenth, maintaining a standard of design, construction and decoration to which other farmers in different parts of the country might aspire but rarely attain. The Wealden houses were indeed the dwellings of yeoman farmers, not gentlemen. Although concentrated in Kent, Sussex, Essex and Surrey, Wealden houses may be seen in other parts of lowland England and an urban version is even more widespread.[6]

Although the Wealden house is the most fully-developed of its type, the arrangement of hall flanked by two-storey wings under a single roof but without the jettied upper storey was widespread through the country.

---

9. WEALDEN AND OTHER OPEN-HALL HOUSES

a. Ground-floor plan showing hall (1), open hearth (2), cross-passage (3) and, opening off it, the buttery and pantry (4 and 5); at the opposite end of the hall are two unheated parlours (6).
b. First-floor plan with upper part of open hall (7) and a solar (8 and 9) on each side and reached by separate staircases.
c. Cross-section through the hall at the cross-passage showing doors to buttery and pantry and to staircase.
d. Cross-section showing the truss in the open hall.
e. Sketch of Wealden house showing the entrance door which leads to the cross-passage, the tall window which lights the open hall, the upper floors here shown jettied to the front at the left-hand end of the building and jettied to front and side at the right hand; the whole is covered by a hipped roof with gablets which would help in evacuation of smoke.
f. Ground-floor plan of a Wealden houses as commonly transformed in the late sixteenth century; a fireplace has been inserted in the cross-passage.
g. Upper part of transformed Wealden house showing chimney stack with fireplace serving the newly-formed chamber over the hall.
h. Sketch of transformed Wealden house.
i. In some Wealden houses the entrance and cross-passage are incorporated in one of the 'wings'.
j. Often the hearth was moved towards the cross-passage, and a partition in the roof truss above created a smoke bay which served as a rudimentary chimney.

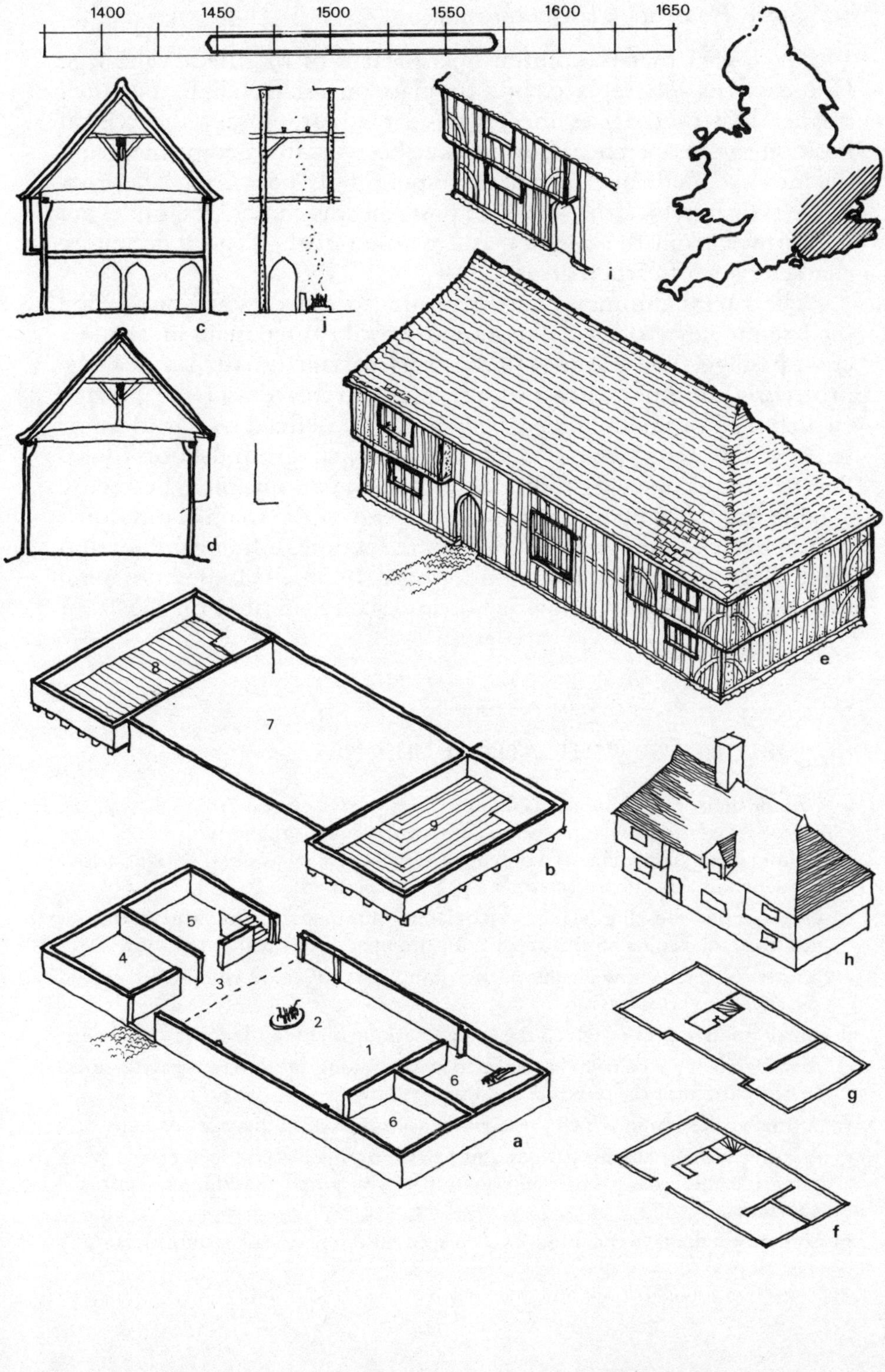
1400
1450
1500
1550
1600
1650
c
j
i
d
e
8
7
9
b
5
4
3
2
1
6
6
a
h
g
f

10. *Small House with lateral chimney*

We have seen that the central open hearth of the medieval Large House was usually replaced by a fireplace on a side wall. In the much smaller hall of the late medieval yeoman or peasant the central position for an open hearth must have been far from convenient and the move to a side or end wall correspondingly beneficial. There is a house type in which the side-wall position was chosen. Examples are not numerous in the country as a whole but the type is definitely characteristic of certain areas.

The lateral chimney house is similar to others which succeeded the late medieval open-hall houses in having three main units and a cross-passage. The entrance to the cross-passage usually lay near the projecting chimney breast of the main fireplace and the passage (which may or may not have been precisely defined by partitions or screens) ran across one end of the principal ground-floor room. Service rooms opened off the passage, and a parlour, often heated by a gable fireplace, opened off the other end of the main room. Such houses had chambers extending over the whole of the first floor and often there were garret rooms in addition. In Small Houses the lateral fireplace was usually, though not invariably, located on the front

---

10. SMALL HOUSE WITH LATERAL CHIMNEY

a. Ground-floor plan showing the living-room (1), fireplace in front side wall (2), cross-passage or cross-entry between opposed doors (3) and with two service rooms (4 and 5) opening off it; beyond the hall or living-room there is a parlour (6) which in this case is heated by a gable fireplace (7).
b. Cross-section showing relationship of lateral chimney stack to the main roof; at this stage the rooms on the upper floor might well be open to the roof.
c. Isometric sketch showing the relationship between lateral chimney stack and entrance into cross-passage.
d. An alternative plan in which the heated parlour is alongside the cross-passage.
e. A variation of the plan having a heated kitchen alongside the cross-passage and a heated parlour at the opposite end of the house.
f. A smaller version in which there are no rooms beyond the cross-passage.
g. A larger version having parlour and service rooms placed together in a wing alongside the cross-passage and a multi-storey porch marking the entrance doorway.
h. Sometimes the lateral chimney was placed on the rear wall as in this plan.

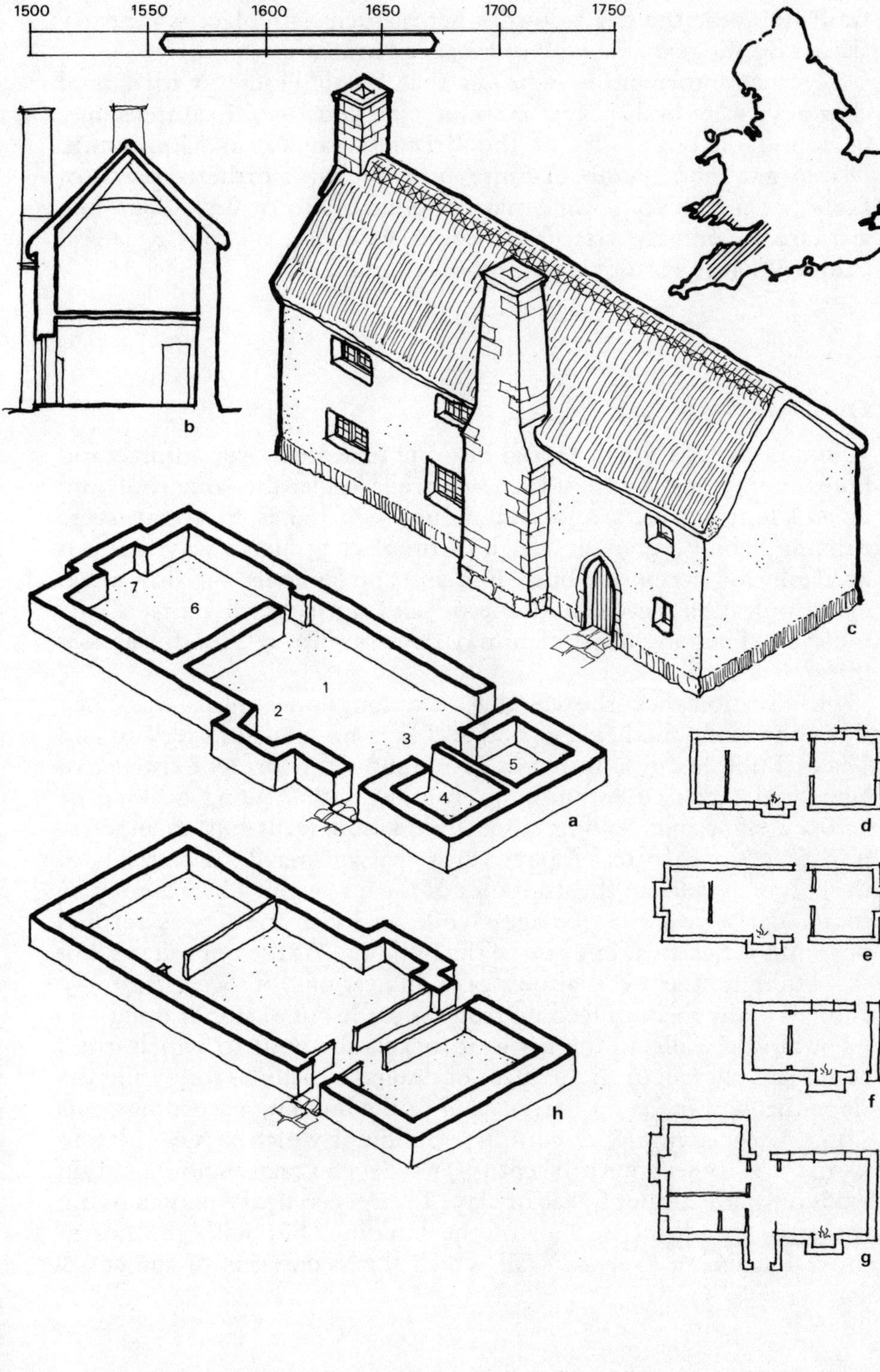
1500
1550
1600
1650
1700
1750
b
c
7
6
1
2
3
5
4
a
d
e
h
f
g

wall, alongside the front door, whereas such a fireplace was nearly always on the rear side wall of a Large House.

Present information indicates that Small Houses with lateral chimneys were built between about 1570 and 1650. Examples may be found on both sides of the Bristol Channel: in Monmouth, Glamorgan and Pembrokeshire and in the northern parts of Somerset and Devon. Some may be found in North Wales, but they are rare in other parts of the country where, of course, lateral chimney Large Houses are common enough.

11. *Longhouse*

A longhouse is a Small House but one in which farm animals and humans are housed within the same walls, under the same roof, and in an elongated rectangular building which has a cross-passage running behind the main hearth or fireplace in such a way that it is available for access by both humans and animals and for inter-communication between domestic and agricultural parts of the building. The longhouse plan may develop through subdivision or through accretion.

Excavation has shown that the longhouse plan was used throughout the medieval period and in many parts of England and Wales. Published results of excavation show the former existence of elongated rectangular buildings running either along a slope or across a slope and having stone foundation walls but an indeterminate superstructure.[7] A paved cross-passage may be detected with the entrance at about the midpoint of the side walls; a hearth may be found fairly near this passage, while an inner room was formed beyond the hearth at one end of the building. At the opposite end of the building the excavations give indications of occupation by animals in the form of feeding troughs made out of stones along one or both side walls, in the form of sockets for posts to which cattle could be tethered, or in the form of drainage channels following the slope through the end or front wall of the building according to its siting. Early examples of complete buildings which survive (dating from the early seventeenth century) have such a plan enclosed within walls of stone, timber frame or clay. They retain the two main living spaces of the domestic half of the building, but with the hearth moved against a fireback wall which forms one side of the cross-

9 *Old Glasson Farmhouse, Thurnham, Lancs.*
The relative positions of doorway and main chimney stack suggest a cross-passage plan, with accommodation for animals to the left and domestic accommodation (originally open to the roof) to the right. The walls are mainly cobbled and the roof was of thatch. (NMR)

10 *House in Worton, Wensleydale, Yorks. W.R.*
Like so many Small Houses in the Yorkshire Dales this has the two-unit plan. The stone walls have widely slobbered pointing and the stone-flagged roof is laid to a low pitch. Steps lead to a granary alongside. (WGM)

11 *Lion Inn, Adleigh, Essex.*
Although now used as an inn this is a good example of an L-shaped Small House. The main range is double-fronted, one room deep and not quite symmetrical; accommodation is extended by means of the wing leading at right angles to the rear. (NMR)

12 *House in Littleborough, Lancs.*
A two-storey house with double-pile plan covered by a low-pitched roof of stone flags. There could have been a continuous run of twelve lights in a mullioned window if the upper floor were ever used for domestic industry. The different character of masonry blocking the window lights from that in the main wall is worth note. (GDB)

passage, and with the 'inner room' divided in some instances between a parlour and smaller space equipped with stone shelves as a dairy. In such buildings cattle are tethered either nose-on to the passage (which presumably served as a feeding passage) or in some other way in an integral cowhouse which has separate external access but which retains intercommunication with the domestic part by way of the cross-passage.

Generally the surviving longhouses have an intermediate floor in the house proper with staircase access to the chambers from the parlour, or from the rear of the living kitchen, or from alongside the hearth. A stage in which the inner rooms were lofted while the living kitchen remained as an open hall was almost certainly included in the development, hence the use of a staircase at the parlour end; though it is rather surprising to find in many examples from the north west of England that the staircase rises from *within* the parlour. Probably the most common arrangement is that in which the staircase rises from the rear wall of the living kitchen – either confined as a mural staircase or, in the later examples, as a double-flight staircase in a rearward projection. The most compact arrangement is that in which a winding staircase enters the fireback wall against the cross-passage and emerges alongside the chimney at first-floor level; such an arrangement was favoured in the southern half of Wales.

In essence the domestic part of a longhouse contained the accommodation of a two-unit Small House and one can see how the rough rectangular building revealed in so many excavations could have been subdivided by walls and partitions, inserted floors and added fireplaces until the fully-developed longhouse emerged. Equally one can see how the longhouse was superseded by a set of distinct buildings: the domestic part becoming the two-unit house and the agricultural part becoming cowhouse, stable, etc. But certain longhouses appear to have been formed as a result of the *addition* of cowhouse, stable, barn, etc., to an existing two-unit Small House, for whenever such a house had a gable entry a cross-passage was formed between house and attached farm buildings in such a way that intercommunication between the two parts was possible even if the farm buildings each had separate entrances.[8] The understanding of the longhouse form is complicated by the practice of alternate re-building wherein the domestic part of a longhouse was rebuilt while the agricultural part was retained and then the improved domestic part was retained while the old agricultural part was rebuilt. In such a process the overall dimensions of the longhouse might remain unaltered and generally the cross-passage retained its original position, perhaps even with its original doorway, but walls in the two parts may be of different materials, roofs of different height, pitch and covering material and the doors and windows might be of different periods.

Surviving longhouses are generally of the late seventeenth or early eighteenth century, but there are some examples, especially in the south-west and West Midlands, which are much older, possibly late medieval, while in the north west, at least, longhouses seem to have been under construction well into the eighteenth century and in Wales longhouses were being formed by accretion throughout that century and possibly later. Longhouses are characteristic of the western half of the country, but examples are also found in East Yorkshire and the former distribution may have been much more widespread.

---

11. LONGHOUSE

a. Ground-floor plan showing living-room/kitchen (1) off which opens an unheated parlour (2) and also a pantry (3); the hearth in its inglenook (4) backs on to the cross-passage (5) which also gives an alternative access to the cowhouse (6). In this instance a winding staircase (7) leads to the upper floor.

b. Cross-section taken through the staircase and showing the chimney hood above the inglenook.

c. Sketch to show the relationship between the two parts of the longhouse and the way in which the cross-passage is associated with the farming part.

d. An alternative plan with living-room/kitchen (8) and parlour (9), all reached by a cross-passage (10) which also serves as a feeding passage for animals (11).

e. Plan based on excavations to show the true longhouse with its cross-passage between parts for humans and animals (12 and 13).

f. Developed plan with parts for humans and animals more clearly separated but with both using the same cross-passage. The house (14) and byre (15) are part of the same structure.

g. Plan to show how cross-passage and farm buildings were added to an existing house of two units which had gable entry. The cross-passage leads to the original house (16) but also serves the cowhouse (17), which has a stable attached (18).

h. Sketch to show a stage of alternate rebuilding in which the farming part is later and of higher quality than the domestic.

i. Sketch to show a stage in which the domestic part is later than the farming part in its reconstruction.

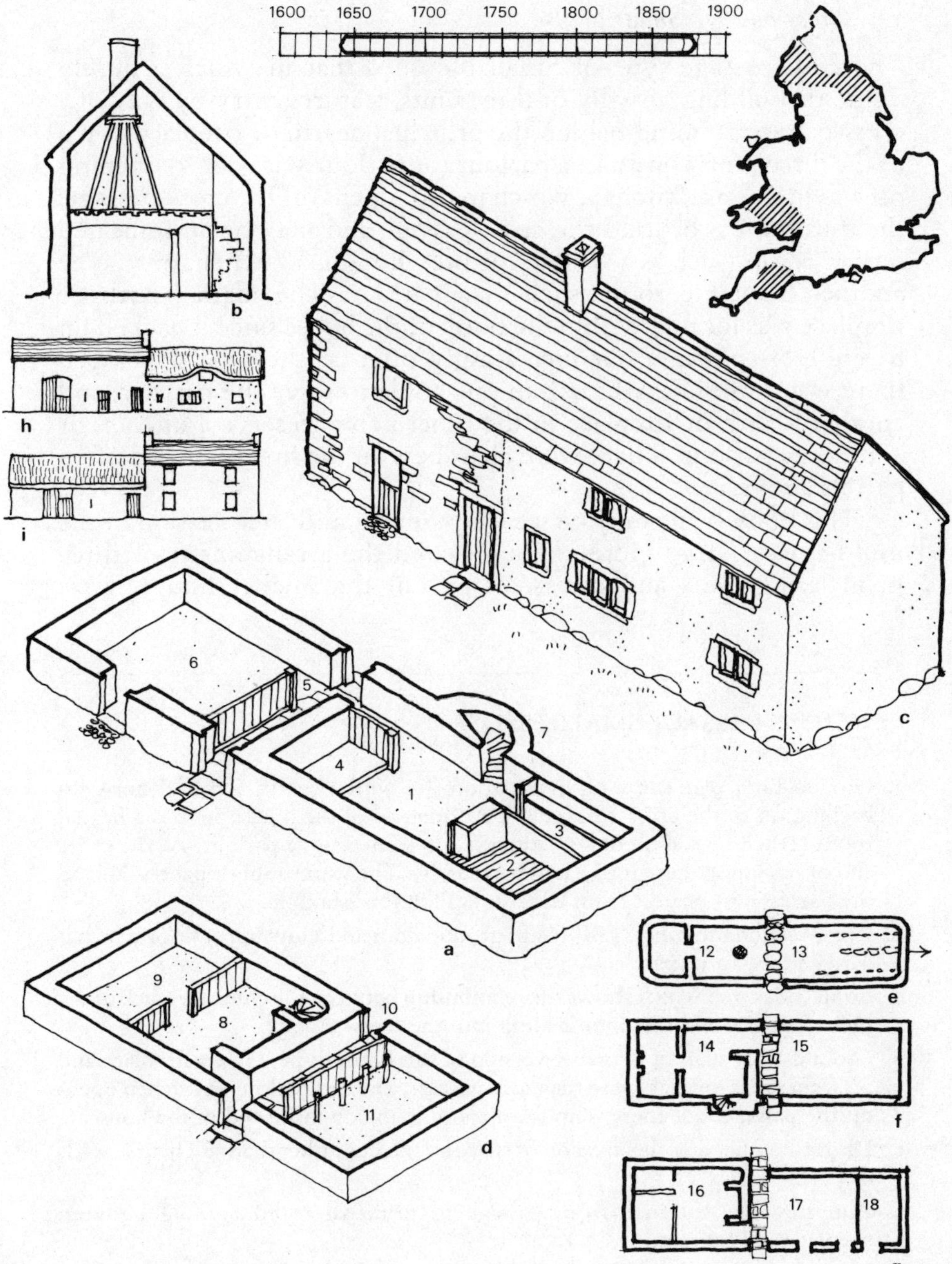
1600
1650
1700
1750
1800
1850
1900
a
b
c
d
e
f
g
h
i
1
2
3
4
5
6
7
8
9
10
11
12
13
14
15
16
17
18

12. *Cross-passage Small House*

The cross-passage type of Small House is that in which a purely domestic building, usually of three units, features entry by way of a cross-passage running behind the principal hearth or fireplace. Two of the three units consist of a parlour (or parlour with dairy) opening off a living-room/kitchen, which in turn opens off the cross-passage; the third unit is beyond the cross-passage and may be an unheated service room (such as a scullery or brewhouse), a kitchen, or maybe another habitable room such as a parlour. The main hearth or fireplace was located within the body of the house since it backed on to the cross-passage, but increasingly often as the type developed there was a subsidiary hearth in one gable to serve the parlour, and another hearth or fireplace in the other gable to serve a kitchen or additional parlour. There were chambers on the first floor and often garrets above.

This house-type may be seen as a smaller and later version of the multi-storey Large House. They shared the arrangement of three main living units and cross-passage but the smaller houses were

---

12. CROSS-PASSAGE SMALL HOUSE

a. Ground-floor plan showing living-room (1) with a hearth and inglenook (2) backing on to the cross-passage (3). At one end of the house there is a heated room (4) which is sometimes a kitchen and sometimes a parlour. At the other end of the house there is a heated parlour (5). The storeroom or pantry (6) and the staircase (7) project from the rear wall in this example.
b. Cross-section showing a full-height ground floor and a low upper floor which is partly in the roof space.
c. Isometric sketch which shows the relationship between the chimney stack of the main fireplace and the door leading into the cross-passage.
d. Ground-floor plan of a smaller version of this house-type. Here a fireplace and adjacent staircase back on to the cross-passage, a heated parlour or kitchen opens off the passage, but there is no third room at the opposite end of the house.
e. Diagram indicating the division of space by screens rather than full height walls or partitions.
f. Plan showing entrance from passage to principal room coming between fireplace and staircase.
g. Plan showing the fireplace centrally placed under the ridge; the staircase projects from the rear wall.

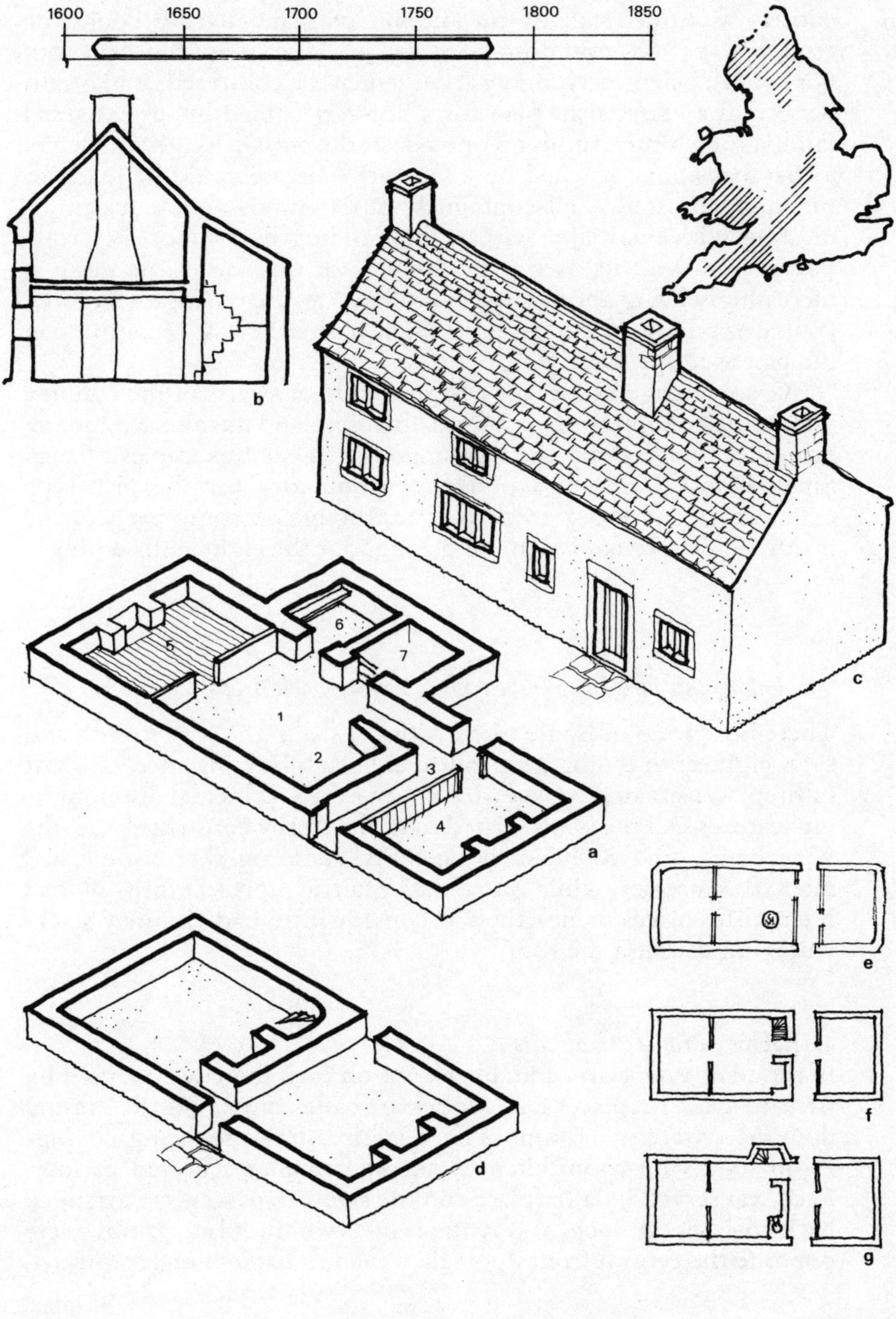
1600
1650
1700
1750
1800
1850
b
c
1
2
3
4
5
6
7
a
d
e
f
g

entirely asymmetrical; by no amount of manoeuvring could the cross-passage and front door be placed in the centre of the elevation, nor could a balanced chimney arrangement be contrived. It may also be seen as a convenient plan for a house occupied by an extended family, for a heated room on one side of the cross-passage which had a chamber above reached by a separate staircase could be made to function almost as a self-contained house-within-a-house, communicating with the major part of the building by way of the cross-passage but with its own entry by way of that same passage. It is increasingly being appreciated that such an arrangement for a retired couple or widow or widower might have been at least as common in the past as it is nowadays.

Cross-passage houses may be seen in many parts of the country with some concentration in the north of England but also with many examples found along the limestone belt. Dated examples of such Small Houses indicate a period of popularity for the plan-type extending from about 1660 to 1740, though in some parts of the north the plan remained in use throughout the eighteenth century.

13. *Lobby entrance house/house with back-to-back fireplaces*

There is a group of house plans widely used in the seventeenth and early eighteenth century which had either a lobby entrance, or a pair of fireplaces situated back-to-back, or both, as principal distinguishing features. All the plans related to multi-storey construction, some were based on two main living units, some on three, some had internal staircases while some had staircase projections, all had internal fireplaces or hearths and consequently had chimney stacks emerging through the roof.

a. *Lobby entrance; two units*

In this plan-type two habitable rooms on each floor were served by back-to-back fireplaces and a lobby or baffle entry. On the ground floor there were two rooms of unequal size, the larger being a living-room (or living-room/kitchen) and the smaller a heated parlour. Each was served by a fireplace and the two fireplaces were arranged back-to-back in such a way that the two fireplace jambs were opposite the central front door; they made a baffle which protected the two rooms from the draughts and so created a small lobby within the front door. On the first floor there were two chambers and one or both might have a fireplace located over the ground-floor fireplaces and with flues combined in a common chimney stack. There were often garret rooms above the chambers. The house was almost symmetrical in elevation, was almost cubiform in mass, and was dominated by this compact block of fireplaces and chimneys.

There were three possible positions for the staircase which linked these various levels: in one, probably the oldest variation, the staircase was apparently considered as part of the double chimney breast, a tight spiral tucked between fireplaces and rear wall; in a second, probably the most numerous, the staircase was a wooden winding or newel staircase fitted into the lobby between the entrance door and the jambs of fireplaces which were pushed back to accommodate it; in the third position the staircase was pushed out into a wing or turret at the rear. Where there was a porch in front of the door as well as a staircase at the rear the plan became a miniature version of the cruciform Large House.

The basic two units were sometimes extended by further rooms at the rear to form a T-shaped or H-shaped plan; but the designers must still have been thinking in terms of a two-unit lobby entrance house, since they maintained on the front elevation the sturdy compact appearance, dominated by the huge chimney stack and its grouped flues.

The two-unit lobby entrance plan was in common use in the eastern half of the country from Lincoln to Essex but is found elsewhere. Most examples appear to date from the first half of the seventeenth century but some may be earlier and others were built later in that century.

b. *Lobby entrance, three units*

The other popular version of the lobby entrance plan had three units instead of two in the main block, presenting an elongated elevation rather than a compact one to the observer.

On the ground floor there were two rooms (usually assumed to have been living-room and kitchen) served by the two back-to-back fireplaces, but a third room opened off the larger of the two principal rooms. Usually this room appears to have been an unheated parlour but sometimes, and especially in later examples, it had its own fireplace in the end wall. However it is possible that in some instances the third room was considered as an unheated service room and the smaller heated room as the parlour. Entrance to the whole building was by way of a door opening on to the lobby against the fireplace jambs and it would have been as easy to make a heated parlour and chamber above into a house-within-a-house as in the corresponding cross-passage houses. There were similar variations in the position of the staircase as found in the two-unit version but with an additional variation when the staircase was placed at the rear of the third room. Examples are widespread in lowland England and Wales and range in date from early seventeenth century to well into the eighteenth century.

c. *Fireplaces back-to-back, entrance away from the fireplaces*
It is perhaps paradoxical to include with this group of house plans one type in which there is no baffle or lobby entry and yet the

---

13. LOBBY-ENTRANCE HOUSE/HOUSE WITH BACK-TO-BACK FIREPLACES

a. Ground-floor plan of a two-unit house with lobby entrance: the living-room/kitchen (1) has a deep fireplace (2) and the parlour (3) has its own fireplace (4) placed back-to-back so that the two fireplaces and chimney stacks make a compact central block; the entrance (5) is into a lobby against the staircase (6) which is squeezed against the jambs of the central fireplaces.
b. Cross-section showing the two full-height storeys and the fireplace in the upper floor joining with the stack from the ground-floor fireplaces.
c. Isometric sketch showing the relationship between chimney stack and doorway.
d. An alternative ground-floor plan with living-room/kitchen (5) and, in this case, an unheated parlour (6) and with staircase (7) located between fireplace and rear wall; the entrance (8) leads to a lobby against the fireplace jamb.
e. Another version of the plan with living-room/kitchen and parlour and back-to-back fireplaces; projecting at the rear is a staircase and at the front a multi-storey porch.
f. Sketch showing the cruciform arrangement dependent on the massive central chimney stack.
g. An alternative plan with a service room projected at the rear.
h. Plan showing a third unit, a kitchen, added to the rear of the two basic units.

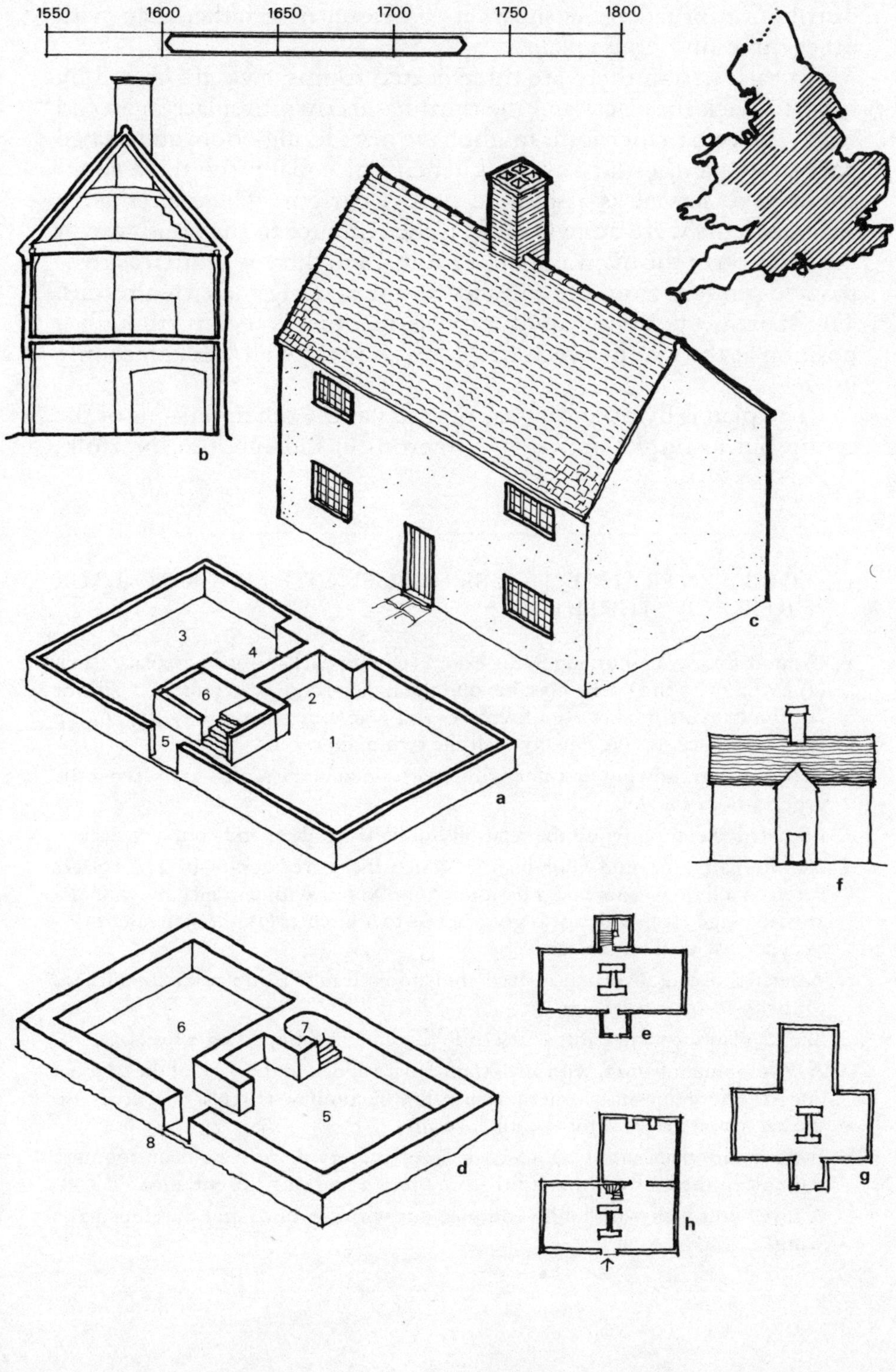
1550
1600
1650
1700
1750
1800
b
c
3
4
6
2
5
1
a
f
e
6
7
5
8
d
h
g

distribution of examples shows it to belong here rather than with other three-unit house plans.

In this version there are three heated rooms: two are heated by back-to-back fireplaces and the third has its own fireplace in an end wall. The two main rooms might have been living-room and heated parlour while the third was a kitchen but equally the third room could have served as a separate heated parlour. These alternative arrangements were quite feasible as the entrance to the house was at the junction of the main and third rooms, and there was often a cross-passage running from the entrance and separating these two rooms. The staircase position could vary as in other versions, though a position at the rear between fireplaces and rear wall was commonly used.

The plan is by no means as common as the other versions of the group but examples are fairly numerous in Lincolnshire, Norfolk,

---

13. LOBBY-ENTRANCE HOUSE/HOUSE WITH BACK-TO-BACK FIREPLACES, THREE UNITS

a. Ground-floor plan showing living-room (1) with back-to-back fireplace block (2) serving also the kitchen (3); beyond the living-room is an unheated parlour (4); the staircase lies between fireplaces and rear wall (5) and the entry (6) is a lobby entrance serving equally well the two main rooms.
b. Cross-section showing first-floor fireplaces added in the same stack serving the ground-floor fireplaces.
c. Isometric sketch showing the relationship between door and chimney stack.
d. An alternative ground-floor plan in which there are back-to-back fireplaces between a living-room and a parlour (7 and 8) but with entrance by way of a cross-passage (10), which also gives access to a kitchen (9): the staircase (11) is associated with the fireplace.
e. A detail showing that back-to-back inglenooks lead to a similar arrangement as for back-to-back fireplaces.
f. Sketch plan showing baffle entry or lobby entry against a single fireplace.
g. A development from f. with an extra fireplace added to the back of the original one – the door does not lie on the centre-line of combined fireplaces; there is also shown here a fireplace for the inner room.
h. A three-unit plan with back-to-back fireplaces serving the two main rooms, a staircase in the lobby and a multi-storey porch marking the entrance.
i. A three-unit plan with lobby entrance but with the third unit developed as a wing.

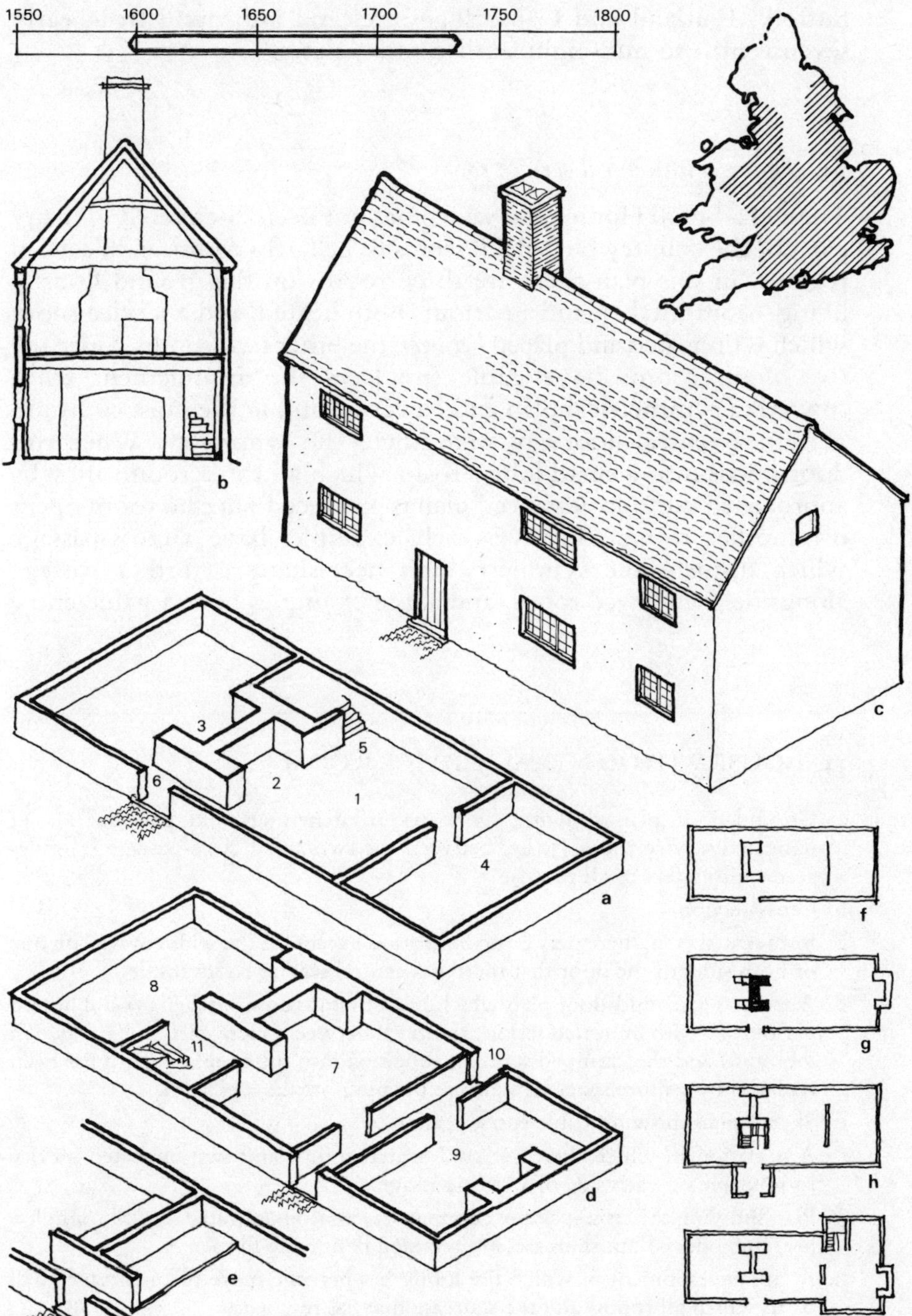
1550
1600
1650
1700
1750
1800
b
c
3
5
6
2
1
4
a
f
8
11
7
10
9
d
g
h
e
i

Suffolk, Rutland and Cambridgeshire, and are found from early seventeenth- to mid-eighteenth-century dates.

14. *House with central service room*

There is a Small House plan which has not been discovered in many parts of the country but which seems to be fairly common in certain regions. In this plan there are three rooms on the ground floor: a living-room/kitchen and a parlour, both heated, and a service room which is unheated and placed *between* the other two rooms. Since the two main rooms have gable fireplaces the arrangement tends towards a symmetrical plan and elevation and in the most common version a central doorway strengthens the symmetry. When this door opens into a small lobby from which all three rooms may be approached quite an advanced plan is produced since no room opens off another room. However early examples have a cross-passage which disturbs the symmetry and necessitates a further passage alongside the service room, and some examples have a gable entry

---

14. HOUSE WITH CENTRAL SERVICE ROOM

a. Ground-floor plan showing living-room/kitchen (1) and parlour (2); an unheated service room (3) lies between the two and a cross-passage (4) gives access ultimately to all rooms.
b. Cross-section.
c. Isometric sketch; there may be no indication except for the width of wall on one or both sides of the door that there is a central service room inside.
d. Alternative ground-floor plan which has a living-room/kitchen (5) and heated parlour (6) with unheated service room (7) between. Here entry is by way of a lobby (8) and the cramped staircase squeezed into the fireplace jamb has been replaced by a more spacious staircase opening off the lobby (9).
e. Sketch plan showing gable entry version.
f. A variation in which there are two heated rooms and two unheated service rooms, one on each side of a cross-passage.
g. Plan showing the cross-passage eliminated; a central unheated service room has been introduced but staircases are retained beside the fireplaces.
h. A late development in which the lobby has become more of an entrance hall from which all rooms and the staircase may be reached.

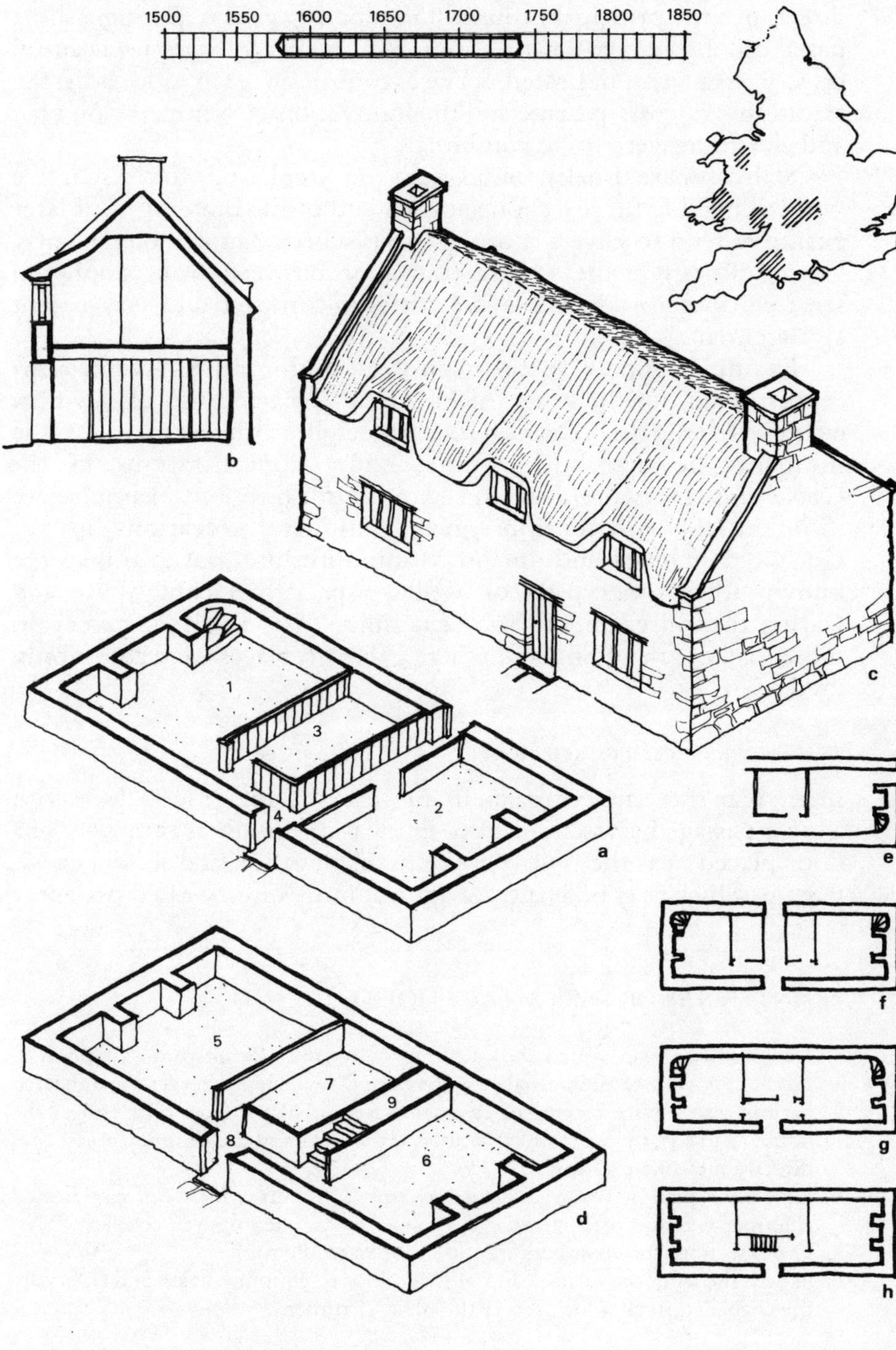
1500 1550 1600 1650 1700 1750 1800 1850
b
c
1
2
3
4
a
5
6
7
8
9
d
e
f
g
h

direct into the principal ground-floor room, again requiring a short passage alongside the service room. In a few early examples a central cross-passage has unheated service rooms on each side as if the tradition of a cross-passage and the innovation of symmetry on plan and elevation were to be combined.

Staircases are usually found with the fireplaces, often a staircase with each gable fireplace, one at each end of the building. But later examples tend to have a more spacious staircase more conveniently located alongside the service room, or between front door and service room, producing a delightfully compact and convenient arrangement.

Examples appear to be mainly of mid- or late-seventeenth-century date but the range of known dated buildings of this plan extends from late sixteenth to early eighteenth century. At the moment the distribution gives some concentrations in the Cotswolds, Dorset and upland Monmouthshire, but examples are moment the distribution gives some concentrations in the Cotswolds, Dorset and upland Monmouthshire, but examples are known from other parts of Wales, especially Denbighshire and Carmarthenshire, and further examples may await discovery in those many parts of England where gable fireplaces were commonly used.[9]

15. *Internal cross-passage house*

In this plan there are two main living spaces on the ground floor with a cross-passage between the two. Entry to the house was by way of a door placed near the centre of the main elevation and so to a cross-passage which may be a true passage but more often was a cross-entry

---

15. INTERNAL CROSS-PASSAGE HOUSE

a. Ground-floor plan which shows the main room, a living-room/kitchen (1), reached by way of an internal cross-passage (2) which also serves the unheated parlour and service rooms (or two service rooms) at the opposite end of the house (3 and 4); the staircase (5) located at the corner of the chimney breast rises directly into one chamber.
b. First-floor plan with an unheated chamber (6) off which opens a heated chamber which is often decorated as a room of some importance (7).
c. Cross-section: the chambers are shown open to the roof.
d. Sketch showing the relationship of front door to chimney stacks and especially the corbelled stack which serves the main chamber.

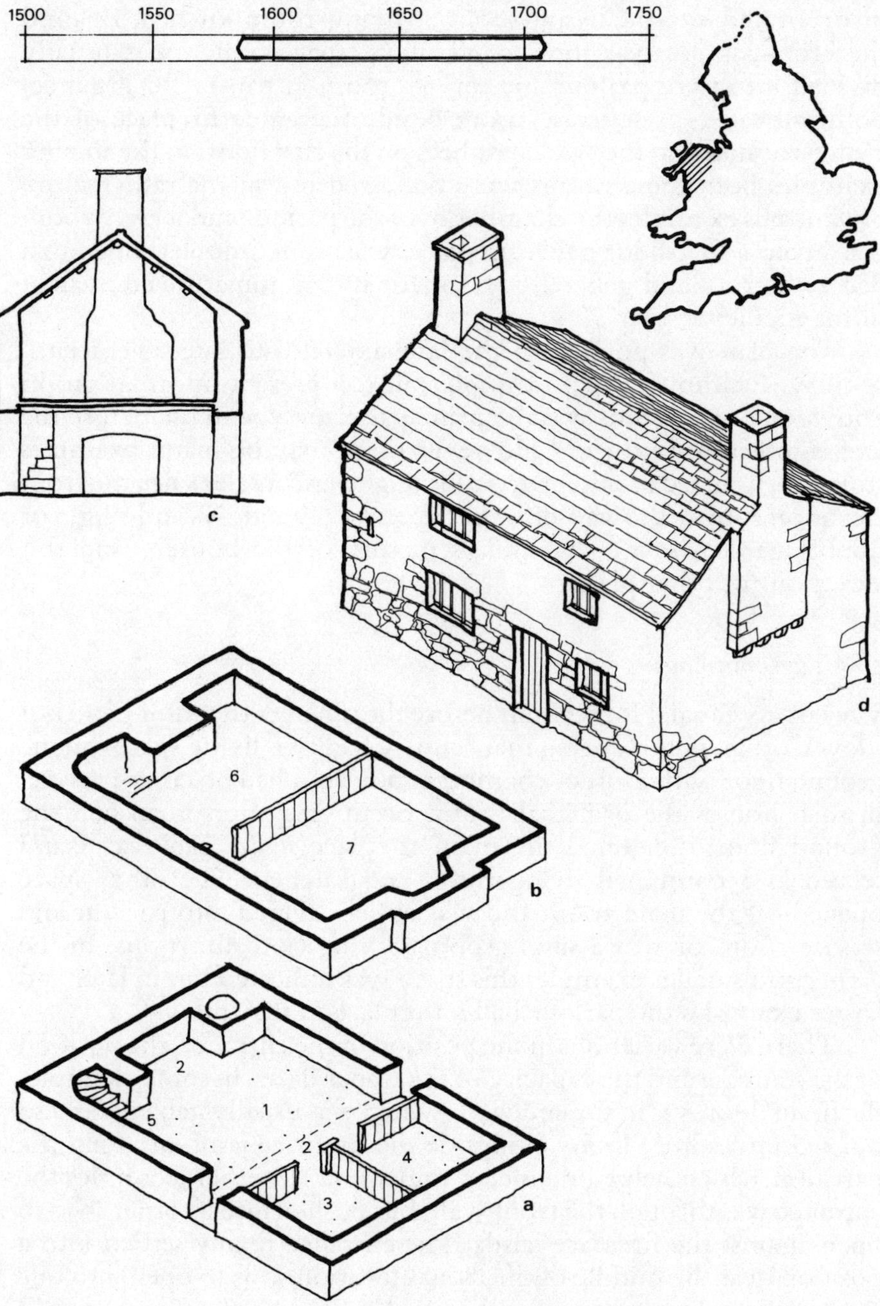
1500
1550
1600
1650
1700
1750
c
d
6
7
b
2
1
5
2
4
3
a

incorporated into the living-room or living-room/kitchen. Beyond the cross-passage was the second living space which was usually divided into two: parlour and service room (a pantry for instance) both unheated. A staircase rising beside the gable fireplace of the living-room led to the two chambers on the first floor. In the smaller examples both these rooms were unheated but in the rather more pretentious examples the chamber over the parlour and service room was given a first-floor gable fireplace, was sometimes left open to a decorated roof and generally was made into a miniature equivalent of the medieval solar.

The plan was popular in the late sixteenth to late seventeenth century. Examples are most numerous (on present information) in Snowdonia where this was the principal plan-type in use before the late eighteenth century.[10] However there may be many examples still unrecognized in other parts of England and Wales since the front elevation simply shows a door between two windows and single or double gable stacks – the child's picture of the house – and this elevation fits other plans.

16. *Two-unit house*

Very many Small Houses built before the nineteenth century and not a few Cottages built during that century had two living spaces on the ground floor with a loft or chambers above but had no cross-passage. In such houses the principal room, occupying more than half the ground floor, contained the main fireplace in its gable wall and served as a combined living-room and kitchen. The other space opened off the main room and was either divided into parlour and service room or was a single room serving both functions. In the earlier and smaller examples this space was unheated but in later and larger examples the parlour had a fireplace in the end wall.

There were variations in the position of the entrance, the position of the staircase and the capacity of the upper floor. In some examples the main door was in the end wall (which was usually gabled), and so opened into a little lobby alongside the fireplace jamb or along the partition which helped define an inglenook. In other examples the entrance was through the front wall, but pushed into a corner so as to open against the fireplace jamb. The entrance finally settled into a position near the middle of the front elevation so as to open into one corner of the living-room/kitchen and against the partition or wall which separated the two living spaces on the ground floor. This

13 *Cottages in Hatfield Broad Oak, Essex.*
This reflected pair of early nineteenth-century cottages illustrates the double-pile single-fronted cottage plan in its minimum dimensions. The decaying rendering reveals walls of clay lump. (JMcC)

14 *Cottages in Styal, Cheshire.*
These cottages are part of the small planned industrial village of Styal. They are raised over cellars which have separate access and could have been used either for industry or habitation. (GW)

15 *Laithe house at Calderbrook, Lancs.*
Set in a characteristically bleak moorland location, this laithe house combines domestic and farming accommodation in approximately equal proportions. Certain mullions have been removed and modern window frames inserted. (RWB)

16 *Castle Street, Ruthin, Denbighs.*
Some wide but many narrow plots have buildings generally with gables to the street. Most of the buildings are timber framed. (RWB)

17 *Market End, Coggeshall, Essex.*
Again, narrow plots are filled with tall narrow houses, but plaster cladding conceals timber-frame. (NMR)

18 *High Street, Lewes, Sussex.*
Frontages are generally wide though continuously built-up; there are cornices rather than gables to the street; timber frame hides behind brick and tile skins. (NMR)

central doorway was in fact rarely placed exactly in the centre of the elevation as such a position would affect the proportions of the two rooms; in the smaller and later examples the door was pushed noticeably to one side, but in the majority of examples the offset was so slight that it has often passed unnoticed.

The staircase might rise from alongside the main fireplace, from within the parlour, by way of a projection from the rear wall, or as a simple timber-framed steeply inclined set of steps within one corner of the main room. The first type was probably the oldest and survived long in the stone-walled houses of upland districts; it was compact and took very little space on either ground floor or first floor, but such a narrow winding staircase became inconvenient. The second type was the most convenient: housed in a projection the staircase intruded on neither floor; being central it conveniently served the first-floor rooms, and the rear projection made a start which was followed for other extensions to the plan. The various staircases became more significant as the upper floor developed from a mere loft lit by gable windows or low dormers into a storey of full height lit by windows at the front.

The two-unit house belongs to the eighteenth century even though examples in the late seventeenth century are quite common and even though smaller versions, really at the Cottage level, were built well into the nineteenth century. Examples may be found in virtually every part of the country, but the two-unit plan was the dominant plan-type for its period in many upland regions such as the southern half of Cumbria.

17. *T-shaped and L-shaped Small Houses*

The general arrangements of the two-unit house plan suited the Renaissance idea of a balanced elevation but could not provide the greater amount of accommodation which was increasingly required as living standards improved. A house which is one room deep and two rooms wide can, up to a point, provide extra floor area but it cannot readily provide extra rooms. Various methods were employed, therefore, to increase accommodation without affecting the appearance of the main elevation.

One way of increasing floor area was to extend at the rear with a wing which produced an L-shaped or a T-shaped plan. The main block retained living-room and parlour with entrance in between,

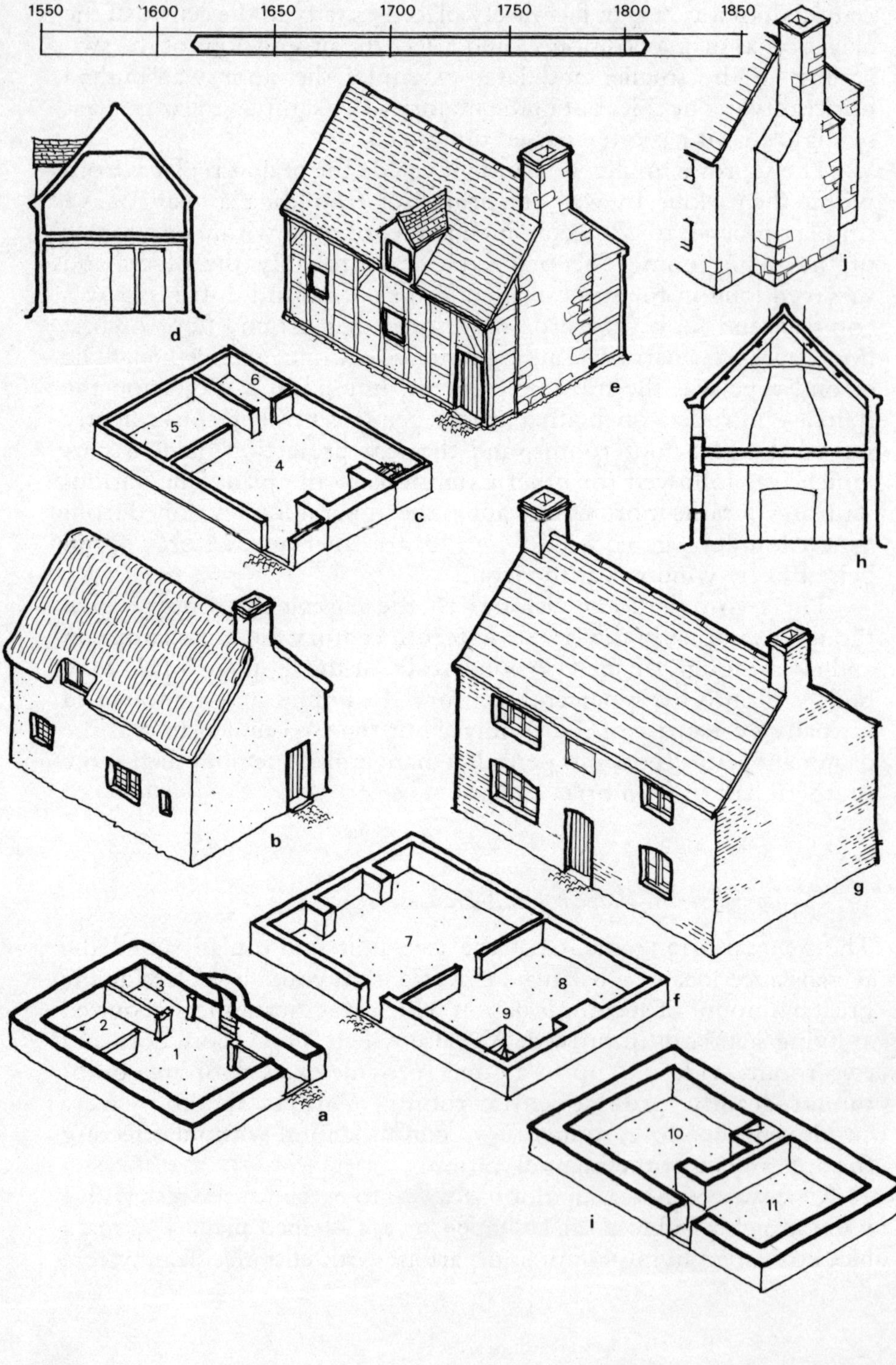

1550
1600
1650
1700
1750
1800
1850
d
e
j
h
c
6
5
4
b
g
f
7
8
9
a
3
2
1
i
10
11

16. TWO-UNIT HOUSE

a. Ground-floor plan of a gable entry two-unit house showing the living-room/kitchen (1) and a second unit here divided between parlour (2) and buttery/pantry (3), both unheated.
b. Sketch to show gable entry.
c. Ground-floor plan of a two-unit house with front entry alongside the fireplace and leading into the living-room/kitchen (4); again the second unit is divided into parlour (5) and buttery/pantry (6).
d. Cross-section showing an upper floor lit by a dormer window.
e. Isometric sketch showing relationship between door and chimney stack.
f. Third version of ground-floor plan with front entry into living-room/kitchen (7) off which opens a parlour (8), which is heated in this case, and from which a staircase rises to the upper floor (9).
g. Sketch to show the central doorway and flanking chimney stacks; this elevation is common to several plan types.
h. Cross-section.
i. A further type of two-unit plan in which entry is into a living-room/kitchen (10) off which opens a heated parlour (11); there is no cross-passage nor does the door make a lobby entrance against a chimney stack.
j. Sketch to show chimney breast and stack projecting from the gable wall.

---

the extension contained a kitchen with its fireplace in the gable wall, possibly a scullery or pantry, and a staircase near the junction of main block and wing and so in a convenient position to serve the three bedrooms on the first floor.

Such an arrangement was quite widely employed during the eighteenth century especially in the brick farmhouses serving the lowland counties of the Midlands.

18. *Two-unit house with an extra bay*

Another way of extending the two-unit house was to add an extra bay to the end of the main block. This meant that the roofing problems involved in the L-shaped or T-shaped plan were avoided and it also meant that a more imposing elevation was produced. Of course it was no longer a symmetrical elevation but the symmetry and significance of the two main living units were marked by devices such as the provision of false quoins or corner stones at the junction of main block and extension.

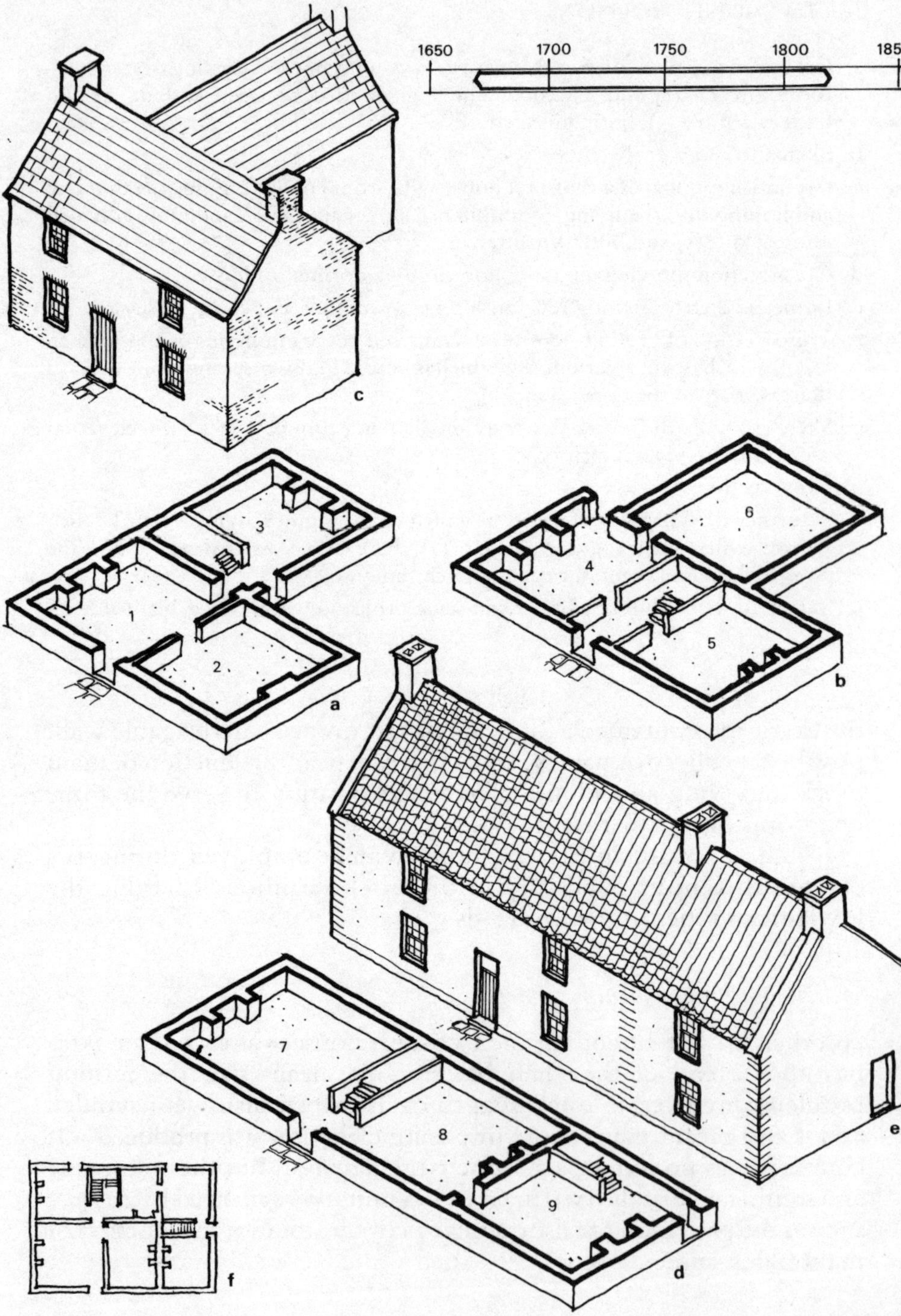
1650
1700
1750
1800
1850
c
1
2
3
a
4
5
6
b
7
8
9
d
e
f

17 and 18. T-SHAPED AND L-SHAPED HOUSES; HOUSE WITH AN EXTRA BAY

a. L-shaped plan with living-room and parlour (1 and 2) and a kitchen (3) at the rear making the leg of the L.
b. T-shaped plan with living-room (4), parlour (5) and the extra room (6), the kitchen, making extra accommodation without affecting the elevation.
c. Sketch of house with L-shaped plan.
d. Ground-floor plan of house with extra bay; the entrance leads to a living-room/kitchen (7) and parlour (8) making a two-unit plan but the extra bay contains the 'men's end' (9) with its own access to a separate bedroom above.
e. Isometric sketch showing the relationship of the extra bay to the main block.
f. Another plan in which the house is two rooms deep and two rooms wide; the extra bay is also two rooms deep.

The extra bay could conveniently serve as a kitchen; but in East Yorkshire at least, and probably in other lowland counties the extra bay became the 'men's end', i.e. the room on the ground floor was the living-room and mess room for the unmarried labourers while the room above, reached by its own staircase, was their bedroom.[11] Access to the 'men's end' was usually from the farmyard at the back of the house, and this distinguishes such a provision from the separately occupied cottage which was often attached to a farmhouse as an extra bay but which had a doorway at the front.

19. *Continuous outshut house*

In terms of the development of Small House planning the most significant type of extension was the continuous outshut running at the rear of the two-unit plan. The addition of ground-floor rooms or extensions to increase accommodation had been common enough in many of the plans already considered: an end extension to a two-room baffle-entry house, for instance, might contain a pantry or a scullery; a rear extension behind a cross-passage house might provide space for similar use; but it was the staircase extension which began the trend which culminated in the continuous outshut house plan.

In the early eighteenth century the narrow, steeply rising, mural staircase tucked into the rear of a two-unit plan was succeeded by the provision of a dog-leg or open-well newel staircase rising in a projection from the rear wall which was covered by an extension of

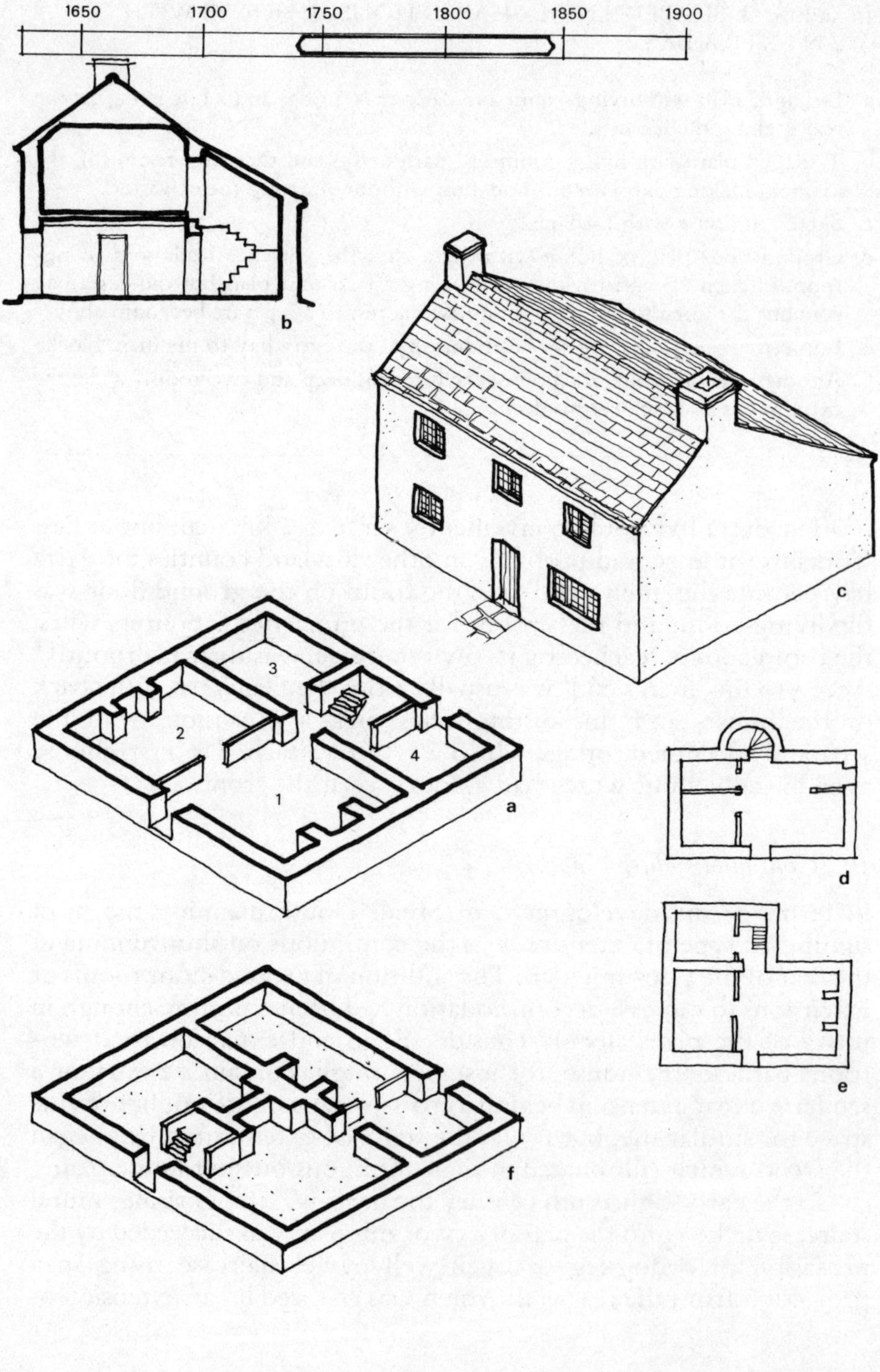

1650
1700
1750
1800
1850
1900
b
c
3
2
4
1
a
d
e
f

19. CONTINUOUS OUTSHUT HOUSE

a. Ground-floor plan showing living-room/kitchen (1) and parlour (2); behind are the dairy (3) and the scullery (4) with staircase between.
b. Cross-section showing the main roof swept down to cover the outshut.
c. Sketch showing the asymmetrical lines of the gable ends.
d. and e. Plans showing how the outshut develops from a rear staircase projection, adding rooms first on one side and then on both.
f. Ground floor plan: back-to-back fireplaces and outshut.

---

the main roof. Such a sweep down from the ridge of the main roof could also cover a scullery or back kitchen behind the living-room and a dairy behind the parlour, one on each side of the staircase. At first these rooms were open to the roof, but later it was customary to insert a ceiling which also acted as the floor to a couple of cramped little storerooms or bedrooms on the first floor. Storerooms were often lit only by borrowed light from the staircase; bedrooms were lit by narrow windows confined between the eaves and floor. The floor level for these rear upper rooms was normally a foot or so below that of the front rooms. The actual depth of the extension depended partly on the form of the staircase and partly on the pitch of the roof: a steep staircase and a steeply-pitched roof meant a narrow outshut, a more gradual staircase and a roof of shallow pitch meant that a generous outshut could be built. Indeed this plan was very popular in the Western and Midland counties where slates or stone flags were the roof covering of the eighteenth century and being laid to a low pitch allowed a deep outshut. The intermediate wall between main block and outshut was considered as a structural wall and the simple forms of roof structure devised for the two-unit plan could equally well be used in this developed version.

This house plan was in use throughout the country from the early eighteenth century well into the nineteenth and may easily be recognized from the asymmetrical end elevation of high eaves at the front and low eaves at the back.

20. *Double-pile house*

The culmination of Small House planning was the double-pile house which had four rooms of equal height on each of two principal floors. At this level, as at the Large House level, the Renaissance ideal of the compact cubiform building matched the functional convenience of well-lit, easily-heated rooms, based on a central communications core of staircase and lobby, taking the least possible space from the main living and service rooms. The double-pile plan may be considered as the farmhouse imitation of the double-pile Large House, or it may be considered as the final development of the continuous outshut plan wherein the rear eaves were raised to match the front eaves and the asymmetrical end elevation was abandoned; but it is probably more accurate to consider it as a happy combination of both influences.

At the Small House level dimensions were more critical than at the Large House, and so the slightly asymmetrical placing of the front door was maintained, and in the older and smaller examples the door led into the main living-room rather than into a passage between the two main ground-floor rooms. Upstairs, the smaller houses could provide space for only two bedrooms at the front, and so a central first-floor window was omitted, or was included in the elevation as a blind window; larger houses could include a third bedroom on the front lit by a central window. Fireplaces were

---

20. DOUBLE-PILE HOUSE

a. Ground-floor plan showing the living-room (1), parlour (2), scullery or kitchen (3) and dairy (4) with staircase (5) in between.
b. First-floor plan showing four bedrooms (6).
c. Cross-section showing eaves at same level front and back; sometimes a cellar at the rear adds to the service accommodation.
d. The sketch shows the symmetrical gables with eaves at the same level.
e. Alternative plan with fireplaces back-to-back on the spine wall rather than on the gable walls.
f. Later examples have entrance into a lobby rather than directly into the living-room.
g. An alternative position for the staircase lit from a gable wall rather than from the rear.

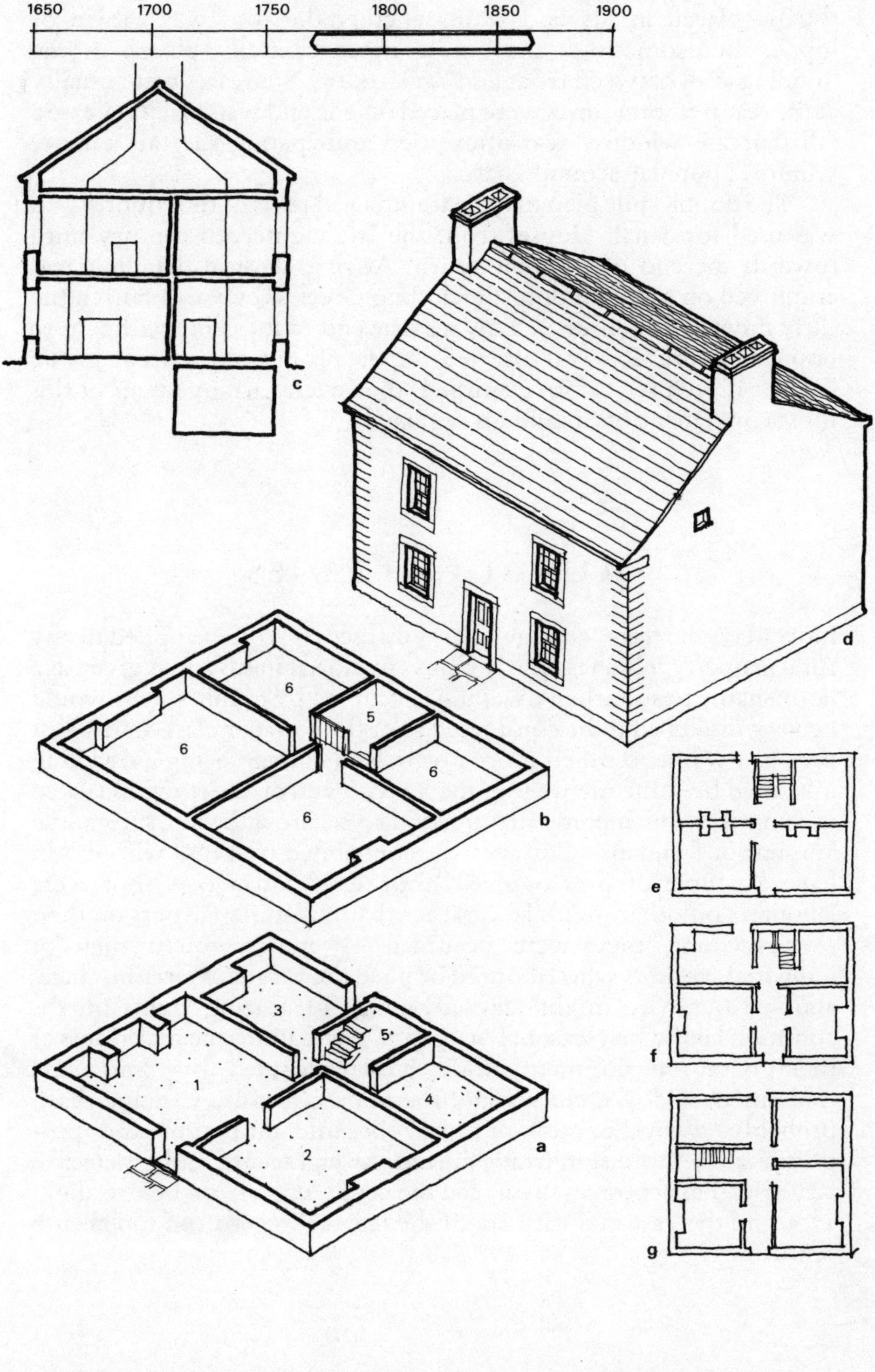
1650
1700
1750
1800
1850
1900
c
d
6
6
5
6
6
b
3
5
1
4
2
a
e
f
g

usually placed in the end walls whether the roof was gabled or hipped but sometimes they were more centrally placed in the dividing wall between front and back rooms. Staircases were usually at the rear but sometimes were placed on one end wall; in either case a tall staircase window was often used anticipating the tall narrow windows popular around 1930.

The double-pile plan may be found in all parts of the country and was used for Small Houses from the late eighteenth century until towards the end of the nineteenth. At first classical detailing was employed on such buildings (including Greek Revival details in the early nineteenth century). Towards the end of the century the more popular Gothic Revival affected the details but not, except in the later or more pretentious examples, the general arrangement of this most convenient of Small House plans.

RURAL COTTAGES

Nowadays the term 'cottage' is loosely used. It is often applied to any rural property which is clearly below manorial status and is given as a house name to suburban dwellings occupied by families who would be very distressed to be considered as of the cottager class. In the past the term was used much more precisely, a cottage being a dwelling inhabited by some member of the lower levels of society who lacked the position which comes from having a secure stake in a substantial amount of farmland. Cottages were inhabited by those who might have a couple of pigs or even 'four acres and a cow' but were labourers on other men's land rather than full-time farmers on their own account; they were occupied by miners, quarrymen or industrial workers who laboured or plied their trade as circumstances allowed but who might take advantage of grazing rights on the common land when seasonal or cyclical fluctuations meant the loss of their main employment; they were occupied by craftsmen, tradesmen, widows, elderly and the poor generally. Cottages have probably always existed but they became numerous and proportionately more significant during the eighteenth and nineteenth centuries. Few cottages survive in the countryside from before about 1700 and the vast majority are of the late eighteenth and nineteenth centuries.

The simplest sort of cottage had one room which served public and private needs, service and storage; but most cottages were designed, like examples of other size-types, around two spaces: one for more public activities, one for more private. The two-room cottage emerged relatively early as a cottage type and, even in the simple one-room cottage, furniture or partitions usually denoted one part as being distinct from the rest. The two spaces thus consisted of one unit, with another, smaller, unit added in some way, or a single unit subdivided. Once cottages came to be built in materials permanent enough to survive, the various stages of improvement followed rapidly, until little more than a century later the cottager could reasonably expect his dwelling to have four rooms – small rooms certainly, but twice the number and double the size of the accommodation which had been considered adequate for so long.

The housing revolution for the cottage dweller occurred mainly in the eighteenth century and practically simultaneously in town and country. The cottager moving to the town was attracted by accommodation as well as employment which was at least as good and probably better than that which he was leaving in the countryside; the cottager who stayed on the land could expect in most areas (and certainly in those where competition for labour by industry was a factor) that newly-built cottages of improved standard would help to encourage him to stay. In some respects the drift or stampede to the towns has been exaggerated in that much of the early Industrial Revolution took place in the countryside: dependent on hand or horse or water power, many of the newly-developing industries, especially in textiles and metal working, were rural rather than urban in basis. Extractive industries such as coal mining, quarrying for iron, tin or lead ore, etc., were necessarily based in the countryside. There was also the uncertainty of the revolution itself. We marvel at the enterprise and optimism of those concerned but we tend to underestimate the caution of those in vulnerable but still viable traditional industries and the pessimism which accompanied business failures and fluctuations in trade. These and other factors make it difficult and a little unrealistic to divide the developments in cottage design between urban and rural. Nevertheless we can see now that towns were to attract an ever-increasing proportion of investment, and that cottages designed or adapted for the needs of town dwellers on urban sites should be considered separately from cottages which continued to serve rural needs.

21. *One-unit cottage*

The one-unit cottage consists of a single room about twelve or fourteen feet square, usually with a further space in a loft above. The single room contained the only hearth or fireplace, and this was sometimes located on the rear wall but more customarily on the end or gable wall. Entry was normally from the front wall, either into a lobby against the fireplace or directly into the single room, though sometimes entry was through the gable alongside the fireplace jamb. The loft space which served as a bedroom was lit through the gable or under a half-hip, or was lit from the front wall by way of a dormer window or a small low window tucked between floorboards and eaves. Access was by a ladder in one corner of the ground-floor room either left open or encased in a sort of cupboard.

Such a one-unit cottage gave the two-part accommodation which was needed even at the most humble level of domestic arrangement, but the two parts were disposed vertically rather than horizontally. These cottages were sometimes built singly but more often were arranged in pairs or short rows or were attached to other buildings. They may be found in practically any part of the country, though their numbers are drastically cut year by year as they are

---

21 and 22. ONE-UNIT COTTAGE; ONE-AND-A-HALF-UNIT COTTAGE

a. Ground-floor plan of a one-unit cottage with front entry into a room with fireplace and ladder leading to a loft above.
b. Ground-floor plan with gable entry.
c. Ground-floor plan with entry away from the fireplace.
d. Ground-floor plan with a tight winding staircase squeezed against the fireplace jambs rather than a ladder set in one corner of the room.
e. Isometric sketch to indicate a one-unit cottage with a loft which is lit by a dormer window.
f. Ground-floor plan of a one-and-a-half-unit cottage showing the half-unit at one end of the main room and the steep staircase in one corner giving access to the loft above.
g. An alternative plan with the entrance near the centre of the main elevation.
h. Sketch showing the extra width which comes from use of this plan.
i. Sketch showing the use of a roof light to serve the loft space.
j. Sketch showing the use of a double-pitch or gambrel roof to permit greater headroom in the loft space.

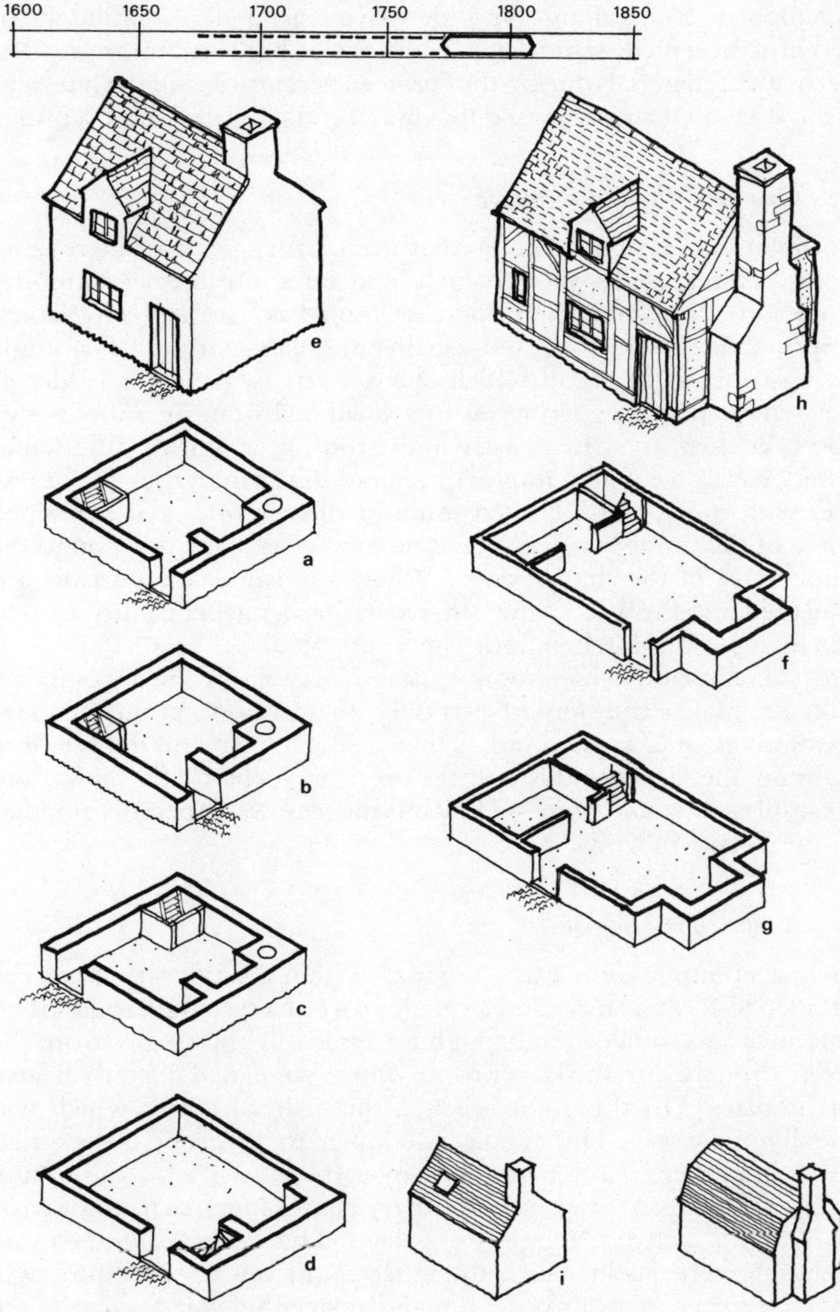
1600
1650
1700
1750
1800
1850
e
h
a
f
b
g
c
d
i
j

abandoned as dwellings and destroyed as useless reminders of recently accepted standards. They were built in more or less permanent materials during the eighteenth century, and the one-unit form was still being proposed for model cottages late in that century.

22. *One-and-a-half-unit cottages*

So small is a one-unit cottage that even a fifty per cent increase in floor area represents quite a small increase in useable accommodation, and yet even such an increase must have seemed a welcome improvement. The one-and-a-half-unit plan consists of a single living-room/kitchen, off which opens a narrow pantry; a ladder or very steep staircase gave access to a small bedroom over the living-room/kitchen, and often partly in the roof space, with a still smaller room, barely a cubicle, above the pantry. The pantry was only a few feet wide and yet it confined some of the activities and contained some of the storage which would otherwise have intruded on to the floor space of the single room. Where the ladder or staircase was squeezed into the back of the half-room then a further intrusion on to the living-room/kitchen floor was eliminated.

The one-and-a-half-room cottage may easily be recognized. Like its smaller counterpart it is only one room deep but the extra space gives an elongated rather than a square plan and the window lighting the pantry adds a little more incident to the elevation. Examples are found quite widely but the plan was especially popular in the West Midlands.[12]

23. *Single-storey cottage*

Here accommodation was contained within a single structural cell divided to form a larger and a smaller part of a rectangular building. Entrance was sometimes through the end wall but usually from the front, directly into the larger room which contained the only hearth or fireplace. Off this room opened the bedroom/store which was usually unheated. The whole was open to the roof except that sometimes there was a loose floor over the inner room, and giving extra storage space or even a subsidiary bedroom in the form of what in Wales is called a 'croglofft' cottage. There were slightly more elaborate versions in which the inner room was divided into two, making a small parlour bedroom and an even smaller pantry. There were also larger versions in which a central inglenook or fireplace served the living-room/kitchen; there was a parlour beyond but there was a third room behind the hearth which could be for domestic use, could accommodate a loom or similar piece of craftsman's equipment, or could house a cow, a horse, or a pig. The larger and later examples of this version approached in size the smaller and earlier of the two-unit Small Houses.

Single-storey cottages survive in relatively small numbers. They were associated with mining and quarrying and with the brief occupation of marginal land. They may be found in practically any building material: stone or brick, timber-frame or clay; they may be found practically anywhere but mostly in remote moorland areas; they are difficult to date but were probably under construction throughout the eighteenth century and, in Wales at least, well into the nineteenth century. They are generally too small and low to adapt to modern housing standards and, indeed, may have been occupied for a comparatively short time. However their long low proportions appeal to the contemporary eye and they are an important element in the rural scene.[13]

24. *Double-pile single-fronted cottage*

Often called the 'two-up and two-down', this cottage type provided a living-room/kitchen and a service room on the ground floor and two bedrooms above. The plan may be considered as a contraction of the double-pile Small House plan or as an expansion of the one-unit Cottage plan. In the former sense such dwellings shared the two-room depth and the rear staircase of the double-pile plan but lacked the extra pair of rooms which lent symmetry to such a house. In the latter sense they represented the culmination of a process of addition and improvement to the simpler cottages. For as the loft space of the cottage was improved to become a bedroom, so the ladder which was inconvenient and encroached on the main living space was replaced by a winding or a double-flight staircase extending from the rear; and as an additional larder or wash-house or other service room was placed alongside the staircase, so a small extra bedroom was added above.

Such cottages were rarely built singly, most commonly they were built in reflected pairs, symmetrical about a centre line which marked two front doors placed together, or symmetrical about a chimney stack which grouped together flues from all the living-

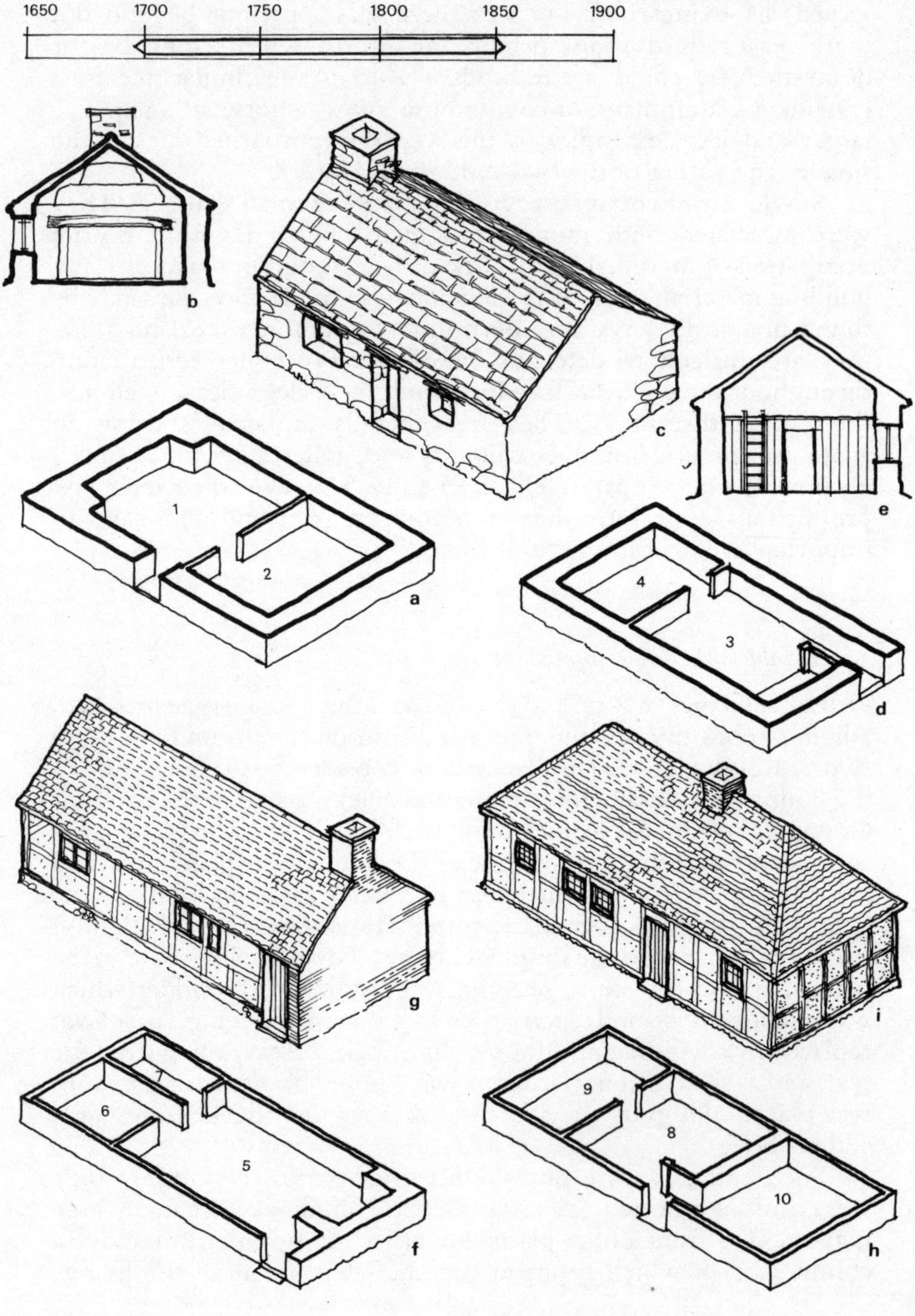
1650
1700
1750
1800
1850
1900
b
c
e
1
2
a
4
3
d
g
i
7
6
5
f
9
8
10
h

23. SINGLE-STOREY AND CROGLOFFT COTTAGES

a. Ground-floor plan with living-room/kitchen (1) and unheated parlour/store (2).
b. Cross-section showing living-room/kitchen open to the roof.
c. Isometric sketch showing low eaves and relative positions of central doorway and single chimney stack.
d. Ground-floor plan with gable entry to living-room/kitchen (3) off which opens the inner room, the parlour/store (4).
e. Cross-section showing the partition which divides off the parlour/store and the ladder giving access to the crogloft or space within the roof and over the parlour/store.
f. Ground-floor plan with corner entry into a living-room/kitchen (5) off which opens the parlour (6) and, here, a separate store (7).
g. Sketch showing the relationship between door and chimney stack.
h. Ground-floor plan of a baffle-entry or lobby-entry cottage; the entrance against the jamb of the fireplace leads into a living-room/kitchen (8) with parlour (9) beyond; a scullery (10) is here shown behind the fireplace.
i. Sketch to show the relationship between doorway and chimney stack.

---

room and bedroom fireplaces. Sometimes they were built in villages in short rows of three or four, sometimes they were built in mining or quarrying districts in long rows to give an incongruously urban effect. Single cottages were, however, attached to larger farmhouses or to farm buildings, and some of the smaller and later 'laithe houses' of the Pennines were really cottages attached to barns.

Cottages of this type are mainly of late eighteenth-, nineteenth- or even early twentieth-century date and may be found in villages or on farms in any part of the country.

25. *Other multi-storey cottages*

Just as the one-unit cottage developed into the double-pile single-fronted cottage plan, so the single-storey cottage had its own development. A common cottage plan had a central door leading to a small lobby, off which opened living-room/kitchen to one side, small parlour or service room to the other and a straight flight staircase to two bedrooms above. This was like the one-unit cottage in being one room deep and more or less symmetrical but, having a second storey reached by a convenient staircase, it was much improved. An alternative arrangement placed the staircase alongside

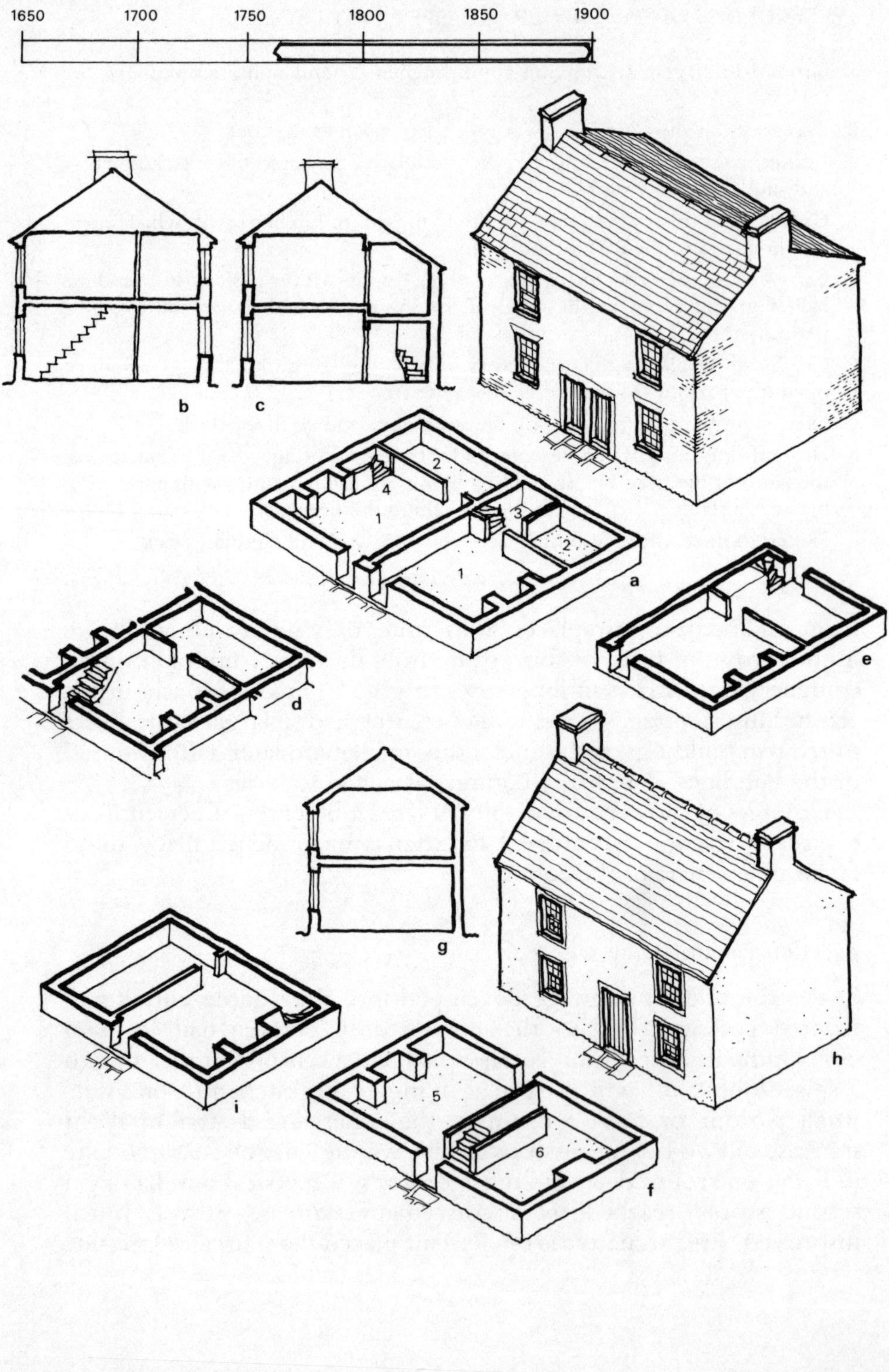

1650
1700
1750
1800
1850
1900
b
c
a
1
2
3
4
d
e
g
h
i
5
6
f

24 and 25. DOUBLE-PILE SINGLE-FRONTED COTTAGE; OTHER MULTI-STOREY COTTAGES

a. Ground-floor plan of a reflected pair of single-fronted double-pile cottages; entrance from the front is directly into a living-room/kitchen (1) with a pantry or scullery (2); one cottage shows a rear staircase (3), the other a staircase alongside the fireplace (4).
b. Cross-section showing the same eaves height at front and back.
c. Cross-section showing the earlier and humbler versions in which the rooms at the rear are even lower than those at the front.
d. Plan of a version in which the straight-flight staircase rises from the front and only door.
e. Plan of a version in which the staircase rises from close to a back door.
f. A common form of multi-storey cottage is one-room in depth and double-fronted or two rooms in width. The plan shows a central door, a central staircase and living-room/kitchen and parlour (5 and 6) on each side.
g. The cross-section shows that the cottage is one room deep.
h. Sketch showing that the cottage looks like a miniature version of the two-unit Small House plan.
i. An alternative plan with the staircase associated with the fireplace; only one room is heated in this cottage.

---

the fireplace, but then the plan had all the characteristics of the two-unit plan as used in Small Houses. Indeed it is sometimes difficult to distinguish between a large double-fronted cottage and a modest two-unit Small House.

SPECIAL PURPOSE HOUSES

26. *Laithe house*

A laithe house consists of a dwelling and farm buildings erected simultaneously, under the same roof and usually of a simple rectangular plan. A laithe house differs from a longhouse in that there is no cross-passage, there is always separate access for humans and animals and there may or may not be intercommunication between the parts of the building. The term was coined by C. F. Stell following his research in the Halifax area during the 1950s and makes use of the dialect word 'laithe', meaning a barn.[14] The term 'coit' had been used by S. O. Addy to include what we now call laithe houses.

Both domestic and agricultural parts of the laithe house are small and unpretentious and there was a tendency for proportions between the two to change during the period in which the building type was used. The earliest recorded example, Bank House, Luddenden, of 1650, is nearly two-thirds domestic; the latest recorded example, Catherine Slack, Hebden Royd, of 1880, is nearly three-quarters agricultural.[15] Typically, the smaller and later example have cottage-type accommodation – a living-room/kitchen and scullery on the ground floor and one or two bedrooms above; the larger and earlier examples have Small House accommodation – living-room/kitchen, parlour, scullery and dairy on the ground floor and four bedrooms above. The agricultural part consists, as a rule, only of barn and cow-house, and these are combined in the one space: typically there is a conventional threshing floor with tall double doors to the front and a smaller winnowing door to the rear. The threshing floor acts as a feeding passage for the cattle tethered longitudinally: sometimes one row of cattle with a storage bay opposite, sometimes two rows facing each other across the floor. In either case there are storage lofts above the cow tyings. The laithe house presents a rather austere elevation, dominated by the tall barn door, but enlivened by the miniature Palladian windows found so often above.

There is some doubt as to whether the barns were intended for corn or hay. Those remaining in use until recently stored hay, and the absence of a winnowing door in some later examples might appear to

---

26. LAITHE HOUSE

a. Ground-floor plan with a house part consisting of a living-room/kitchen (1) a parlour (2), scullery (3) and pantry (4) and a farming part consisting of a threshing floor (5) and cattle stalls facing.
b. First-floor plan with bedrooms (6), and lofts (7) over the cattle stalls.
c. Cross-section through the threshing floor.
d. Sketch showing the two parts under the one roof and the Palladian window over the barn doors.
e. A variation with a small proportion of farming space to domestic space.
f. Equal proportions of farming and domestic accommodation but on a smaller scale, the house is only one room deep.
g. A variation with a small proportion of domestic to farming space.

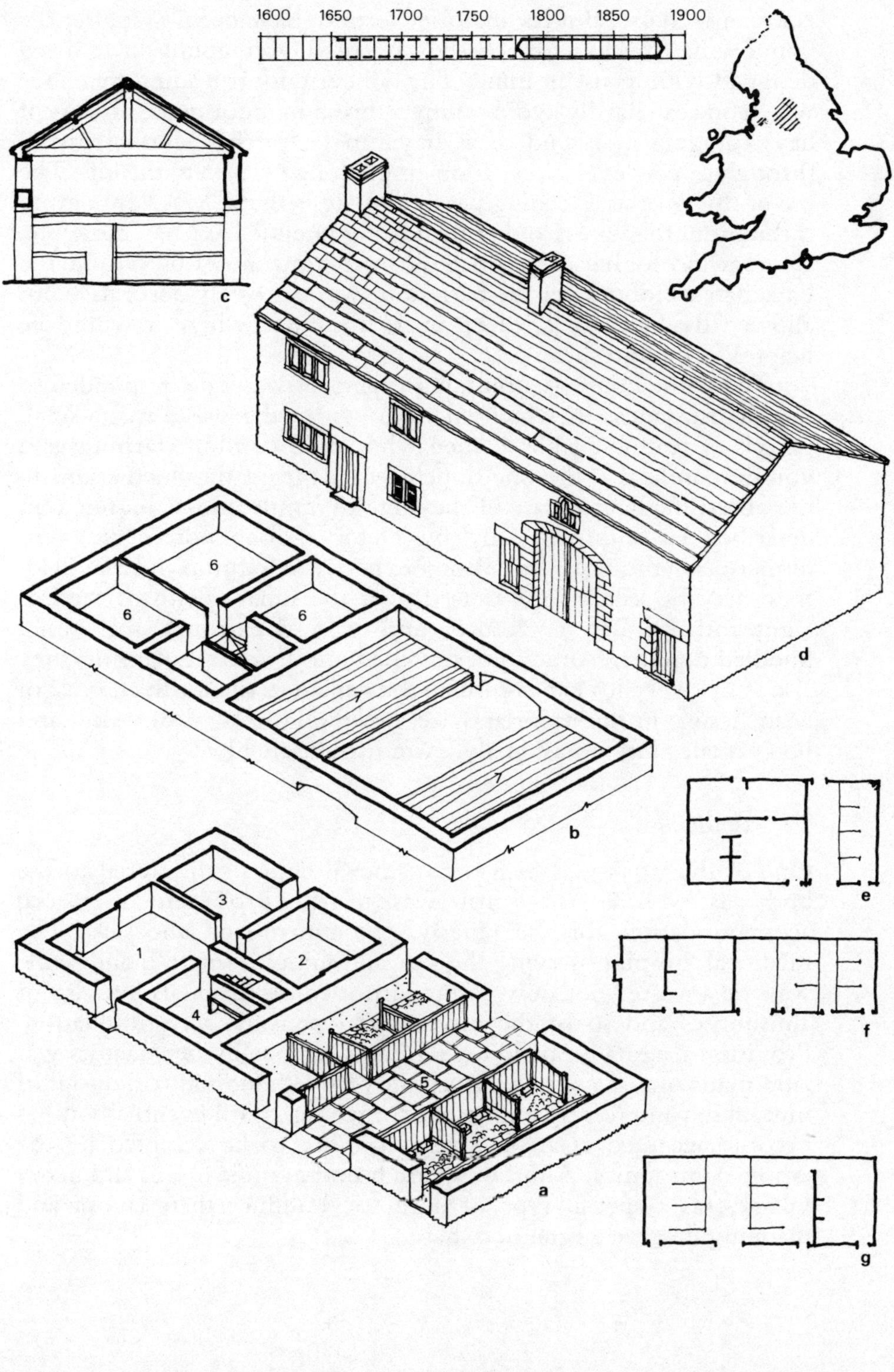
1600
1650
1700
1750
1800
1850
1900
c
6
6
6
7
7
d
b
3
1
2
4
5
a
e
f
g

confirm such use. But the majority seem to have been built after the winnowing machine had been invented and could have been designed with its use in mind. The tall barn doors leading to a floor which one can hardly avoid calling a threshing floor make no sense if hay storage was intended, as hay can be pitched perfectly well through upper-level access doors or pitching eyes on to the loft. The use of the floor as a feeding passage suggests that it was kept empty throughout the winter rather than being intended as a hay mow (i.e. a storage bay for hay). To clinch the matter one must observe that the Palladian window over the barn door was not solely decorative but allowed daylight to fall deep on to the floor where it would be helpful to the threshers.

The laithe house as a building type seems to have responded to the circumstances in which enclosure from the waste made small parcels of land available to men who could combine farming and domestic industry, the one hopefully balancing the fluctuations in the other: the happy state of the integral family and economic unit described so enthusiastically by Defoe. Laithe houses are very numerous in the Yorkshire Pennines between Skipton and Sheffield; they may be seen singly, dotted over the square fields of the late eighteenth-century enclosure, and in little groups sometimes huddled together, sometimes stretched out in an irregular line; they also stray over into Lancashire, in the valleys to the north and east of Manchester, in the moorland areas of the Forests of Bowland and Rossendale, and, occasionally, even further afield.

27. *Almshouses*

One of the ways in which the medieval church ministered to the body as well as the spirit was in the provision of special accommodation for the elderly, the infirm and the sick. The medieval 'hospital' serving the sick and injured, the frail and senile was the ancestor not only of modern medical hospitals but also of almshouses and so of the modern old persons' accommodation. Provision originally made for religious reasons by benefactors was later made out of a sense of social duty by rich individuals, or out of mutual self-interest by guilds and companies, until eventually it has become accepted as a social responsibility to be accepted by the whole community. Almshouses are found in most towns and many villages; as a special type of domestic building their layout and planning deserve a brief note here.

The earliest examples of provision for the aged or infirm have a hall with a chapel on the long axis at the east end, as may be seen at Chichester and Glastonbury. There was provision for communal living, including eating and sleeping, in the hall as well as for communal worship in that extension of the hall which was the chapel. There were obvious disadvantages in the hall and chapel arrangement: lack of privacy, lack of comfort, difficulties in lighting and heating, waste of space in the huge draughty upper levels of the hall; and these were presumably among the factors which led to the abandonment of this arrangement.

The successors in the late medieval period followed the precedent of the college rather than the hall; they had the combination of chapel, hall, kitchen and individual rooms which we recognize most easily in the older English universities. Before the Reformation, some almshouses were arranged as colleges: Ewelme, founded in 1437, is the best surviving example. The ancient Hospital of St Cross at Winchester, reorganized in 1445, includes cottages for the brethren arranged with the earlier church and the refectory to make a self-contained collegiate community.

The foundations of medieval almshouses, like those of chantries, usually required prayers to be said for the souls of dead benefactors; and so during the Reformation, from 1547, they became liable to dissolution. Some were spared, some were re-founded, others were superseded by the almshouses based on existing buildings or on new sites. Dwellings for elderly couples or single people were arranged around a courtyard which also included a chapel, as at Leycester's Hospital at Warwick, or simply a hall, as at Cobham College, Kent. The dwellings looked inwards towards the courtyard, which was entered by a narrow passage and so was cut off from the noise and bustle of the street. Other examples included Whitgift Hospital, Croydon, of 1596–9 and, on a much smaller scale, there was the little Hospital of St Mary Magdalen at King's Lynn, rebuilt in 1649. The pattern of enclosed quadrangle with or without a chapel remained in use for the many almshouses founded during the seventeenth century.

Towards the end of that century, the quadrangular plan was opened out to give a three-sided composition, probably under the influence of the great royal foundations of Greenwich and Chelsea, and this modification may be seen at the quite palatial Kirkleatham Hospital of 1742 in North Yorkshire. The Geffrye Almshouses at Shoreditch in London of 1710 provide a large-scale example; Ward's

Hospital at Buntingford, Herts., endowed in 1684, and the Marlborough Almshouses of St Albans are on a more usual scale. All are on three sides with a wide fourth side open to the street and with some pediment or other architectural emphasis of the centre.

Another arrangement popular from the early eighteenth century onwards consisted of a narrow elongated courtyard, one end giving on to the street and the other end occupied by a chapel or hall so that the dwellings faced each other in two long parallel rows over a paved, cobbled or grassed courtyard. Tomkins' Almshouses of 1718 at Abingdon in Berkshire provide one example; Penny's Almshouses, Lancaster of 1720 provide another.

Throughout the period in which these substantial ranges of almshouses were built there were many small sets of almshouses consisting simply of a row of cottages: two, three or four as a rule, sometimes rather more. Usually these rows had some sort of architectural emphasis at the centre, less often the eighteenth- and early nineteenth-century examples were arranged in a three part composition with the ends of the row marked as well as the centre. Almost always they can be distinguished from other cottages in the village by signs of conscious composition, however elementary, by the use of rather more up-to-date architectural details, and by the careful architectural setting provided for the plaque commemorating the founder.

Except for the hall and chapel foundations almshouses were usually designed as groups of cottages with fairly conventional plans. No doubt in the earliest halls there were no fixed divisions to define

---

27. ALMSHOUSES

a. Medieval arrangement of hall and chapel.
b. Late medieval collegiate layout.
c. The closed quadrangle developed from the collegiate layout.
d. The open-fronted wide quadrangle: centre block and short flanking wings.
e. The narrow courtyard, long ranges facing each other, chapel or hall at the end.
f. The simple range of the village almshouses.
g. Communal living in the hall.
h. The one-roomed almshouse cottage.
i. One room and a loft, two of various fireplace positions.
j. One room and a pantry, bedroom above.

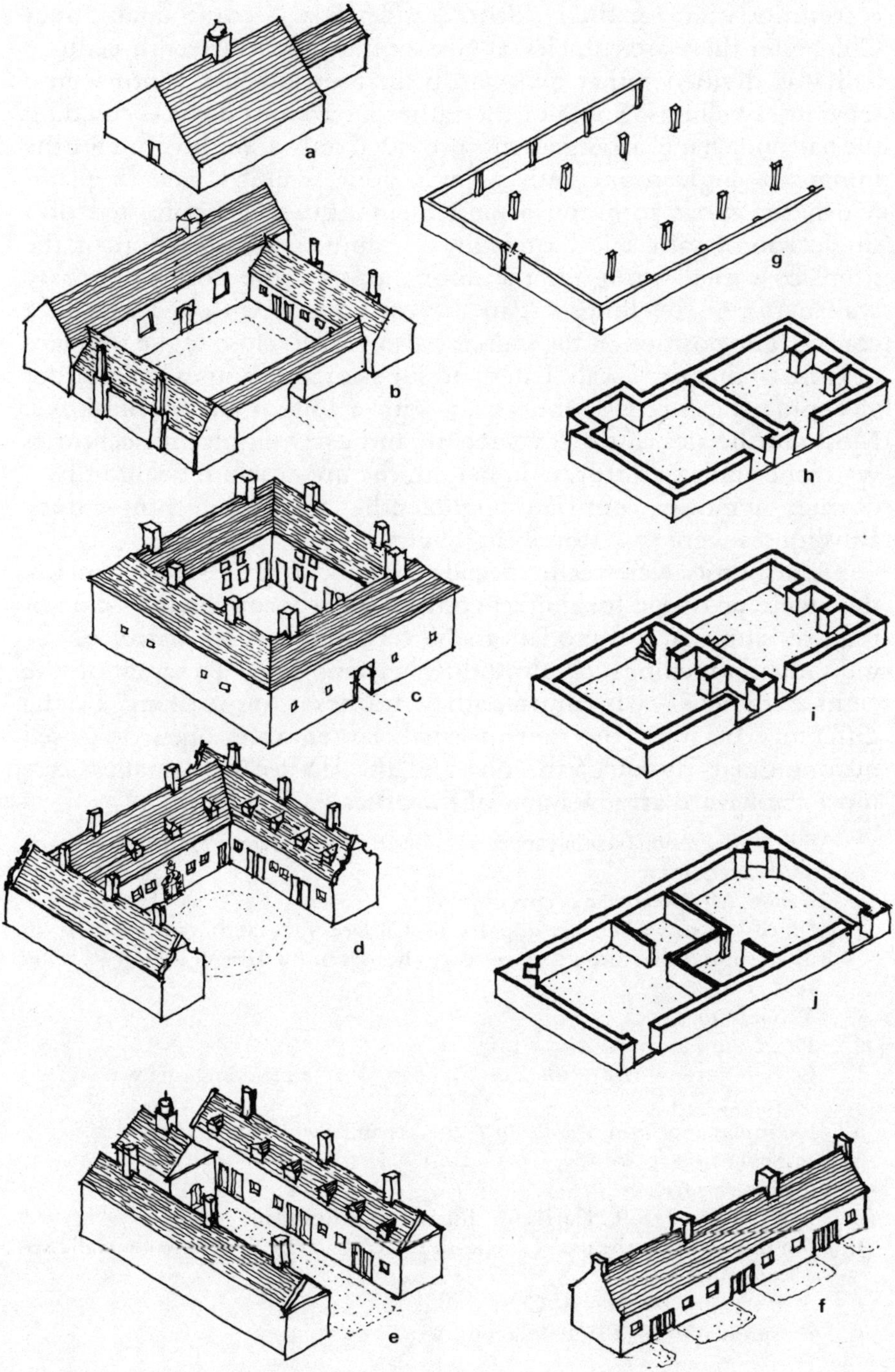
a
b
c
d
e
f
g
h
i
j

accommodation for the residents: residence was communal; but at Chichester there are cubicles, at Glastonbury the fourteenth-century hall was divided rather awkwardly in the sixteenth century into separate dwellings. Some of the rather later almshouses succeeding the hall and chapel arrangements provided only a single room for the inmate, a single room with a single door, window and fireplace. Much the most common arrangements, however, consisted of a single room with a loft or bedroom above. The position of the fireplace varied: alongside the door, opposite the door on a party wall between dwellings or, in the early eighteenth century, in a corner. The position of the staircase also varied: close to the fireplace or close to the party wall. Later and superior almshouses had a larder alongside the living-room, again with a loft or bedroom above. Most almshouses of the seventeenth and early eighteenth centuries were one and a half storeys in height, the upper room being lit by a dormer window, but late eighteenth- and nineteenth-century almshouses were two storeys in height.

Almshouses were really special types of cottages. Since normally they were provided for single people or elderly couples they did not require family accommodation. Nevertheless the similarity of the individual dwellings in almshouse groups with cottages of the eighteenth and early nineteenth centuries is as striking as the difference between the more formal, larger scale, open or closed quadrangular layout of the one and the less formal, smaller scale more haphazard arrangement of the other.

1. Further discussion on siting appears in *Roberts 1978* and *Beresford and St Joseph 1979*.
2. *Michelmore 1973*.
3. *Ramm, McDowall and Mercer 1970*.
4. Much on tower houses appears in *Curwen 1913* and *1965*; there is an interesting distribution map of tower houses in the British Isles in *P. Smith 1975*, 338.
5. *P. Smith 1975*, 232.
6. Rigold in *Foster and Alcock 1963*.
7. G. Beresford in *Med. Arch.* Vol. 23, 1979, 98–158 including turf walling.
8. *Mercer 1975*, 42.
9. Examples appear in *Machin 1978*, 68–91, and *Smith 1975*, 232.
10. *P. Smith 1975*, 158.
11. see *Neave 1971*.
12. I am indebted to R. Harris for discussion of this plan.
13. For discussion of the use of single-storey cottages in Yorkshire generally see *Newton 1976*.
14. *Stell 1965*, 20, *Addy 1975*, Ch. 4.
15. P. Smith 1963, 432 and Stell 1965, 21

CHAPTER THREE

Urban Houses

The evolution of urban house plans

The town house was intended to serve different needs from the house in the countryside, it was subject to greater restrictions on design, and surviving examples have suffered more alterations; so it is hardly surprising that town houses usually differ materially in appearance from those of the countryside and that they deserve separate study.

The housing of animals was not, of course, a matter of prime importance in the design of a town house – although it might include a stable and carriage house, perhaps even a pigsty or a stall for a cow in its outbuildings. On the other hand many town houses were not exclusively residential, being designed to incorporate workshops, retail shops, warehouses, space for cottage industry, accommodation for lodgers etc.; and each non-domestic use brought its own architectural requirements.

Most town houses were built on restricted sites subject to the distinct legal restraints of the urban system of land tenure. The classic medieval urban site consisted of a narrow strip fronting on to a market place or shopping street and stretching back into gardens and so on to a river, perhaps, or a piece of common land. Plots were usually about twenty or thirty feet wide and stretched back two hundred and fifty or three hundred feet: in Taunton and Oxford about thirty feet was a standard width, though some plots were subdivided into strips no more than ten feet wide; in Totnes and York by the mid-fifteenth century the characteristic width was twenty feet, but again there was some subdivision and some amalgamation. The narrow width meant that houses built on a single plot could be only one room wide; the great length meant that from the narrow width a passage had to be taken in order to give access to the greater part of the plot. Because the shape available for building was so awkward town houses were built several storeys high at a time when houses in the countryside were commonly only one or two storeys in height; but this multi-storey construction was limited through the need to provide light to the rooms at the rear of the building by way of courts or light wells which might themselves be overshadowed by adjacent property. Multi-storey construction was also limited by the need for staircases and chimney stacks, required at each level but taking up valuable floor space.

Like houses in the countryside most of the older town houses have been rebuilt or re-faced, extended and re-roofed several times during their period of existence, but the town house sites have generally been subject to over-building to a much greater extent than those in village or open country. Pressure on space either because of the physical limits of a city wall or, more commonly, because of the legal difficulties in expanding into the collar of common land which encircled many towns meant that the orchards and gardens, paddocks and cesspits along the length of the urban plot became building land, especially during the late eighteenth and early nineteenth century when expansion of urban population was so rapid. These developments intensified the difficulties in house design for convenience and privacy.

At the same time not all town houses were subject to these restrictions. Powerful landowners acquired large plots on which they could build houses similar to conventional types in the countryside. The church owned large compact tracts of land in every town and a religious establishment might develop the fringe of one of its properties to provide shallow plots of relatively wide frontage for fairly spacious cottages or small houses: examples occur in York and Tewkesbury for instance. After the Reformation many pieces of church land became available for building. While all the towns were developed to high density in the prime commercial areas, in few towns was there a high overall density. Even in cities such as York and Chester whose medieval walls still survive, the overcrowded zones were limited and many streets outside the commercially desirable area were available for relatively unfettered domestic construction. Then again suburban development along the roads which extended from the town gates was practised whenever conditions were safe and frontage of ample width was available. The effects may be seen on streets such as Blossom St. in York or North Bar Without in Beverley. So the conditions of the eighteenth and nineteenth centuries which led to intensive development of the medieval urban core also led to the more extensive ribbon development of at least part of the periphery.

During the period to about 1700 two principal methods of extending down the length of a medieval plot were developed: a continuous range along one side of the plot and a series of buildings alternating with courts along the length of the plot. The first method allowed easy access from one room to another by means of an internal corridor or open-fronted gallery, but the width of room provided was limited by the width of the plot and the need for penetration of light, especially into the ground-floor rooms. The second method gave limited space for ground-floor rooms since part of the width of the plot had to be reserved for the continuous corridors linking court with court; but at first-floor level the whole width could be used unless, as was often the case, a gallery was provided; there was no restriction on the depth of the room, the only limitation being the area of court needed to provide some useful daylight, especially for the ground-floor rooms. Since medieval houses in the countryside often consisted of several buildings only loosely associated on the site and without covered access from part to part, the use of separate buildings along the length of the medieval urban plot would hardly have been considered a great handicap to domestic life.

The influence of the Renaissance during the seventeenth and eighteenth centuries led to a different concept of what was appropriate for the urban site, and the terrace, with its variations in square and crescent, represented in examples to be found in practically every town, reflected the new attitudes to siting of urban houses. Long rows of houses built to regular design and with classical details were erected in Great Queen Street and Lincolns Inn Fields in London during the 1630s. The layout of Covent Garden at the same time transformed the terrace into a formal square. The idea of making each house in the terrace part of a grand palatial composition, reducing its individuality but enhancing its share in the greater whole, was developed during the late seventeenth century and early eighteenth century in examples such as Bloomsbury Square and Grosvenor Square in London. With the Circus, and especially with the Royal Crescent of 1767–75, the Woods of Bath developed the flat terrace into the livelier crescent to the great benefit of urban design in Britain. Indeed, well into the nineteenth century, many humble cottages were given dignity as part of a terrace or vitality as part of a circus or crescent.

Town house plans may be divided into three main groups with subdivisions within each group. The general sequence will be considered here and then each type will be separately described.

The first group consists of medieval houses in which at least one room is a hall open to the roof. Some examples, of very narrow frontage, have the hall running at right angles to the street; others, of rather wider frontage, have the hall running parallel to the street. There are also a few surviving first-floor halls. Many of the medieval houses included workshops or retail stores opening off the street and capable of separate access and separate letting, and plans were varied

---

URBAN HOUSES: SUMMARY OF MAIN PLAN-TYPES

A: *Earlier houses: including an open hall*

1. Narrow frontage, internal hall, undercroft
2. Wide frontage, first-floor hall
3. Wide frontage, lateral hall, behind shops
4. Wide frontage, cross-passage, single-ended ground-floor hall
5. Narrow frontage, cross-passage in hall, 5a with wider frontage
6. Narrow frontage, long passage incorporated in the house
7. Narrow frontage, small hall

B: *Later houses: multi-storey throughout*

8. Wide frontage, back-to-back fireplaces
9. Wide frontage, L-shaped or T-shaped houses
10. Wide frontage double-pile houses, end-wall fireplaces, 10a. central fireplaces
11. Narrow frontage, longitudinal passage, back-to-back fireplaces
12. Narrow frontage, longitudinal passage, end-wall fireplaces
13. Wide frontage, central stair, end-wall fireplaces
14. Universal terrace houses
15. London terrace houses, rear stairs
16. London terrace houses, central stairs
17. Narrow frontage, central stairs between fireplaces

C. *Cottages*

18. Longitudinal passage within one-room cottage
19. One-room cottage, no passage within
20. One-room cottages, back-to-back
21. Houses for cottage industry
22. Two-up and two-down cottages, rear stair
23. Two-up and two-down cottages, central stair
24. Tunnel-back cottages

URBAN HOUSES: EARLIER

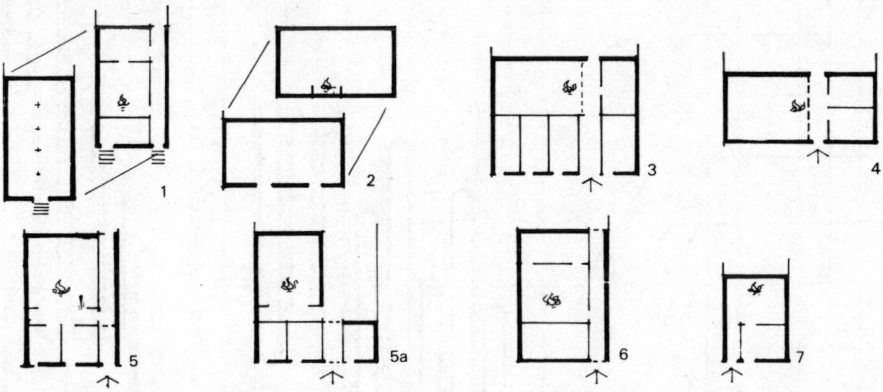

URBAN HOUSES: LATER

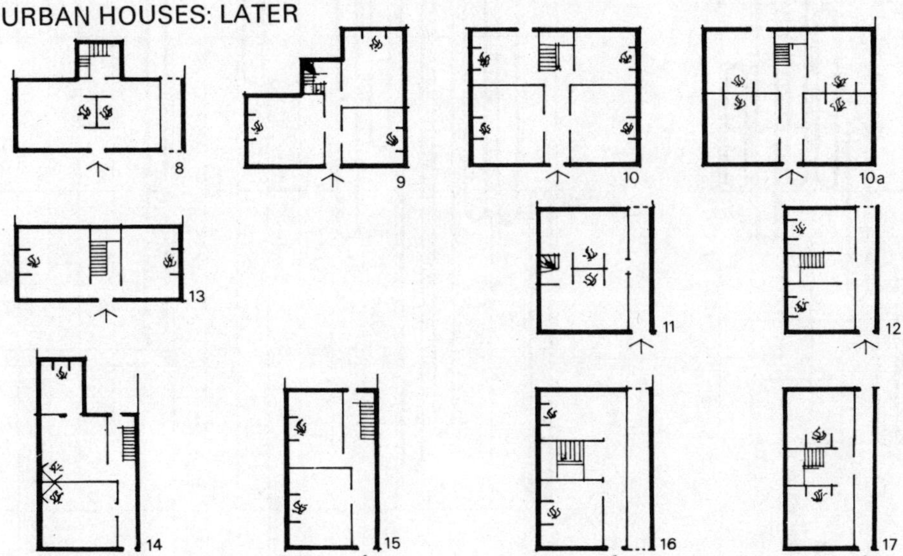

URBAN COTTAGES

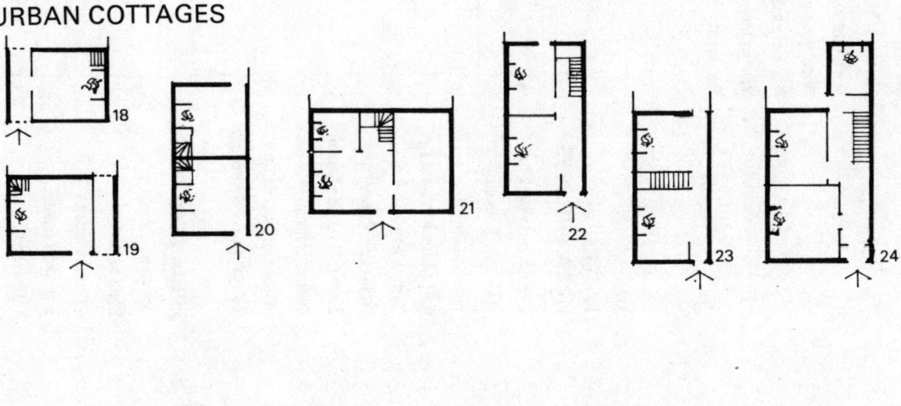

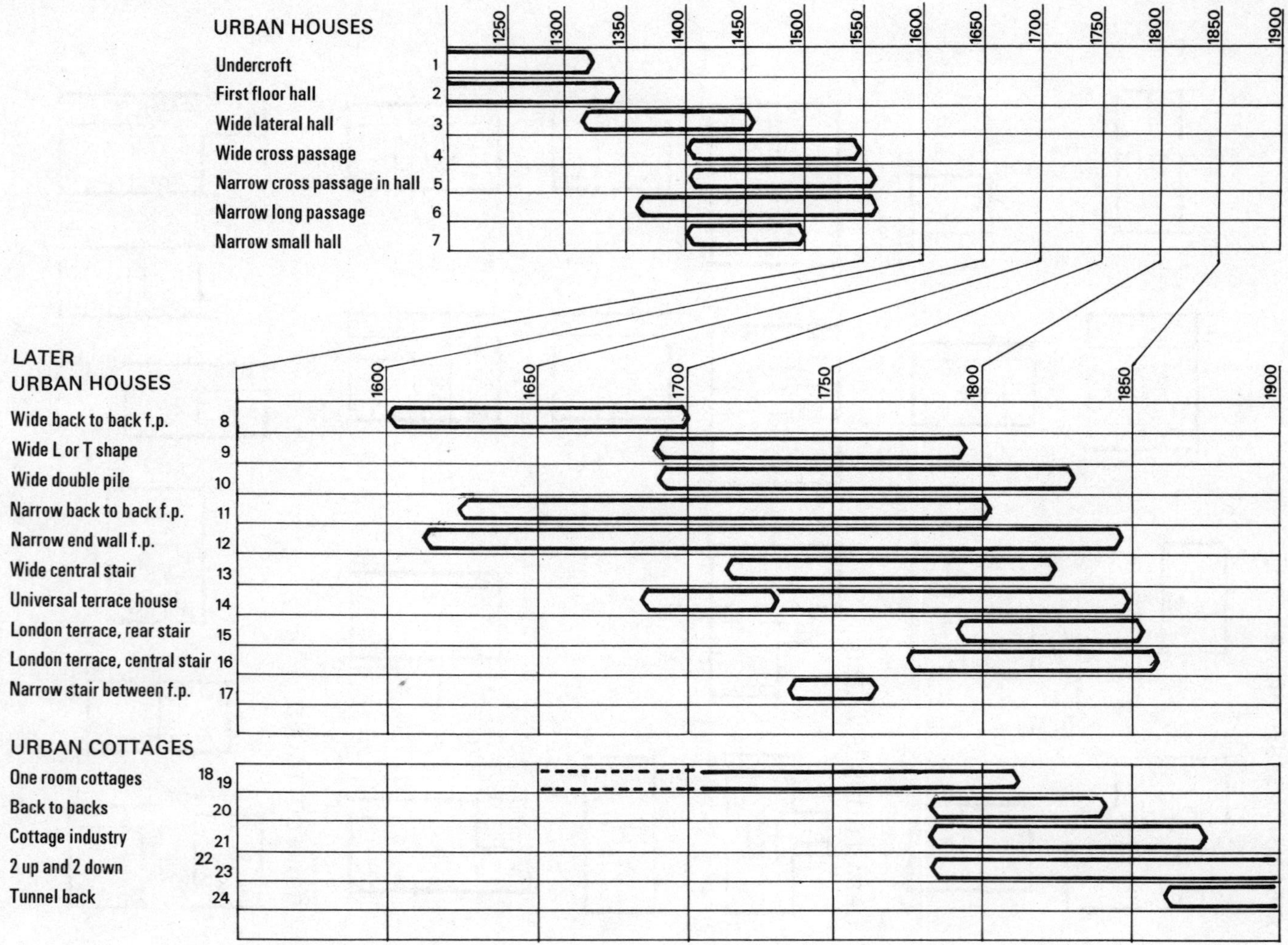
URBAN HOUSES
1250
1300
1350
1400
1450
1500
1550
1600
1650
1700
1750
1800
1850
1900
Undercroft 1
First floor hall 2
Wide lateral hall 3
Wide cross passage 4
Narrow cross passage in hall 5
Narrow long passage 6
Narrow small hall 7
LATER
URBAN HOUSES
1600
1650
1700
1750
1800
1850
1900
Wide back to back f.p. 8
Wide L or T shape 9
Wide double pile 10
Narrow back to back f.p. 11
Narrow end wall f.p. 12
Wide central stair 13
Universal terrace house 14
London terrace, rear stair 15
London terrace, central stair 16
Narrow stair between f.p. 17
URBAN COTTAGES
One room cottages 18 19
Back to backs 20
Cottage industry 21
2 up and 2 down 22 23
Tunnel back 24

to allow this and to permit upper-level domestic rooms to extend over these shops.

The second group consists of multi-storey houses: dwellings which lacked open halls but had several storeys of rooms conveniently reached by a single staircase and adequately served by fireplaces and flues. Again there was a distinction between narrow frontage and wider frontage properties, in the one case leading to rooms one behind the other while in the other case leading to rooms side by side. Fireplaces were either back-to-back, giving a compact stack which kept the heat within the house, or were arranged separately in the party wall. Staircases were either compact and within the house, or extended and at the rear. The group ranges from the large many-storeyed houses of London, Bristol and Bath to the humbler two-storey houses of the smaller provincial towns.

The third group consists of the urban cottages, generally of quite late date and generally consisting of developments from the simple cottage of one room and a loft which filled so many spaces in medieval towns to the comparatively spacious and well-equipped narrow frontage cottage of the nineteenth century.

A fourth group, not included on this diagram but worth a mention, includes the suburban houses and cottages of two storeys and bungalows built especially in the period 1920–39.

EARLIER URBAN HOUSES

1. *Narrow frontage house with internal hall, undercroft*

Among the earliest types of town house is that in which an open hall and its attendant rooms are raised over a vaulted undercroft. Such houses were usually built on narrow plots, only twenty feet or so in width. At the street front one flight of stairs led down to a half-basement which extended the whole length of the main building and was used as a workshop, warehouse, retail shop etc. according to the occupation of the householder or tenant; another flight of stairs led up from the street to the main entrance, giving access often to a smaller shop and through it to the hall, parlour and chambers. The hall was raised like the other rooms over the cellar on a stone vault and was of conventional medieval type, open to the roof and presumably with a central open hearth to provide heat in the winter time, and, where the site permitted, with a cross-passage at one end. Off the hall opened a parlour, and above parlour and shop there were chambers reached by narrow internal staircases and sometimes linked by a gallery running along the upper part of one of the walls of the hall. Beyond the parlour there would be a courtyard which led to the detached kitchen and to other service rooms.

In this plan the provision of daylight was difficult: it was impossible to light the undercroft except by what little daylight could penetrate the low front wall, and the hall could only be lit by borrowed light from any convenient courtyards provided by adjacent owners. The houses usually presented a gable to the street and there was no problem in lighting chambers and garrets.

This plan-type has been most thoroughly studied in Southampton but examples are also known from Exeter and Stamford.[1] The 'rows' of Chester may have been developed from some version of it. Its general period of use is believed to be the thirteenth and early fourteenth centuries.

2. *Wide frontage house with first-floor hall*

The hall raised to first-floor level was employed simultaneously with the ground-floor hall in early medieval towns as well as in the countryside, though few examples actually survive. Probably the best-known are the two 'Jews Houses' in Lincoln but other so-called 'King John's houses' may be found here and there – at Southampton for instance.

---

1. NARROW FRONTAGE HOUSE WITH INTERNAL HALL, UNDERCROFT

a. General view showing two examples together, one cut away on the long axis; entrance to long passage (1), to shop (2), hall (3), parlour (4), chambers (5).
b. Cross-section showing undercroft (6), shop (7), passage to hall (8), chamber (9).
c. Undercroft with steps down from street (10), piers supporting floor above (11).
d. Ground-floor plan with long passage (12), shop (13), hall (14), parlour (15), kitchen (16), steps up from street (17).
e. Upper-floor plan showing chambers (18) and upper part of hall (19).
Note heating provision and position of internal staircases not determined

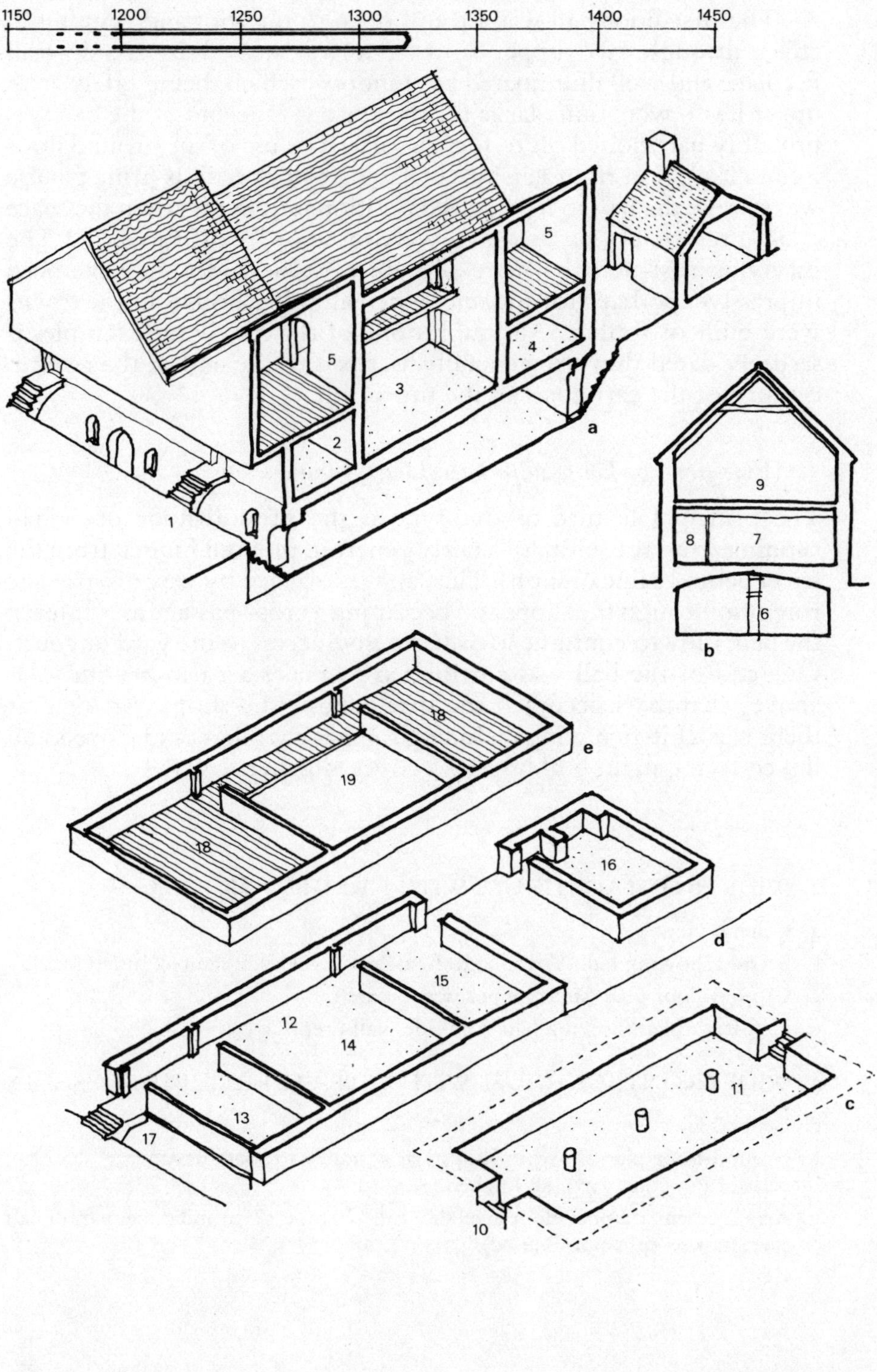
1150
1200
1250
1300
1350
1400
1450
1
2
3
4
5
5
a
9
8
7
6
b
18
19
18
e
16
d
15
12
14
13
17
11
c
10

The first-floor hall was a room open to the roof and running in effect through two upper storeys; it was heated by a side-wall fireplace and well illuminated by windows which, being safely at an upper level, were quite large for the period. One end of the hall was probably partitioned off to form a solar. The use of the ground floor is not clear; as in rural versions of the first-floor hall its principal use was to raise the hall to its required position; but in the town the space could presumably be used as a warehouse or let off for shops. The surviving first-floor halls are all built of stone and must have been impressive, perhaps formidable, when all other houses in the towns were built of timber. Although none of the surviving examples is securely dated they are generally ascribed to the end of the twelfth century or the early part of the thirteenth.

3. *Wide frontage house with lateral hall, behind shops*

The principal feature of this type is the ground-floor open hall running *across* the width of a fairly generous plot but hidden from the street behind a line of shops. The hall was reached by way of a passage running through the shops and becoming a cross-passage as it entered the hall, only to continue in order to give access to the yard or court. One end of the hall was partitioned to make a parlour with solar above; chambers occupied the space above the shops. At the rear there was a kitchen wing including further chambers and garrets and linked to the main building by a covered gallery.

---

2. WIDE FRONTAGE HOUSE WITH FIRST-FLOOR HALL

a. General view.
b. Section showing hall (1), raised to first-floor level over vaulted undercroft (2).
c. Ground-floor plan (staircase positions varied).
d. First-floor plan showing hall with side wall fireplace (3).

3. WIDE FRONTAGE HOUSE WITH LATERAL HALL, BEHIND SHOPS

e. General view.
f. Ground-floor plan showing shops (4), entrance to cross-passage (5), hall (6), parlour (7), courtyard (8), kitchen (9).
g. Arrangement at upper-floor level showing chambers (10) and upper part of hall (11) (staircase positions varied).

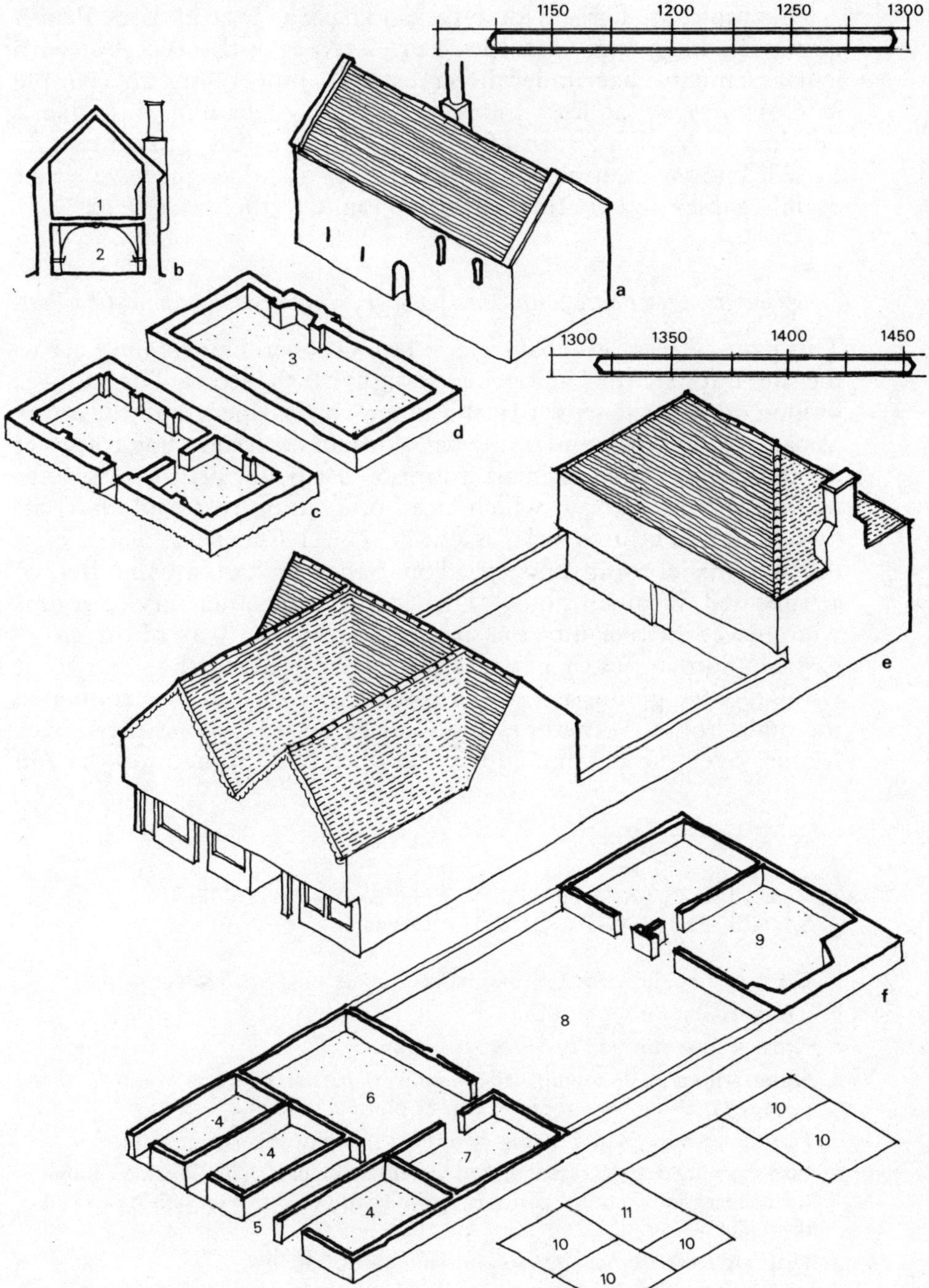

1150
1200
1250
1300
1300
1350
1400
1450
a
b
c
d
e
f
1
2
3
4
4
4
5
6
7
8
9
10
10
10
10
10
11

Examples are fairly widespread and have a range of dates. Pantin quotes Tackleys Inn, Oxford *c.* 1291–1300 as of this type but with half-basement cellars under the shops; S. R. Jones quotes an example in Coventry as 'at least fourteenth century'; Faulkner ascribes a building in Market Square, Faversham, to mid-fifteenth century.[2]

All known examples are timber-framed and might have either double gables or a continuous jettied range to the street front.

4. *Wide frontage house with cross-passage, single-ended ground-floor hall*

This plan-type is also characterized by an open hall running across the site, but here the hall opened straight off the street. The hall was single-ended in the sense that subsidiary rooms opened off the cross-passage at the lower end of the hall with no corresponding rooms at the upper end. The subsidiary rooms could be for private or service use but the small room which faced on to the street could have its own door and be used or let as a shop. The chamber was placed over the two smaller rooms and jettied on to the street, giving the effect of a truncated Wealden house. The kitchen and other service rooms were placed further into the site and reached by way of the cross-passage. Sometimes there was a line of shops along the street front with an entry giving access to a courtyard which in turn contained the main house. Sometimes the solar extended beyond the service rooms, over the passage and so into the hall. Sometimes the full

---

4. WIDE FRONTAGE HOUSE WITH CROSS-PASSAGE, SINGLE-ENDED GROUND-FLOOR HALL

a. General view showing shop and hall entrances and jettied upper storey.
b. Cross-section through hall.
c. Cross-section through two-storey portion.
d. Ground-floor plan showing hall (1), shop (2), parlour or service room (3), cross-passage (4) also giving access to rear of plot.
e. Part upper-floor plan showing chamber (5) and upper part of hall (6).
f. Plan showing double-ended hall on wider frontage; as in the Wealden houses of the countryside there is a parlour (7) and chamber above located at one end of the hall.
g. Diagram to show a chamber occupying part of the hall.
h. Diagram to show the hall behind a range of shops.

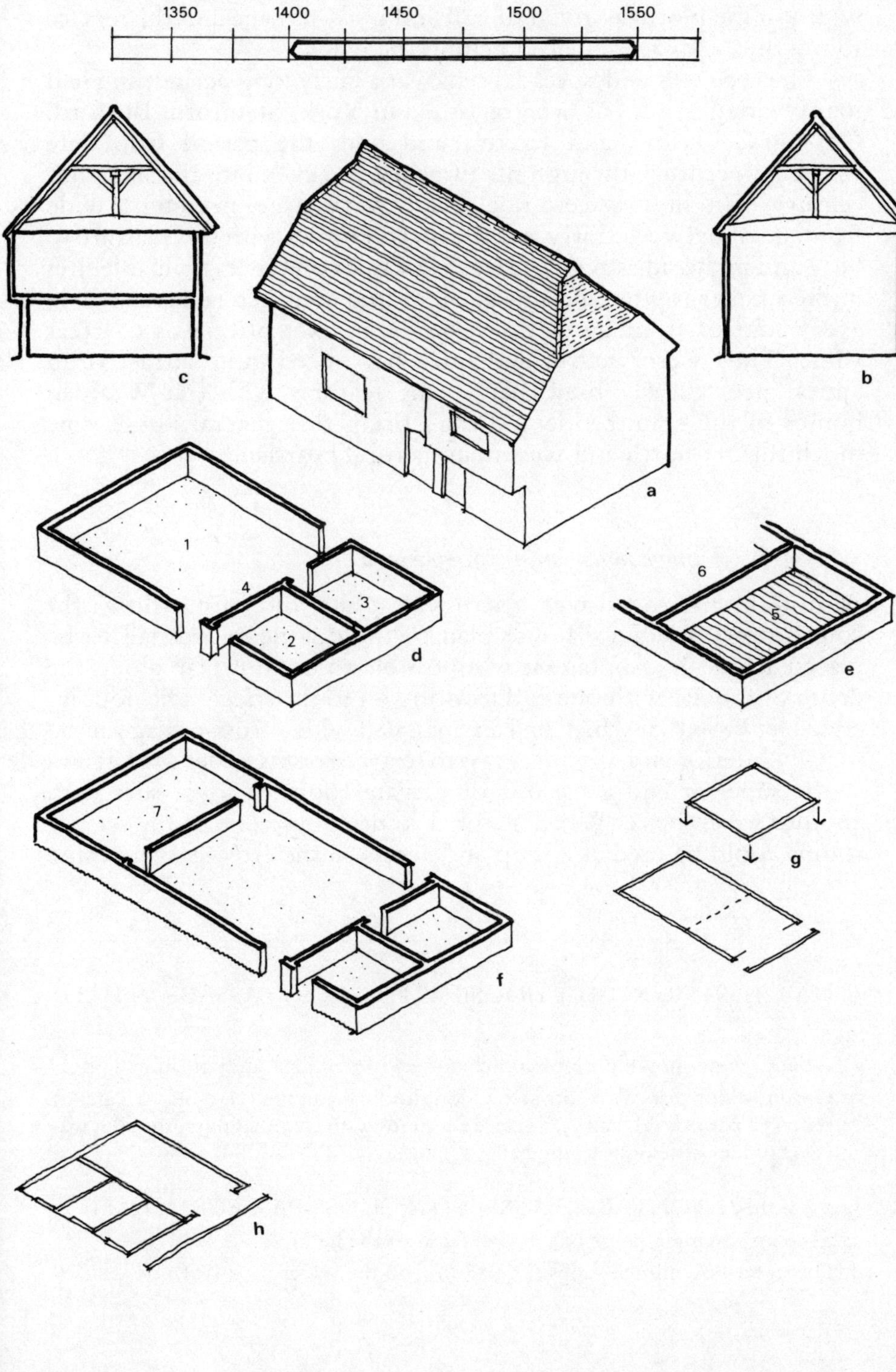

1350
1400
1450
1500
1550
c
b
a
1
2
3
4
d
5
6
e
7
f
g
h

width of the plot was given to hall and cross-passage and the service rooms and solar were placed behind the hall.

The type was widespread, used over a fairly long period, and had many variations. It has been recorded in York, Stamford, Burford, Coventry, Oxford and Exeter, and over the period from late fourteenth century through the fifteenth and even into the sixteenth century. The houses were not usually very large; needing a wide frontage of between thirty and fifty feet. Houses with this plan are to be found in the side streets of larger towns or on the less valuable sites in the smaller towns, and not in the prime commercial areas where every foot of frontage to the street or market place was of great value. They were well lit and must have been quite attractive in appearance. Clearly they share some features with the Wealden houses of the countryside and they bring this general house type much further north and west than its rural heartland.

5. *Narrow frontage house with cross-passage*

Although the narrower medieval plots did not allow the conventional medieval house plan of the double-ended hall to be placed across the frontage it was possible to use this plan along the depth of the site with one end fronting on to the street. The double-ended hall was that which had an open hall with a cross-passage at the socially inferior end, giving access to service rooms under a solar, and at the superior end a parlour or private room of some sort with another solar above. When adapted to urban use one of the service rooms could be used as a shop and access to the cross-passage came

---

5. NARROW FRONTAGE HOUSE WITH CROSS-PASSAGE IN HALL

a. General view showing shops and chambers roofed separately from hall.
b. Ground-floor plan with entrance to longitudinal passage (1), cross-passage (2), shop (3), parlour (4), hall (5), service room (6) with chamber over; the alleyway (7) provides little light to the hall.

5a. WIDER FRONTAGE HOUSE WITH CROSS-PASSAGE IN HALL

c. Sketch showing a range of shops in front of the hall.
d. Diagram showing the shops (8), hall (9) and the wider yard (10).

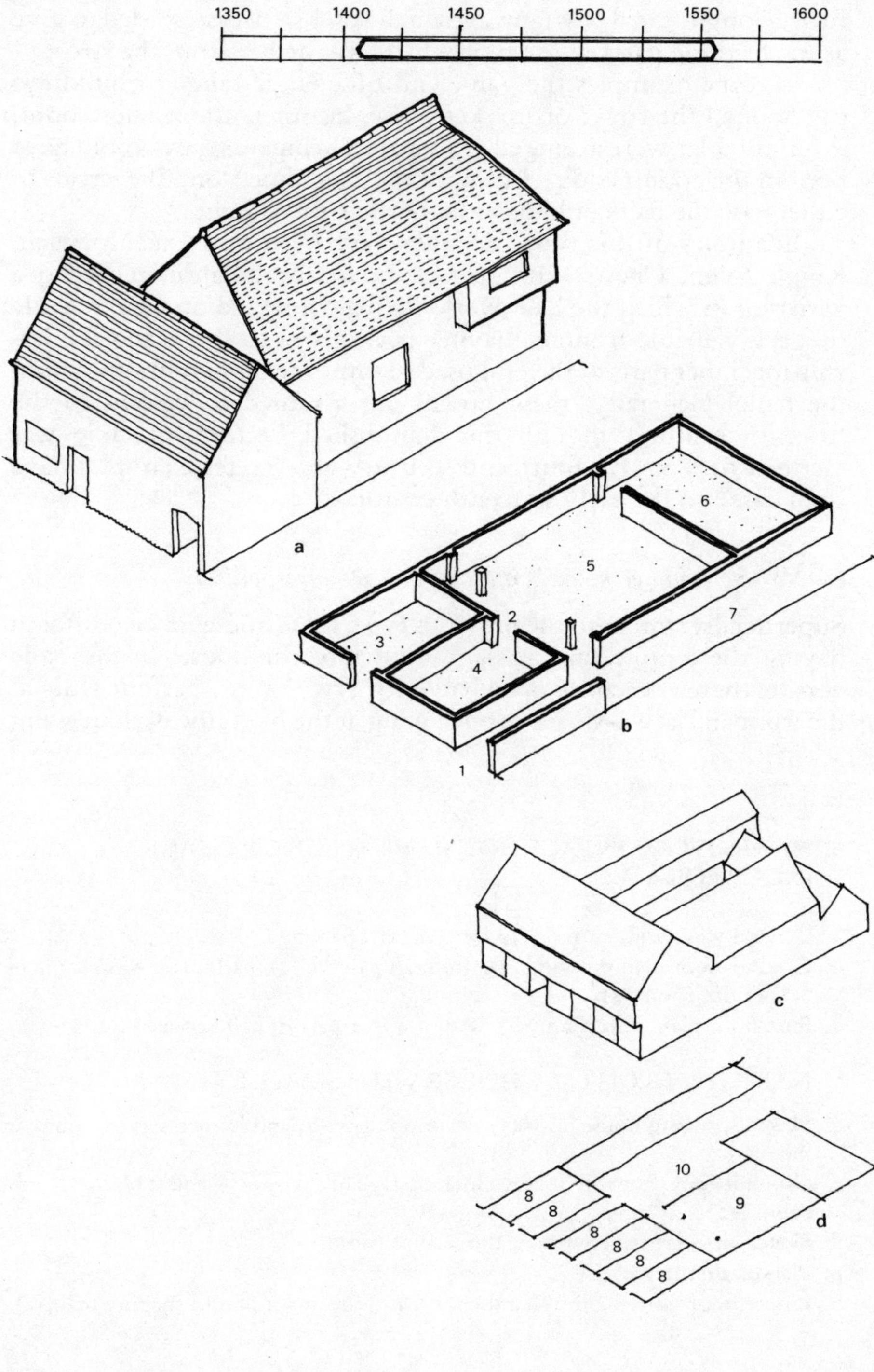
1350
1400
1450
1500
1550
1600
a
b
1
2
3
4
5
6
7
c
d
8
8
8
8
8
8
9
10

from a longitudinal passageway which was in any case needed to give access to those parts of the plot which lay further from the street.

In some examples the gable end of a single range of buildings overlooked the street or market place, in others the service room, shop and solar were arranged as a separate wing – as they would have been in the countryside – but with the eaves line along the street. In either case the hall could have had little natural light.

Examples of this type of house have been noted in Norwich, King's Lynn, Chester and Exeter. In Oxford, Pantin recorded a variation in which the hall overlooked a courtyard on a fairly wide site; the valuable frontage having been given to shops and the less valuable inner parts of the plot used to improve the conditions within the hall.[3] Generally, these houses are assumed to belong to the fifteenth century, though the demolished Oxford example was ascribed to the early fourteenth century and Exeter examples have been dated to the early sixteenth century.

6. *Narrow frontage house with long passage incorporated*

Superficially similar to the previous type, these houses in fact differ in having the longitudinal passage built into the house. In the basic version there is a central open hall with a two-storey parlour wing at the front and a two-storey service wing at the back; the parlour wing

---

6. NARROW FRONTAGE HOUSE WITH LONG PASSAGE INCORPORATED

a. General view with entrance to longitudinal passage (1).
b. Ground-floor plan showing longitudinal passage (1), parlour or shop (2), hall (3), service room (4).
c. First-floor plan with chambers (5) and upper part of hall between (6).

7. NARROW FRONTAGE HOUSE WITH SMALL HALL

d. Sketch showing house door (7) and shop door (8) and lean-to service room at the rear.
e. Ground-floor plan with longitudinal passage (9), shop (10), hall (11) and service room (12).
f. Sketch of alternative without the service room.
g. Plan of alternative.
h. Upper floor showing the chamber (13) and the upper part of the tiny hall (14).

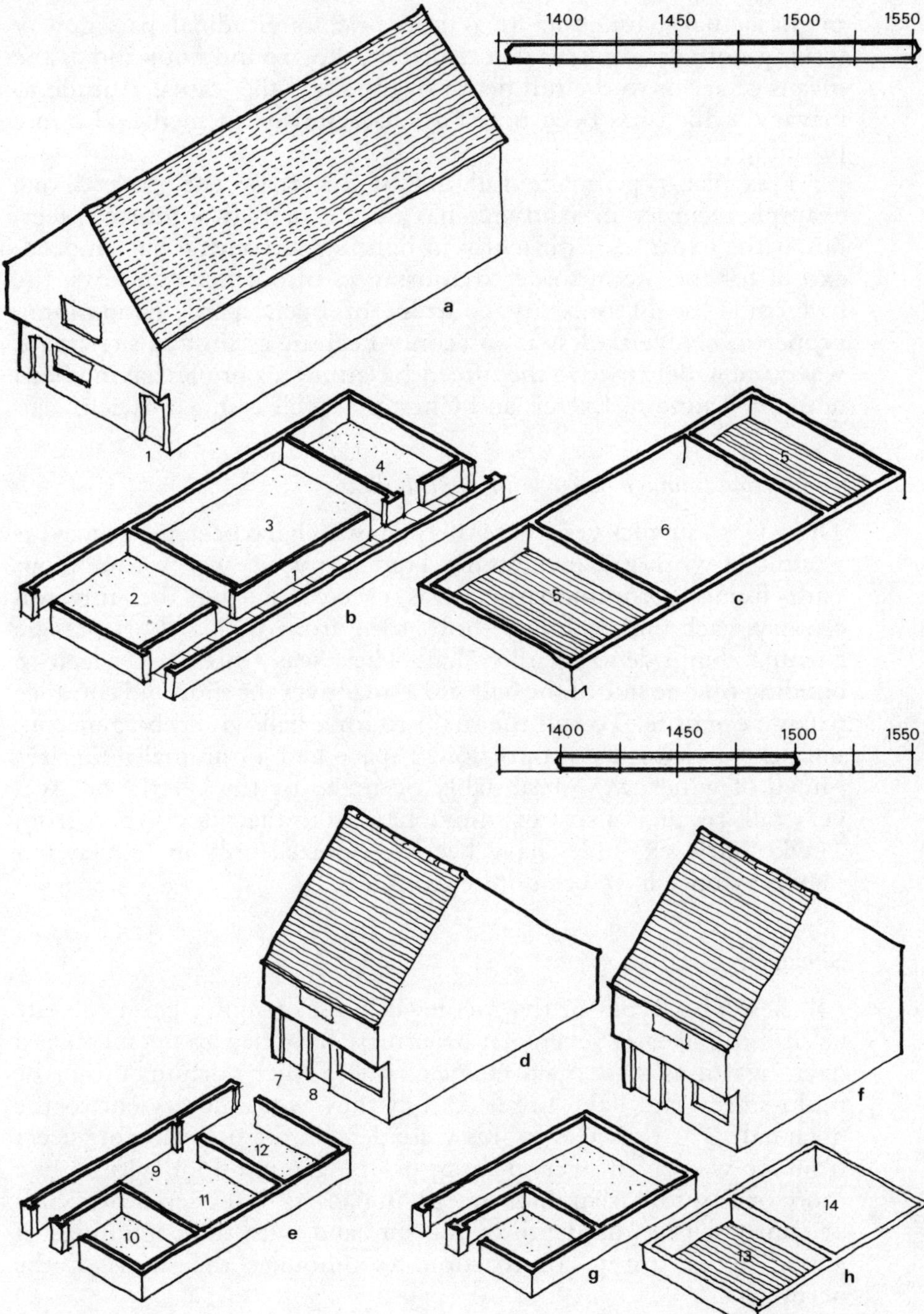
1400
1450
1500
1550
a
1
2
3
4
1
b
5
6
5
c
1400
1450
1500
1550
7
8
d
f
9
12
11
10
e
g
14
13
h

might actually function as a shop; the longitudinal passageway serving both as an internal corridor on the ground floor and as the means of access to the full depth of the site – the 'casual attitude to privacy' which has been noted as characteristic of medieval house planning.

This plan-type made full use of a narrow site (indeed one example recorded in Sandwich has a site as narrow as fourteen feet) but at the expense of difficulty in lighting the central hall. Indeed, except for the use in some circumstances of dormer windows, the hall could be lit only by courtesy of open space in adjoining properties. Nevertheless as an economical use of limited site area it was quite widely used in the fifteenth century, examples having been noted in Taunton, Exeter, and Chester as well as in Sandwich.

7. *Narrow frontage house with small hall*

There was a smaller version of this plan which has been recognized as a result of work in Tewkesbury. Here a row of twenty-four shops with living accommodation was erected during the fifteenth century, each unit having a shop at the front with a short passage running alongside to a shallow hall. There was a kitchen in a lean-to building off one side of the hall and a solar over the shop and entrance passage opposite. To call the main room a hall would be generous since the awkwardly-proportioned space had a minimal floor area (much of which was presumably occupied by the hearth) but was very tall, rising as a sort of smoke bay up to the ridge. Apart from Tewkesbury, examples have been recognized only in Exeter, but they may once have been quite common.

Summary

All these plan-types of the medieval house, ranging from the late twelfth to the early seventeenth century, have had an open hall and open hearth as their main characteristic. Other portions might be multi-storey and have fireplaces but they were subservient to the open hall. The principal rooms were deep in the site; valuable street frontage was given over to shops on the ground floor with only a more or less utilitarian doorway giving access to the series of rooms or courts within the depth of the site, and with the beginnings of jettied upper storey construction to announce the status of the occupants.

LATER URBAN HOUSES

8. *Wide-frontage house with back-to-back fireplaces*

By about 1500 the open hall had fallen completely out of favour and houses built during the sixteenth century and later were of several storeys connected by staircases (which were given steadily greater architectural importance) and heated by fireplaces which gained increasing significance in house planning. Since the narrow plots of the medieval urban core in each town were already occupied, the newer houses of the sixteenth and seventeenth centuries were built on wider plots on the fringes. This tendency continued through succeeding centuries, but some houses were built as replacements on existing narrow plots and some plots were even subdivided when pressure on the most favoured sites made such land ever more valuable.

The basic multi-storey town house consisted of two rooms on each floor heated by fireplaces which were placed back-to-back and whose flues rose to a huge central chimney stack. The rooms were served by a staircase which either projected from the rear or was tucked into the baffle-entry lobby against the chimneys. There were usually two main floors and an attic or garret storey lit by dormer windows. This house plan was introduced into Oxford and Stamford at least during the early seventeenth century, adopted for houses built either in brick or stone, and remained a popular plan especially for smaller dwellings until well into the nineteenth century.

As an alternative, houses were designed for a wide frontage but with the central entrance giving on to a staircase hall and the two principal rooms on each floor having gabled fireplaces (see universal terrace houses, p 134).

9. *Wide frontage L-shaped or T-shaped house*

Since the plot width of a town site was limited, extra accommodation could be provided only by increasing the height or the depth of the house. One way was to add a third heated room on each floor in a wing projecting from the rear to give an L or T shape. The three rooms on each floor were connected by a staircase, usually of quite a generous size, located in the angle between the wing and main block.

10. *Wide frontage double-pile house*

The end of the seventeenth century and the early years of the eighteenth saw the introduction of the double-pile house plan, an event as significant in the development of urban house planning as it was in the planning of houses in the countryside. The essential feature of the plan was that there were four rooms on each floor: two at the front and two at the back. Double-pile houses were two rooms in width, two rooms in depth, and usually two rooms in height if one discounts garret and cellar spaces.

---

8. WIDE FRONTAGE HOUSE WITH BACK-TO-BACK FIREPLACES

a. General view showing how central fireplaces rise to a compact grouped chimney stack halfway along the ridge. In the sketch there are deep dormer windows lighting the topmost storey.
b. Plan showing the back-to-back fireplaces serving hall (1) and parlour (2) with newel or dog-leg staircase at the rear (3).
c. Alternative plan with back-to-back fireplaces serving hall and parlour but with newel staircase tucked between front door and fireplace jambs.

9. WIDE FRONTAGE L-SHAPED OR T-SHAPED HOUSE

d. Sketch showing a house one room deep with gable fireplaces and chimney stacks and a rear projection making an L-shaped plan.
e. Plan with entrance passage between hall (4) and parlour (5) and with a projecting kitchen (6) and newel staircase (7) in the angle.

10. WIDE FRONTAGE DOUBLE-PILE HOUSE

f. General view of a double-pile town house showing the depth of two rooms, in this instance covered by two parallel roofs drained by a valley gutter.
g. Plan showing entrance and staircase between hall (8) and parlour (9) and kitchen (10) and rear parlour (11); the fireplaces are on the end or party walls.
h. The plan of Type 10a, the similar general arrangement but with fireplaces on the internal or spine walls.

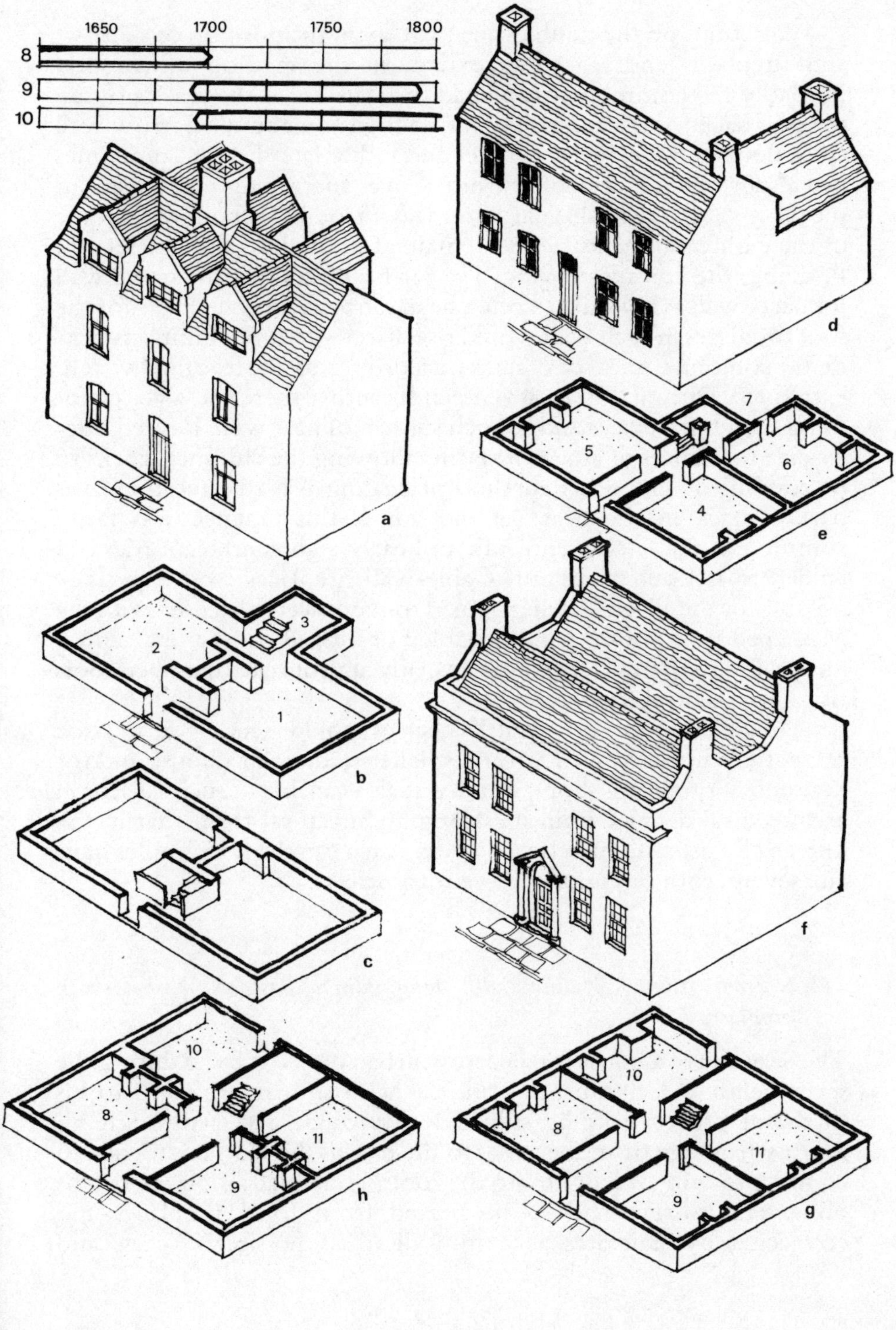
1650
1700
1750
1800
8
9
10
a
1
2
3
b
c
d
4
5
6
7
e
f
8
9
10
11
g
h

Variations on the double-pile plan lay in the position of staircase and fireplaces and, to some extent, in the method of roofing. Probably the commonest type had the staircase at the rear between the two back rooms and rising in two flights or about a narrow well from floor to floor, but the larger and rather later houses sometimes had a staircase at one side, lit from above, and giving more space to the rooms at the rear; this variation was introduced about the middle of the eighteenth century and remained in use into the nineteenth. Probably the commonest location for fireplaces was the gable wall (or party wall as it would so often be in the town house). Flues for the four fireplaces in each wall would rise directly to four chimney stacks or be combined into two stacks according to the roofing system employed. During the late seventeenth century there was a vogue for using corner fireplaces and so such sources of heat were located side-by-side in corners of adjacent rooms allowing the chimney stacks to be combined. The other method of heating was to have fireplaces back-to-back in the heart of the house: this practice was fairly common in the late seventeenth and early eighteenth centuries but tended to fall out of favour. Gable-wall fireplaces were especially suitable for the all-embracing gabled roof but were also used with the M-shaped roof of two parallel gabled or hipped roofs and a central gutter. Internal fireplaces were especially appropriate to hipped roofs rising to a central flat area.

This plan was so versatile that it could serve for a large pretentious house as well as for a smaller tradesman's house and for houses incorporating shops; but it was also capable of such variety in architectural detail within its strong architectural form that it was universally used and practically every town can show examples in its late seventeenth or eighteenth-century streets.

11. *Narrow frontage house with longitudinal passage, back-to-back fireplaces*

The designer of a house for a narrow urban plot was faced during the seventeenth and eighteenth centuries with similar problems to his medieval predecessor: he still had to provide access through his narrow frontage from the street to the rear of the plot; he still had to contrive to bring daylight into the rooms, but in addition the rooms on several storeys had to be heated from fixed fireplaces and connected by staircases as commodious as possible. Access and daylight entailed longitudinal corridors and rear courtyards; fireplaces and staircases gave opportunity for more variety in arrangement.

Many houses built in towns after the early part of the seventeenth century had two fireplaces set back-to-back on each floor with a spiral staircase or a very tight newel staircase rising alongside. On the ground floor there was a longitudinal corridor or passageway which gave access from street to yard, as well as providing internal communication, and the staircase was confined between passageway and fireplace jambs. Where two rooms on each floor would suffice the plan was neat and compact and gave no serious problems in daylighting. There were some problems in roofing, however: the obvious method was to present a gable to the street and have a ridge running along the depth of the house, but this was a medieval type of roof, unfashionable in the seventeenth century and more commonly a hipped roof was provided, partly concealed behind a front parapet. An alternative solution was to run a ridge across the house, the deep roof being used for attic rooms and a gambrel section giving more headroom to these attics. A more complex roof had an eaves to the front with ridge across the site and a gable to the rear terminating a longitudinal ridge. Where more than two rooms were required on each floor the plan was not satisfactory and extra rooms had to be built as pavilions along the length of the site, leaving small courtyards or light wells to allow daylight into the rear rooms of the main building.

After its introduction early in the seventeenth century this type remained popular and examples may be found in smaller towns well into the nineteenth century. The plan was used mainly in the southern half of England, examples having been recorded from Oxford, Harwich, Taunton, Blandford, Exeter and Totnes. The variation found in York, for example, in which a staircase splits the fireplaces, is noted as 17 below.

12. *Narrow frontage house with longitudinal passage, end-wall fireplaces*

The association of staircases and fireplaces was never very convenient. This tightly packed block in the centre of the house dominated each floor and gave little freedom in floor or room planning. The staircase tended to be narrow, tightly turning, and generally cramped. As the fashion developed for taller and taller rooms it became more and more important to allow space for the

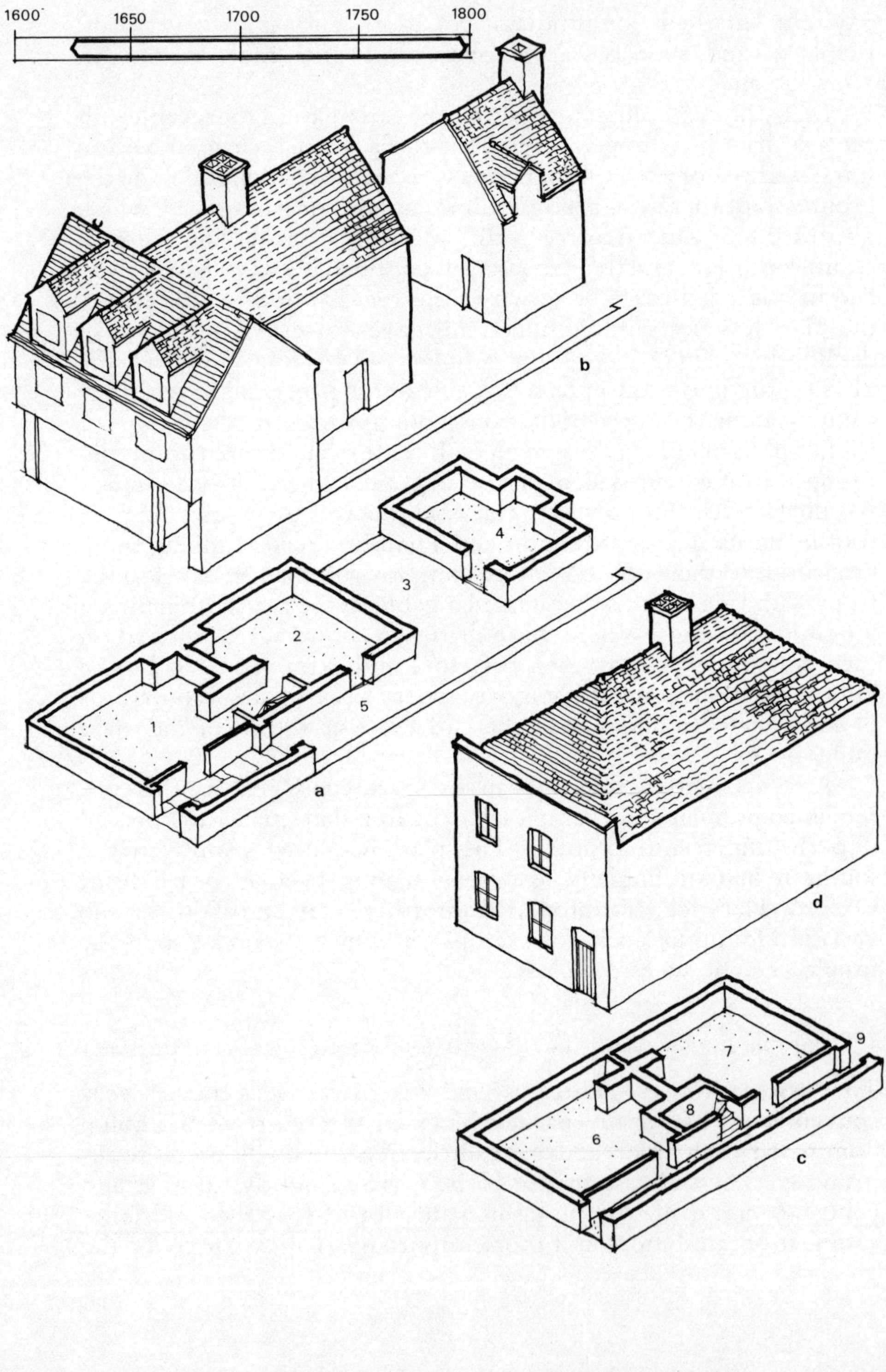
1600
1650
1700
1750
1800
a
b
c
d
1
2
3
4
5
6
7
8
9

11. NARROW FRONTAGE HOUSE WITH LONGITUDINAL PASSAGE, BACK-TO-BACK FIREPLACES

a. Ground-floor plan showing a parlour or shop (1) and living-room (2), then an open court (3) which allows light into living-room and outside kitchen (4); access is by means of a passage through the front part of the house and so along an alleyway (5) which leads to the rear part of the site.
b. Isometric sketch showing the whole frontage of the site occupied by the front part of the building; there is an eaves line along the street, and dormer windows light an attic storey; the remaining part of the site has buildings roofed at right angles to the street.
c. Ground-floor plan of a smaller house with parlour (6) and living-room (7) having fireplaces back-to-back; there is a staircase against the fireplace jambs (8); the passage (9) is incorporated within the house but also gives access to the rear of the plot.
d. Isometric sketch of plan c. Here there is a front parapet which partly conceals the low-pitched roof.

---

staircase, to take the fireplaces away, and to place them where they could be in proportion to bigger and more spacious rooms. Since front and back walls were required for windows, the only other location for the fireplace was the end or party wall. The advantages of the central staircase conveniently serving rooms on each floor and reached from a longitudinal corridor were retained and the disadvantages minimized when fireplaces, flues and chimney stacks migrated to the party walls.

Such a plan was introduced into Exeter and Totnes during the late sixteenth century and early seventeenth century, was known in Stamford in the early eighteenth century and in York rather later, and it was used in these and other towns right through the eighteenth century and well into the nineteenth. Earlier examples had a gabled roof but from the end of the seventeenth century the use of a hip or a complex roof with ridge parallel to the street may be observed.

Not all urban plots even in central areas of ancient towns were of the long medieval type; some were short because they were extensions to existing streets or because they were carved from the depth of some large plot. But it was still important to make the most use of a narrow frontage and so many of the eighteenth- and early nineteenth-century town houses were only one room in depth, had a short passage running from front to back between the single room on each floor and the straight flight staircase, and rose up two or three floors, often with rooms in the roof space in addition. It was virtually inevitable in such a plan that the fireplace would be on a gable or party wall.

13. *Wide frontage house with central stair, end-wall fireplaces*

While one way, and the earlier way, of handling a wide frontage was to employ fireplaces back-to-back as has been noted, another way, and ultimately a way which was preferred, was to arrange a central entrance opening on to a staircase hall and to provide two principal rooms on each floor, fireplaces in the end or party walls serving each room. The compactness of the central common stack was lost but better proportions were gained for the various rooms and a better approach: it can hardly have been comfortable or satisfying to enter from the street against the blank wall of a fireplace jamb. Such a house was less spacious and less compact than a double-pile house but it was just as imposing when set within an urban terrace and gave an

---

12. NARROW FRONTAGE HOUSE WITH LONGITUDINAL PASSAGE, END-WALL FIREPLACES

a. Ground-floor plan showing a parlour or shop (1) living-room (2) and detached kitchen (3) with a courtyard (4) lighting kitchen and living-room; the fireplaces are on the end or party wall and the staircase (5) is between the main rooms. The passage (6) leading from the street is incorporated in the ground floor of the house.
b. Isometric sketch showing a gable to the street and, in this instance, jettied storeys as from a timber-framed front wall.
c. Ground-floor plan of a house which is on a similarly narrow frontage but is also only one room in depth. The fireplaces are on the end or party wall and the entrance lobby also serves as a passage to the rear.
d. Sketch showing, in this example, an eaves line along the street and dormer windows lighting the attic rooms.

13. WIDE FRONTAGE HOUSE WITH CENTRAL STAIR, END-WALL FIREPLACES

e. Plan showing the house taken through 90° as permitted by the wide plot. There is a living-room (9), a parlour (10) and a staircase between (11); the fireplaces are on the end or party walls. A short passage (12) serves the rear of the plot and the bedrooms would be built over this passage.

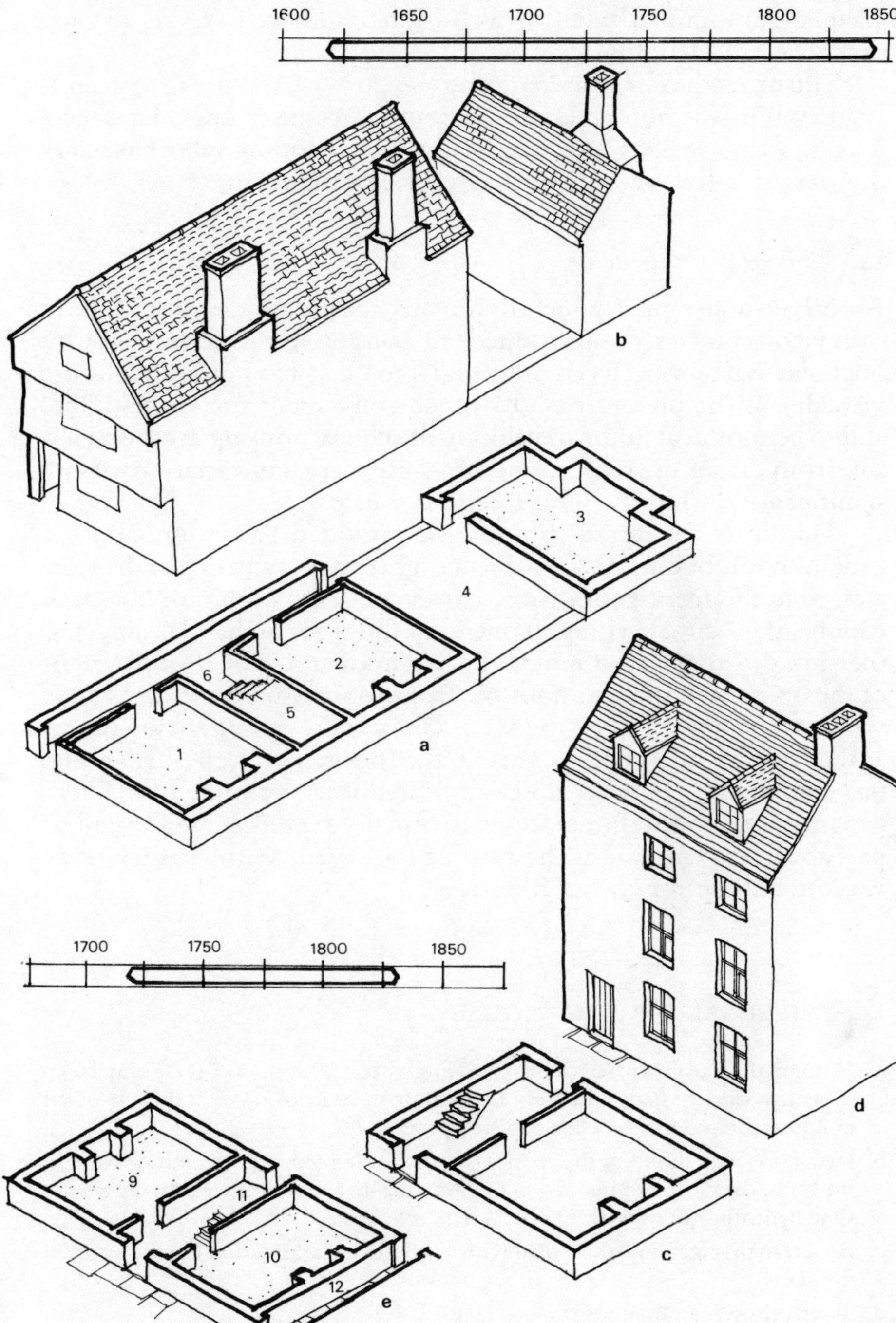
1600
1650
1700
1750
1800
1850
b
3
4
2
6
5
1
a
d
1700
1750
1800
1850
9
11
10
12
e
c

adequate amount of well-lit, well-heated and well-served accommodation on each floor.

The plan was introduced during the early part of the seventeenth century but was not generally used until a century later. Examples may be seen in what were then the newly developing suburbs such as those outside the walls of York, Beverley or Chester.

14. *Universal terrace house*

An urban house plan which dominated domestic design for more than two centuries was introduced in London in the houses built by Nicholas Barbon between 1670 and 1700 and has continued in use virtually to the present day. It was so convenient for domestic life and so economical in the development of new housing areas on land free from earlier site restrictions that there were few variations of any significance during the whole period of its use.

The universal terrace house plan provided two rooms on the ground floor, one at the front and a slightly narrower one at the rear; alongside the front room is the entrance lobby; alongside the back room is the staircase rising in one long flight to the half landing and then in a shorter return flight to the first floor and so up the full height of the house. On the first floor the front room usually ran the whole width of the house but on the second floor there might be two rooms at the front to give three rooms on that floor. The earliest examples had a small single-storey 'closet' or heated study opening off the rear ground-floor room. Fireplaces were usually placed along the end or party wall except that at the turn of the seventeenth century there was the fashion for corner fireplaces.

---

14. UNIVERSAL TERRACE HOUSE

a. Ground-floor plan with parlour (1), dining-room (2) and a closet (3) which was sometimes heated in order to serve as a study; the staircase (4) is at the rear of the building; fireplaces are in the gable or party walls.
b. First-floor plan showing the room (5) which extended over the whole front of the house and came to be used as the drawing-room or principal living-room. One bedroom (6) is on this floor, others are above.
c. An alternative ground-floor plan with similar accommodation but with corner fireplaces.
d. Sketch showing one house in a terrace.

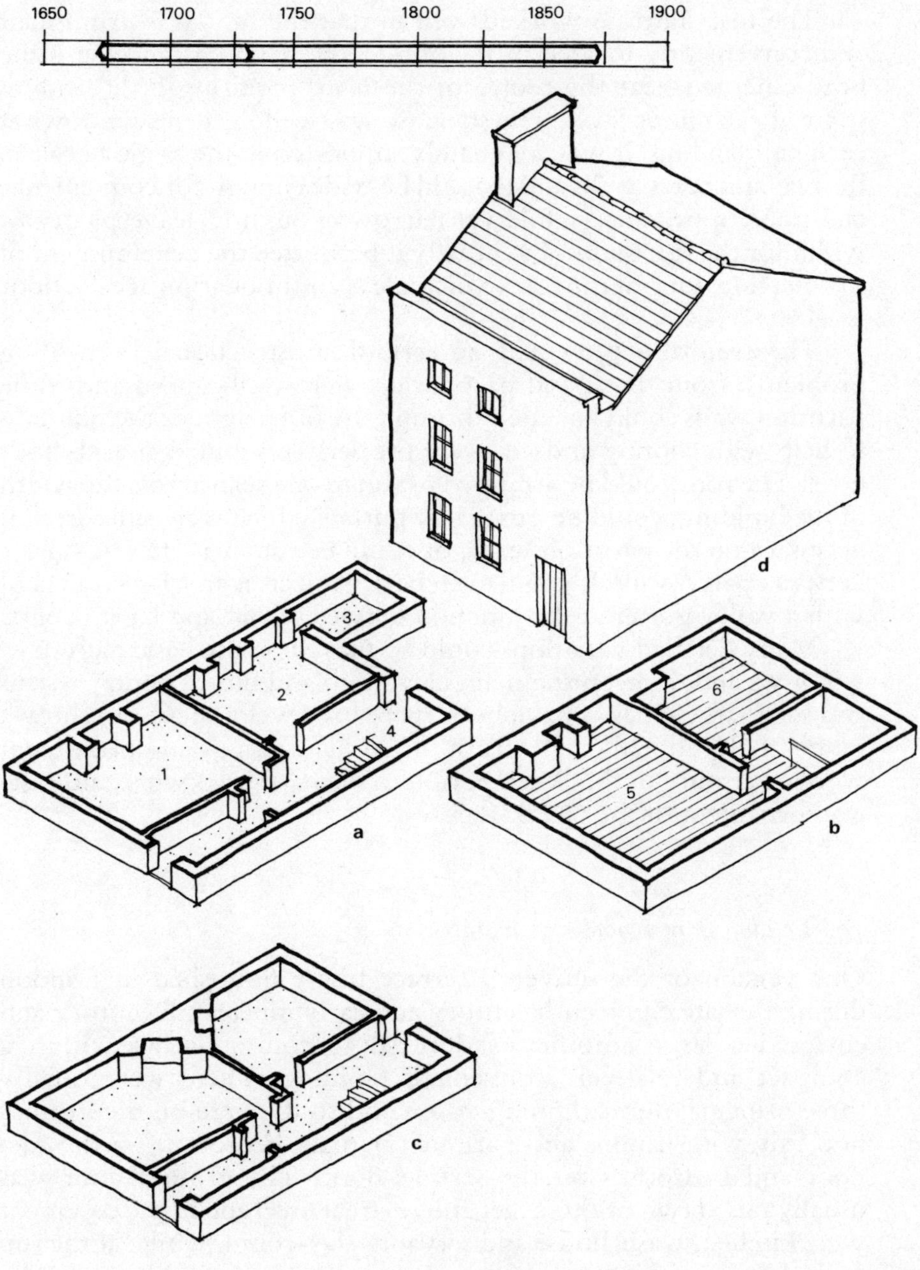
1650
1700
1750
1800
1850
1900
1
2
3
4
5
6
a
b
c
d

The rear staircase worked well in that the foot was prominent and conveniently located in relation to the main entrance, and the head emerged near the centre of the plan, requiring little landing space at each floor level. The staircase was well lit from windows at each half landing; it was adequately supported in the angle between the rear and party walls and it could be wide enough for convenience and good appearance while yet narrow enough to leave plenty of width for the rear room. Eventually it permitted the development of a projecting wing at the rear to increase accommodation at each floor level.

The plan also presented no serious constructional or roofing problems: front, back and party walls were well-braced and some partition walls could be raised through the full height of the building to help with roofing and yet were properly restrained at each floor level. The roof could be arranged to run in one span across the width of the building, could be carried by purlins which were supported if necessary on the partition walls, or could be run in a series of valleys between party walls. It could even be organized as an M-section roof with a valley gutter at the junction between front and back rooms.

Many detailed variations could be played on the basic pattern of windows and door on the main elevation, and most country towns and such large cities as have been spared redevelopment can show a range of elevational details from the stone dressings and prominent wooden cornice of the Wren period to the hard brickwork and cast-iron ornament of the Greek Revival.

15. *London terrace house, rear stairs*

One version of the universal terrace house flourished in London during the late eighteenth century and early nineteenth century and enclosed a large amount of domestic accommodation within a compact and relatively convenient building. There were usually three principal floors. Dining-room and study were on the ground floor, drawing-rooms and parlour (or main bedroom) on the first floor and bedrooms on the second floor. The ground floor was usually raised two or three feet above street level and in the basement were kitchen, wash-house and servants' day-room, while, at the top of the house, within the roof space, were the servants' bedrooms. The basement rooms at the front of the house were lit from an 'area' i.e. an open light well within the curtilage of the house which also gave access to coal cellars under the footpath. Servants and tradesmen reached the area by way of steps from the pavement railings, for, in the absence of any other means of access to the house at the rear the area stairs was the tradesman's entrance and general means of servicing. Since the artificial road level was often several feet above the natural ground level the rear basement rooms might open directly on to a garden at the rear of the site. This, incidentally, allows what in other circumstances might be called cellar dwellings to be quite legitimately termed 'garden apartments' in houses which have been subdivided. The rooms within the roof were true attic bedrooms in that the double-pitch gambrel roof which was often provided was above the cornice line and behind a parapet. Since every room from basement to attic had a fireplace, the party walls were a honeycomb of flues and the simple, even austere, lines of the elevation were relieved by the dozens of chimney pots which once contributed so much to the visitor's impression of London.

The side staircase was usually lit from a window or series of windows at each landing level, and light penetrated down the well between the two flights which formed each stretch of the staircase and along the short corridors which served each floor.

16. *London terrace house, central stairs*

The central staircase plans of the seventeenth century were never entirely superseded by the rear staircase or universal terrace house plans. The central staircase plan had a renewed period of use in the late eighteenth and early nineteenth centuries but with fireplaces on the party wall, and, in London especially, was used for some of the most magnificent town houses of the late Georgian and Regency period.

The disposition of rooms floor by floor was similar to that of the London terrace house, with side stair already described, but the central staircase, top-lit from a lantern in the roof, wound gently around a generous open well to give light and movement in a part of the plan which would otherwise have been dark and rigid. The whole of the rear wall was available for lighting an important room on each floor, and by interposing an ante room behind the stairs and between the principal rooms an attractive architectural sequence of spaces on each floor could be contrived.

The very generosity of the space allocated to the staircase meant

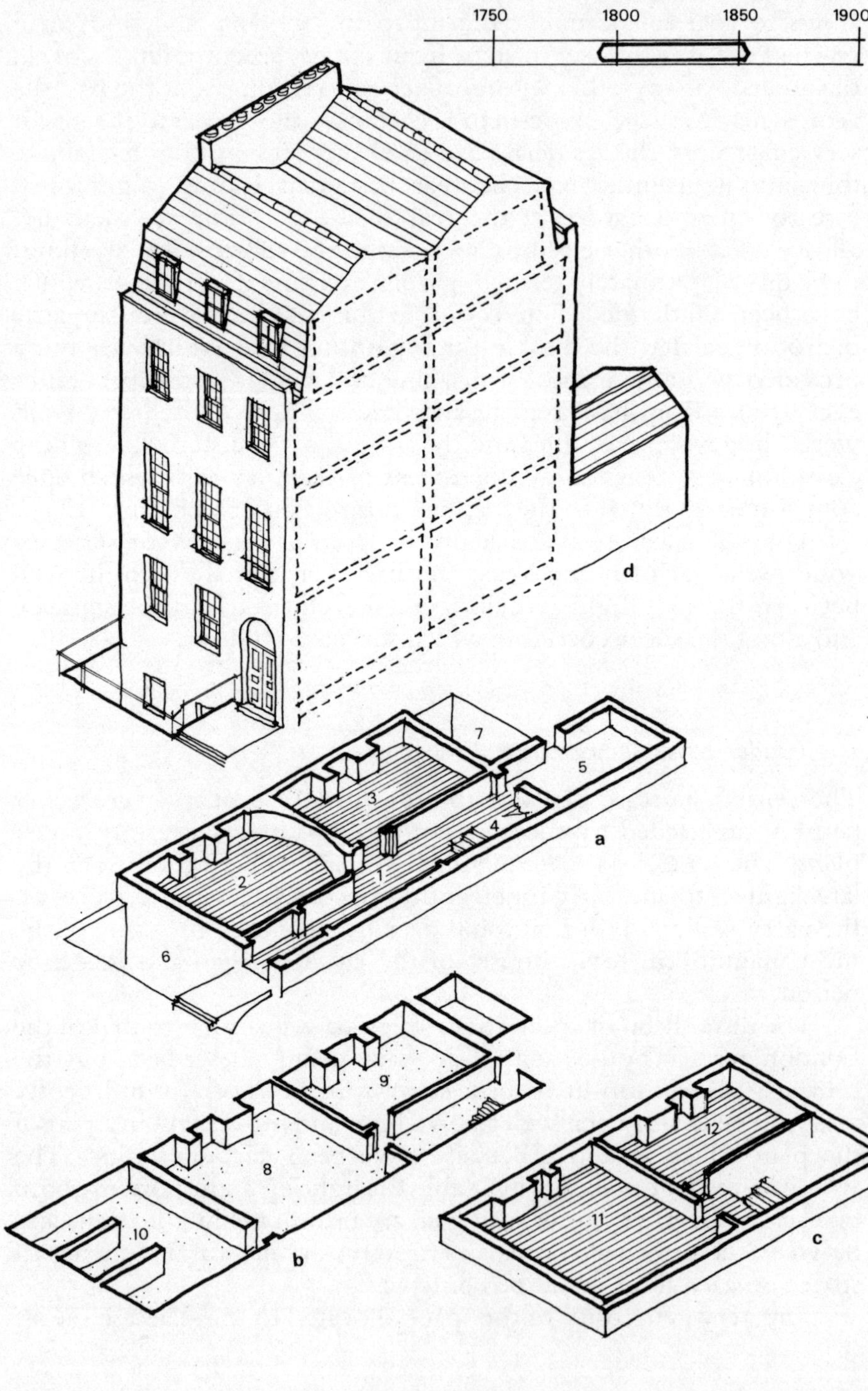
1750
1800
1850
1900
d
7
5
3
4
a
2
1
6
9
8
12
11
10
b
c

15. LONDON TERRACE HOUSE, REAR STAIRS

a. Ground-floor plan showing the entrance lobby (1), parlour (2) and dining-room (3) with a double-flight staircase (4) at the rear; there is a service room (5) projecting into the main yard; at the front of the house an area (6) gives light and access to basement rooms; in this instance another area (7) has been provided to light basement-rooms at the rear.
b. Basement plan showing kitchen and staff rooms (8 and 9) lit from the front and rear areas; the front area also gives access to coal bunkers under the footpath (10).
c. First-floor plan with the drawing-room (11) stretching across the front and a bedroom (12) beside the staircase.
d. Sketch showing the building as a tall narrow slice from a terrace. Here there are front parapets with attic storeys and a collection of chimneys in a huge stack in a party wall.

---

that this plan was not quite as economical as its counterpart with the rear staircase, but for the larger houses the architectural gains were presumably considered worth the slight loss in economy.

As in other terraced houses there was the problem of access to the rear of the plot to be solved. In smaller examples the only access might be through the house, though usually an open corridor was provided between houses; in larger examples access was by way of the basement. Where there was a rear service road or alleyway then access was readily provided, and for larger houses so favoured there was often a mews consisting of coach house and stable with coachman's quarters above.

The London terrace house plans were convenient and economical up to a point. Their many fireplaces, several reception rooms and many bedrooms were on a number of floors and, while this was economical in construction and compact at each floor level, the family for some of the time and the servants for much of the time must have found flight after flight of staircase something less than a convenience. It was an arrangement which often drew comment from Continental travellers more accustomed to the wide and spacious 'hotel' or the flat all on one level.

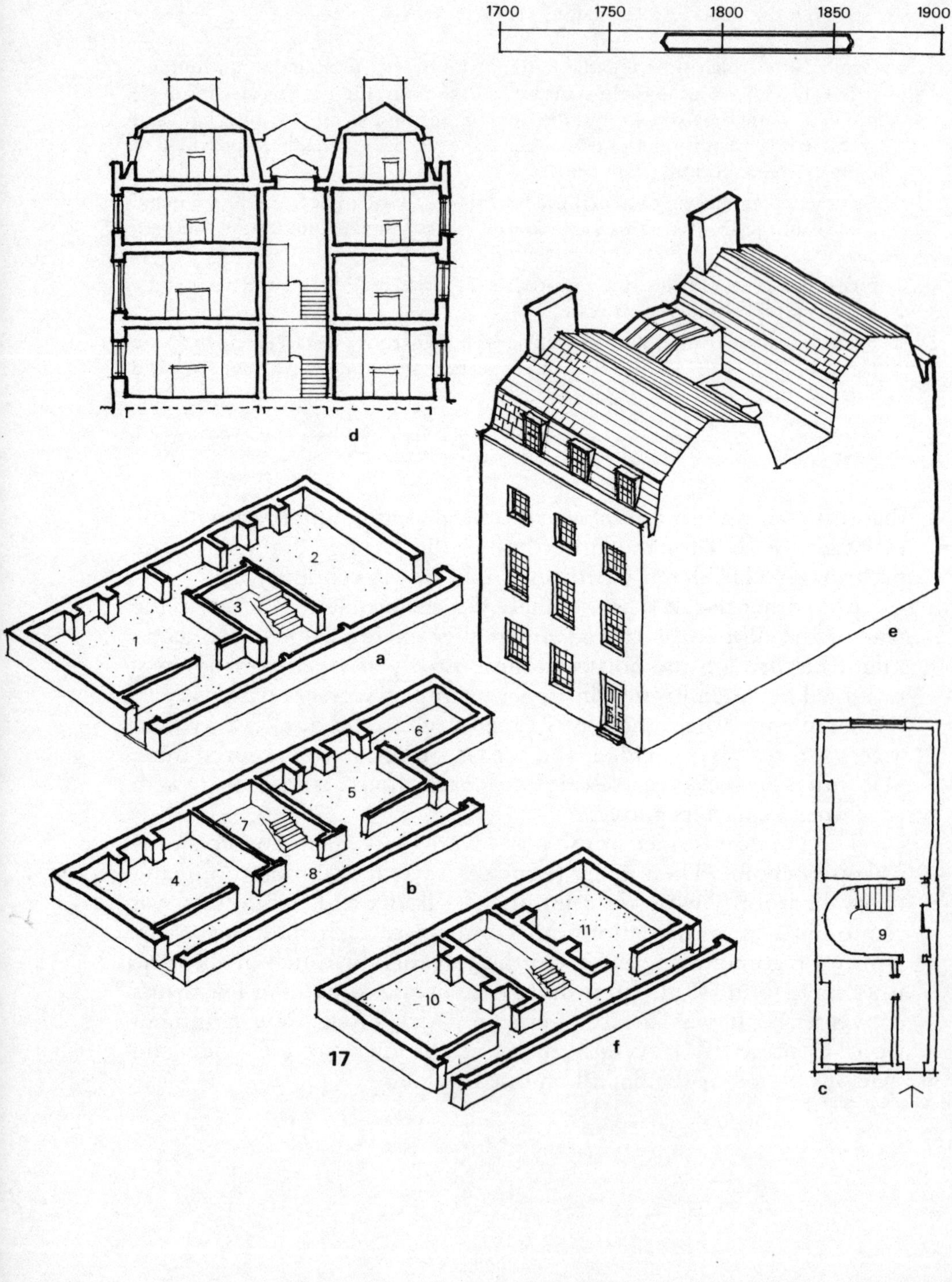

17

17. *Narrow frontage house with central stairs between fireplaces*

This plan, which has been particularly noted in York, has a room at the front and a room at the back on each floor, a staircase between the rooms, a longitudinal passage linking rooms and staircase and sometimes serving also as the link through from street to rear of the plot, but is unusual in having fireplaces backing on to the staircase walls. The arrangement gives rooms which are well-proportioned, well-lit and as spacious as restricted sites of narrow frontage will allow; it gives a staircase which rises easily and graciously about two equal flights to a landing which serves the rooms on the upper floors with the minimum of wasted floor space. The central staircase, as in all similar plans, frees the front and back walls for windows to the principal rooms, but in the darkest part of the plan can itself be lit only from a lantern. The split back-to-back fireplaces require two separate closely adjacent chimney stacks or a complicated gathering together of flues in the roof space, and so it is hardly surprising that the plan did not have very widespread use.

---

16. LONDON TERRACE HOUSE, CENTRAL STAIRS

a. Ground-floor plan showing the two main entertaining rooms (1 and 2) with the staircase (3) in between; fireplaces are in the party wall.
b. Alternative ground-floor plan found in some smaller houses with parlour and living-room (4 and 5) and a service room (6); the staircase (7) lies between the two main rooms: the passage (8) acts as an internal corridor and also gives access to the rear of the site.
c. A ground-floor plan as found in some larger houses and indicating a spacious staircase (9) lit from a lantern above.
d. Cross-section showing how the lantern lights the staircase. A subsidiary staircase would give access to servants' bedrooms in the attics and another to the kitchens etc. in the basement.
e. Sketch to show the full depth of the house, the narrow double-pitched roofs often used and the lead flat roof between.

17. NARROW FRONTAGE HOUSE WITH CENTRAL STAIRS BETWEEN FIREPLACES

f. Ground-floor plan showing the two main entertaining rooms (10 and 11) heated by fireplaces split by the central staircase.

URBAN COTTAGES

Documentary evidence has suggested that medieval towns were full of independent families of relatively poor people: labourers, minor tradesmen, artisans and the elderly who lived in dwellings which were basically of a single cell. Virtually nothing remains of such dwellings, though their foundations are being revealed in excavations on sites in such towns as Winchester, York and Carlisle. Only occasionally, as in cottages in Goodramgate, York, have special circumstances preserved such dwellings, otherwise they have been demolished or incorporated in later structures, because neither in size nor in construction did they meet the standards of the seventeenth and eighteenth centuries let alone the nineteenth. As towns expanded during these centuries so more and more cottages were needed and they were built initially on such plots as were available within the gardens or yards of older houses. Later they were built on small virgin plots as new land became available to be incorporated in the towns. Until recently virtually every small town of medieval foundation included its crowded section of cottages tightly packed along narrow alleyways hidden from the streets and reached by way of narrow and often low passageways through the buildings on the main frontage. But a combination of central area redevelopment and campaigns to clear slums lacking adequate light and ventilation however full of history has left few such areas to be seen and appreciated. Standards of accommodation certainly did increase swiftly until the nineteenth century saw very substantial cottages built in terraces in the expanding urban area. In its way the developed 'two-up and two-down' urban cottage plan was as ingenious and adaptable as that of the universal terrace house.

18. *Longitudinal passage within one-room cottage*

Among the very few surviving early cottages are those in which a passage runs from the street to the back yard and gives access to a single ground-floor room. This passage is incorporated within the single-cell structure of the cottage: the door on the street is really the entry door to the site for the front (and only) door to the dwelling opens off the passage. In the very smallest, single-storey examples, the one room comprised the whole dwelling though in England and Wales, as distinct from Scotland, few single-storey cottages of any plan survive. Where found they tend to be associated with certain occupations: the fishermen's cottages of Cullercoats come to mind; or they survive from villages which have been engulfed in the nineteenth-century spread of towns such as Bradford.

19. *One-room cottage*

When small cottages were built, from about 1700, in a more permanent form than their predecessors, they still retained what was basically a single cell. The principal room was about twelve or fourteen feet square, with a door near one corner, a fireplace in a party wall, and a steep narrow staircase leading to the remaining accommodation which was a loft in the roof space. This plan remained in use throughout the eighteenth century and into the early part of the nineteenth. Cottages had to be sited on the least valuable pieces of land: on roadsides at the extremities of the town or within the former gardens and yards of other properties near the centre of the town. In fact the single-cell plan of these cottages made them suitable for infilling narrow medieval plots: a plot twenty feet wide could take a row of cottages having a twelve-foot room depth and still leave six feet or so for access and a token amount of daylight. Unlike other house plans there was no possibility of through ventilation, but few earlier houses and cottages of shallow depth actually had such ventilation and it was not until the association of disease and lack of ventilation was assumed that this absence was apparently considered important.

Improvements to the single-cell house took the form of greater floor to ceiling heights (including a full height first floor instead of lofts in the roof space), greater dimensions, slightly easier staircases, more fireplaces and chimneys, until the improving cottage merged with the smaller and meaner versions of the universal terrace house plan to produce the standard single-fronted double-depth cottage of the mid-nineteenth century. Before this merger took place there was a variation of the single-cell house in the form of the back-to-back cottage plan, which was quite extensively used, and, although often condemned, may still be seen here and there in the industrial towns.

20. *Back-to-back cottage with narrow frontage and wide frontage*

As well as the very narrow backlands behind existing houses, the newly expanding towns had some plots which were empty or could be cleared. These also tended to be long and narrow and so the only feasible way of developing such sites with single-family dwellings of what was considered a reasonable density was to place two rows of single-cell dwellings back-to-back. Such cottages were not inferior to those inhabited by workmen generally, either in size or construction, and, with the help of savings made in the costs of external walls and roofs, might be built to let at rents which

---

18. LONGITUDINAL PASSAGE WITHIN ONE-ROOM COTTAGE

a. Plan showing the one-room cottage reached from a passage which also serves the rear of the site; a ladder in one corner of the room rises to the loft above.
b. Sketch showing the door which serves passage and cottage; the dormer lights the loft.

19. ONE-ROOM COTTAGE

c. Ground-floor plan showing the cottage opening directly off a street or alleyway; access to the rear of the plot would be from a separate back lane or by way of a passage alongside the cottage.
d. Sketch of the cottage; in this instance the gable facing the street allows a window to light the loft space.
e. A similar plan but with ladder access to the loft.
f. Sketch showing the eaves running along the street elevation and a dormer serving the loft space.

20. ONE-ROOM COTTAGE, BACK-TO-BACK

g. Ground-floor plan showing two cottages placed back-to-back; each has a single exposure to the outside air; fireplaces are in the longitudinal party walls; one cottage has a staircase near the fireplace, the other has a staircase running alongside the lateral party wall.
h. Sketch to show the deep plan covered by a roof of shallow pitch.
i. An alternative plan with the staircases rising alongside the longitudinal party walls and the fireplaces back-to-back on the lateral party walls.
j. Here the plan shows the urban equivalent of the one-and-a-half-unit cottage of the countryside, but organized as back-to-back cottages.
k. Sketch of this wider plan.

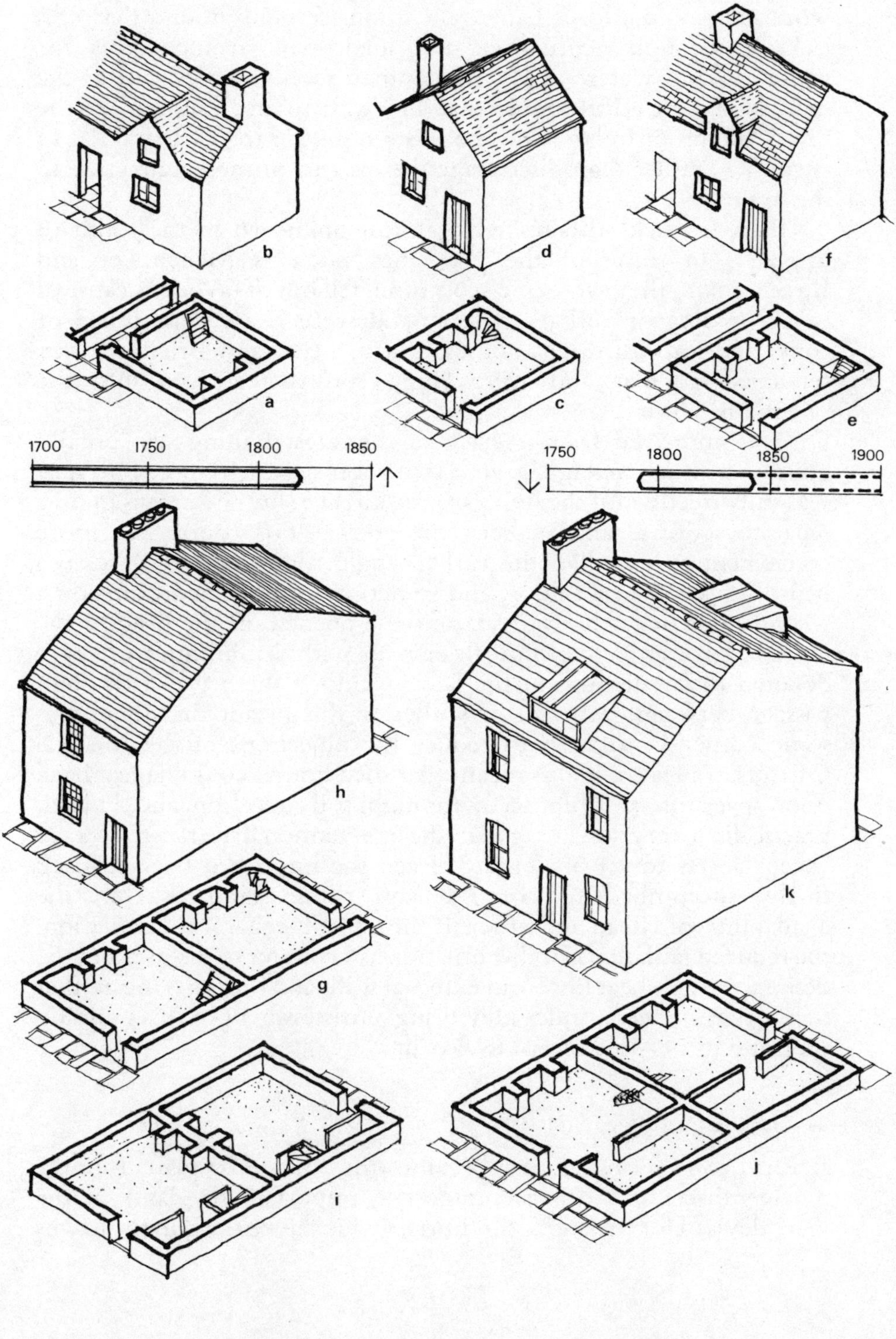
b
d
f
a
c
e
1700
1750
1800
1850
1750
1800
1850
1900
h
k
g
i
j

workmen could afford. Later generations certainly found that size, lack of through ventilation, and inadequate arrangements for sanitation and water supply condemned such cottages, but at the same time there is little doubt that they were so much superior to the flimsy hovels of Ireland and the more remote parts of Britain as to encourage rather than discourage the drift from the countryside to the towns.

Back-to-back cottages were almost unknown in the south of England. In some of the big cities, such as Manchester and Birmingham, they were once common, fell out of favour because of overcrowding or sanitary defects, and were either demolished or converted into 'through' houses. But in Leeds and Bradford they remained popular and were being constructed even into the twentieth century.

The improved back-to-back of the West Riding was usually built on a wide frontage, giving two rooms to each floor. Entrance was still directly into the living-room/kitchen, but the provision of a separate staircase and scullery meant that this room was more convenient to use than the earlier single room. There were two bedrooms on the first floor, and sometimes further bedrooms on a second floor or in the roof space; these opened off the head of the stairs to give an economical floor plan with a minimum of space devoted to circulation. In the later examples there was a through passage between each pair of sculleries: this meant that there was some corner ventilation to reduce the objections of the Medical Officers of Health; it also meant that such houses could have a back door, space for a dustbin, access for night soil collection, and, indeed, practically every advantage of the conventional terraced cottage except access to a private yard. Even the improved back-to-back finally succumbed to criticism and rising standards, but the availability of cheap and efficient means of mechanical ventilation, the reduced faith in natural ventilation as a counter to disease, and the desire to reduce heat loss from external walls and roofs has meant that the virtues and economies may bring a reassessment of this building type and its possible return to favour.

21. *House for cottage industry*

Before considering what became the standard plan for the nineteenth-century urban cottage it is important to glance at the plans devised for the cottage industries which developed in the towns as well as the countryside towards the end of the nineteenth century and whose representatives survive, though now adapted purely for domestic use, in many parts of the North and Midlands.[5]

Various branches of the textile trades made the greatest demands on cottage industry: silk in Manchester, Stockport, Macclesfield and Leek, types of cotton working in the Manchester area such as fustian cutting in Lymm and Irlam, lace-making in Nottingham, hosiery in Nottingham and Leicester. Various metal trades also made their demands, however: jewellery in Birmingham, lock-making in Willenhall, horse tackle in Walsall, items of builders' ironmongery in many parts of the Black Country. Each dwelling had some provision for domestic requirements and some workshop provision. The workshop might be above, below or alongside the dwelling; it might be used by the cottager or let separately to a craftsman who had to reach the workshop without intruding too seriously on the privacy of the family. The buildings might be erected in ones and twos or in great numbers so as to dominate a whole quarter of an industrial town.

Probably the best-known arrangement is that in which the workroom was placed above the domestic accommodation. This arrangement is easily recognized by the elongated 'weavers' windows' of archaic pattern which contrast with the more up-to-date windows of the house. The workroom (or 'loomshop') usually ran without interruption from front to back of the building, the roof being carried on purlins which spanned from party wall to party wall. For many textile operations – weaving and frame knitting for example – adequate headroom was important and this could be most conveniently obtained on the top floor. Within the roof space the 'cock loft' immediately under the ridge was used for storage. As the machinery of the period was light in weight and made of wood and wrought iron no heavy loads were imposed on the floor, and as assembly within the workshop was customary there was no difficulty in taking the parts up a domestic staircase. In the standard arrangement each workroom ran over a separate cottage and between party walls, but in later examples several rooms were run together, perhaps along the length of a whole terrace, roofs were carried on trusses rather than party walls, a single access point was provided at the end of the terrace and, in some instances at least, power was transmitted by way of shafting and belts from a steam engine, so that individual workmen in small-scale enterprises could make some attempt to compete with the large factories.

Another convenient arrangement was that in which a workshop was included with domestic accommodation within a two-storey structure. One common practice was to have a single ground-floor room running the whole depth of the building with living-room/kitchen and scullery alongside and bedrooms above. This meant that separate access was easily provided for any craftsman tenant and the extra bedroom space could be let to lodgers – an important consideration during the period of swift urban expansion – or could be used temporarily as a loomshop if trade so required. Sometimes the workshops can be recognized as such through the use of archaic window details or through the special provisions required for certain processes (some silk weaving, for instance, demanded large windows but no ventilation), though the special windows might be confined to side or rear with conventional domestic type

---

21. HOUSE FOR COTTAGE INDUSTRY

a. Ground-floor plan of a cottage which has a loomshop above; entrance from the street is directly into the living-room/kitchen (1) and there is a scullery/wash-house (2) at the rear; the staircase (3) which leads to the bedroom floor is adjacent to the back door.
b. Plan of the loomshop, which was generally on the second floor; working space (4) was reached by a ladder or steep staircase which rose from the first-floor landing into the darkest part of the room.
c. Cross-section showing the loomshop lit by windows at front and back and with a storage space within the roof.
d. Sketch showing the 'weavers' windows' lighting the loomshop floor just beneath the eaves; many such cottages have conventional windows lighting the front of the loomshop and the special, horizontal, windows lighting the rear.
e. Ground-floor plan of a cottage which incorporates a loomshop at ground level; entrance is directly into the living-room/kitchen (5) from which is entered the loomshop (7) lit from front and rear; there is a small scullery (6) and a staircase at the rear of the cottage.
f. Sketch to show the domestic and industrial parts of the elevation – though room uses would vary with the fluctuations in trade.
g. Ground-floor plan of a cottage with basement workshop; entrance is made over an area into the living-room/kitchen (8) and scullery (9); separate steps lead down to the area (10) from which the workshop was entered.
h. Sketch showing the cottage above the workshop; there was usually no intercommunication between the two parts of the building.

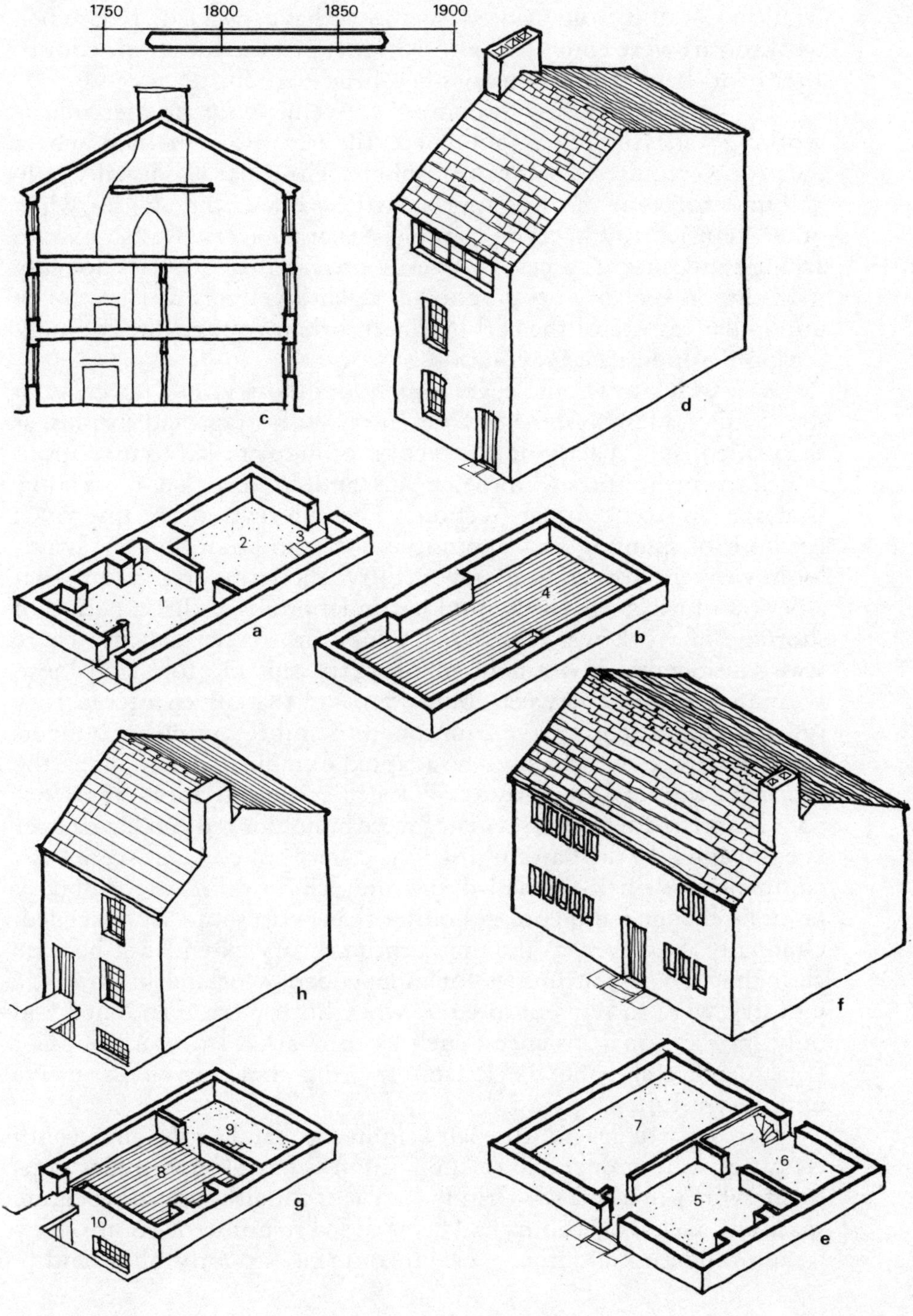
1750
1800
1850
1900
c
d
1
2
3
a
4
b
h
f
9
8
10
g
7
6
5
e

windows at the front. Often windows have been altered, when workrooms were converted into parlours or other domestic rooms, after hand-based craft industries had been abandoned.

The cellar workshop was most convenient for heavier metal-working trades but it was found in textile areas also, especially where the process required a damp atmosphere. The cellar was usually only half underground and was approached by steps from an area while other steps led to the cottage above. Separate access was so easy to arrange and internal access was rarely provided, and so it is not easy to distinguish cellar workshops from cellar dwellings which were an unpopular feature of the early years of urban cottage development during the Industrial Revolution.

As is well known, the development of industry, and especially of the textile trades, was one of alternation of shortage and surplus, as the inadequate capacity of one section of industry led to inventions which turned shortage into surplus and in turn led to relative shortage in some other section. The alternation in improved methods of spinning and weaving is a case in point. For the hand-loom weaver or other domestic operative there was no certainty that a period of great activity would last indefinitely or that a period of shortage of work was necessarily temporary or permanent. There was considerable investment in property suitable for hand-loom weaving especially between about 1770 and 1840. Even after factory processes appeared to have triumphed the more optimistic builders erected cottages which could be adapted to industrial use: not all the blocked weavers' windows of the Pennine terraces represent conversion to domestic use: many were built blocked and have never been opened. In the hatting districts, terraces of cottages were built complete with half-formed doors and windows in case millinery fashions changed and cottages rather than workshops were needed. Gradually, however, as the nineteenth century extended it became clear that few opportunities for independent working in domestic industry were to remain: integral workshops were abandoned and only in occasional instances, such as the back-yard workshops of Leicestershire and the Black Country, did these activities survive until recent times.

Urban cottages of the late eighteenth and early nineteenth centuries were vulnerable to the fashion for large-scale redevelopment which marked the decade of 1960–70: although often quite spacious, once workrooms had been added to domestic rooms, they lacked modern sanitation, were in some cases poorly built, and in many cases had been neglected. Most such buildings have gone or are about to go, but here and there, in pockets both in smaller towns and the big cities, the tell-tale indications of design for cottage industry may still attract the observant eye.

22 and 23. *Two-up and two-down cottage*

Just as the double-pile house developed from its seventeenth-century introduction to become first a standard Large House plan of the early eighteenth century and then the standard plan for Small Houses of the late eighteenth century and much of the nineteenth, so its reduced counterpart, the universal terrace house, may well have influenced the design of the single-fronted 'two-up and two-down' urban cottage which was equally ubiquitous and whose examples are even more numerous. This plan-type consists of four rooms: a living-room/kitchen and a scullery/wash-house on the ground floor and two bedrooms on the first: it had a staircase which ran either along or across the plan.

It is clear that one line of development leading to this plan originated in the single-cell cottage. Just as Small Houses one room in depth had been extended and made more convenient and comfortable by adding a staircase and service room at the rear, so the single-cell cottage gained improved access to a full-height bedroom through the introduction of a dog-leg or a winding staircase alongside a small pantry or other service room at the rear. The cottages were further improved when the first floor accommodated two separate bedrooms and the ground-floor service room became nearly as big as the main room. Another line of development may have been the 'filtering down' the social scale of the universal terrace house plan with its staircase in one long flight and another shorter flight at the rear alongside the secondary living-room. However, a third possible ancestor of the two-up and two-down plan is the urban house two rooms deep with central staircase: early nineteenth-century pairs of cottages in Stamford, for instance, have central staircases of two return flights in small-scale imitation of those introduced nearly two hundred years before. For the smallest cottages, the easy double-flight staircase was evidently considered an extravagance, whether located at the rear or in the centre of the plan, and a steep single-flight staircase was generally used instead. While room heights were comparatively modest, not to say actually low, such a staircase could be accepted within the smallest cottages, but difficulties arose as room heights increased.

Once adopted, the two-up and two-down plan in either of its variations remained without fundamental change. Architectural fashion and enthusiasm for hygiene did lead to ever-increasing room heights: many otherwise unpretentious late nineteenth-century cottages have ground-floor rooms as much as twelve feet tall as against the current standard of seven feet six inches; cheap coal and improved living standards led to the use of three or four fireplaces in the meanest cottages; demands for greater privacy led to the formation of a lobby or passage running between the front door and staircase; these, however, were simply refinements to the basic plan.

Two-up and two-down cottages are often misnamed back-to-back from the common and reasonable layout of terraces facing on to a street for public access and backing on to a footpath or alleyway for

---

22. TWO-UP AND TWO-DOWN COTTAGE WITH REAR STAIRS

a. Ground-floor plan showing the living-room (1) and kitchen (2) with the staircase alongside (3).
b. Alternative ground-floor plan with living-room (4) and dining-room (5); the staircase (6) which is at the rear is approached by a lobby leading from the front door; in such a cottage there would be a kitchen in the basement or as lean-to at the rear.
c. Sketch showing the parapet and hipped roofs which were much used in the smaller London terrace houses and cottages.

23. TWO-UP AND TWO-DOWN COTTAGE WITH CENTRAL STAIRS

d. Ground-floor plan with living-room/kitchen (7), scullery/wash-house (8) and a steep staircase in between.
e. Cross-section showing the tall floor to ceiling heights of the rooms.
f. Sketch of the house with the characteristic arrangement of door and windows.
g. 'House over house' with the house at the lower level built into the slope.

24. TUNNEL-BACK HOUSE AND COTTAGE

h. Ground-floor plan showing the living-room (10) and parlour (11) with kitchen or scullery (12), pantry (13) and coal-house (14) projecting from the rear.
i. The sketch shows the rear projection and the way in which the living-room windows are lit by a tunnel-like recess between the adjacent projecting scullery blocks.

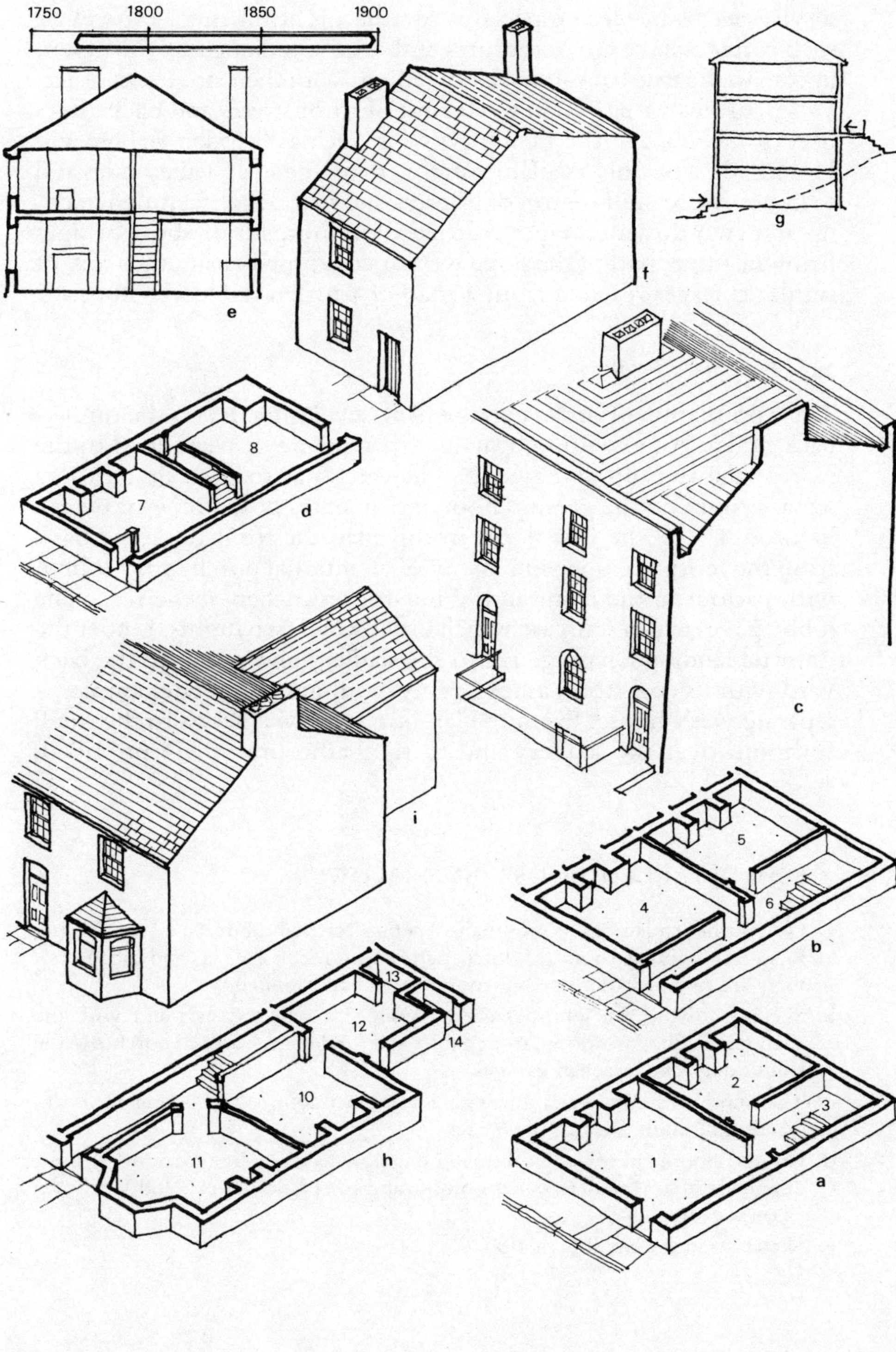

1750
1800
1850
1900
e
f
g
8
7
d
c
i
5
4
6
b
13
12
14
10
11
h
2
3
1
a

service access needed, especially for the nightsoil men. However, such cottages have two exposures and so are fundamentally different in plan to the true back-to-back dwellings with their single exposure.

A curious variation on the layout of front streets and back alleys occurs in certain of the Pennine towns, such as Hebden Bridge and Holmfirth. The only available sites were on the steep valley sides and so houses were built on top of houses: one row of conventional two-up and two-down cottages reached by a footpath or short bridges from the upper part of the slope was superimposed on another row of similar cottages reached from a road or path on the lower slope.

24. *Tunnel-back cottage*

The culmination of urban cottage plan development was the tunnel-back house. An extension, usually of two storeys, was added to the rear of the two-up and two-down plan so as to provide an extra service room on the ground floor and an extra bedroom – or even a bathroom – on the first floor. In this plan the front door, set back from the footpath, opened by way of an internal porch into a lobby, with parlour in the front and living-room/kitchen at the rear. The lobby gave on to a staircase which usually had two flights. Under the staircase landing a passage led to the scullery and so out to the back yard with its coal store, ashpit, privy, and, in the better examples, a separate wash-house. From the landing there was access to the small bedroom over the scullery and to the bathroom where provided.

SEMI-DETACHED HOUSE, BUNGALOW

a. Ground-floor plan of a typical pair of semi-detached suburban houses having lounge (1), dining-room (2), kitchenette (3), staircase hall (4) and garage (5); there are two bedrooms, a 'boxroom' and a bathroom above.
b. Sketch showing the semi-detached houses as a reflected pair and with the characteristic bay windows, front gables as if for dormers, arched porches to the front doors, and attached garages.
c. The 'sunshine house' variation with a combined lounge and dining-room (6) running through from front to back.
d. Ground-floor plan of a typical small bungalow having a living-room (7) and a dining kitchen (8) with two bedrooms (9 and 10), bathroom (11) and W.C. (12) all on the same level.
e. Sketch of such a small bungalow.

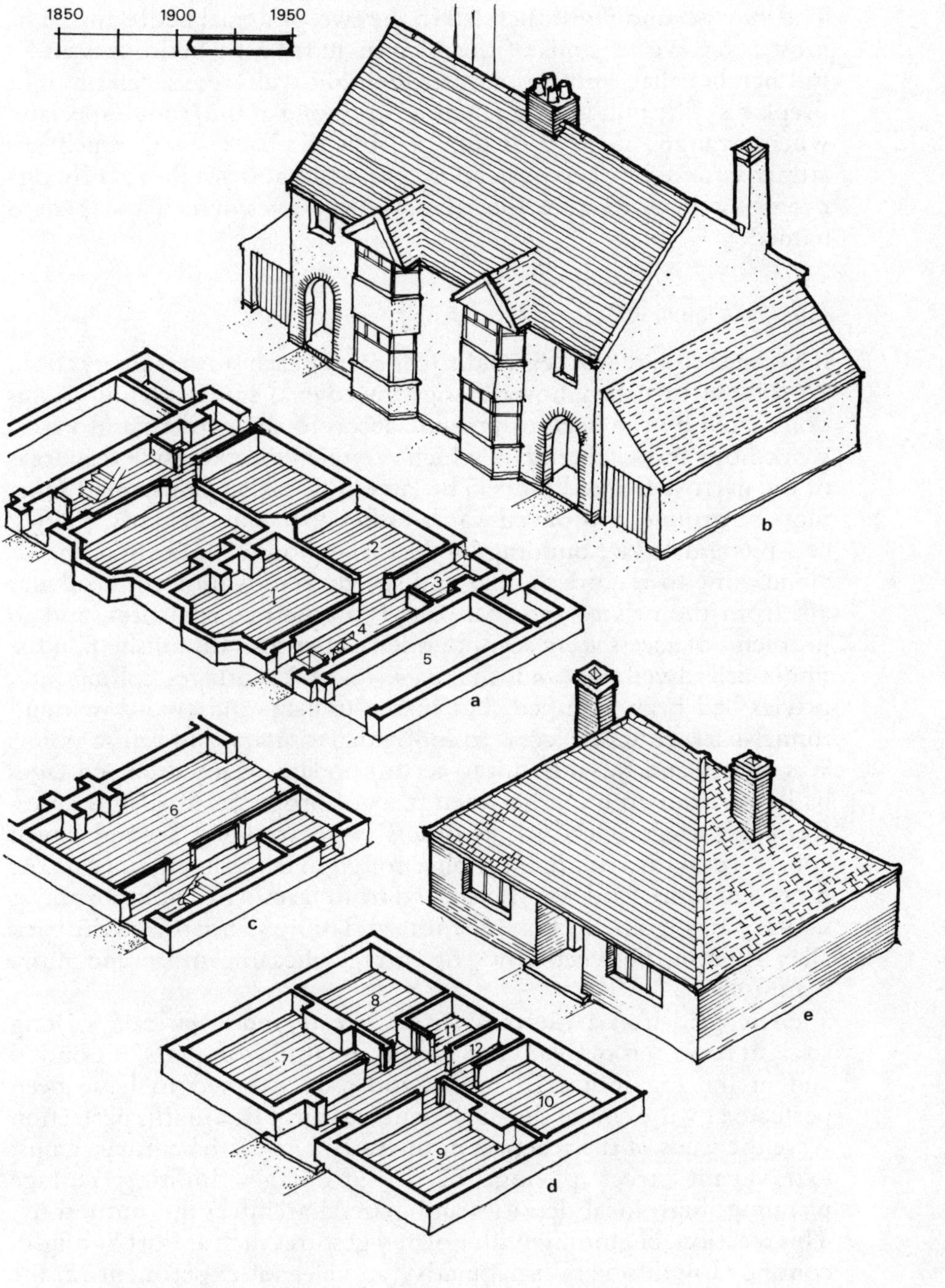
1850
1900
1950
1
2
3
4
5
a
b
6
c
7
8
9
10
11
12
d
e

The short second flight then led to the two principal bedrooms. The most extensive versions of this plan included attic bedrooms and a full-height cellar, and such a cottage might well have seven or eight fireplaces. The buildings were most imposing at the front, especially when arranged in pairs or terraces, but the backs were much less attractive and the deep projections cut off light from the rear living-rooms/kitchens to give the tunnel effect after which the plan is named.[6]

Later developments

It has been seen that access to the rear part of each site has always been a problem in urban house design. Medieval house planning was dominated by the need to provide access to the gardens and yards, workshops and kitchens etc. which occupied the extensive rear areas of the narrow fronted plots. The later and smaller houses had short plots of ground and paved yards rather than the orchards, stables, cess-pits and service buildings of the earlier houses, but sanitary needs alone came to require regular and speedy removal of nightsoil and ash from the privies and increasingly numerous coal fires, and so problems of access were compounded rather than diminished. In the single-cell dwellings and the back-to-back cottages ashpits and privies had been grouped, but in the two-up and two-down and tunnel-back cottages access to individual sanitary and refuse points was needed and was difficult to accommodate. Many urban cottages had a corridor running between pairs of properties to afford access from the street at the front; others were arranged around paved courtyards with a single entry big enough to take a horse and cart. As more and more land was transferred from farming to housing and as sanitary arrangements became more and more standardized the back alley running between rows of cottages became more and more common.

The grid-iron pattern of front streets and back alleys, long straight rows and regular cross-streets so familiar in parts of London and in the big industrial towns and cities seemed to have been perfected by the end of the nineteenth century. But in this perfection were the seeds of the reaction of the early twentieth century against extravagant street paving, narrow frontages limiting cottage planning, high local densities and general architectural monotony. This reaction, beginning with isolated gestures such as Port Sunlight, continued with several imaginative and elegant experiments in the first decade of the century, but led to the rash of suburban houses of the interwar period, solving some of the architectural and planning problems but creating their own monotony.

1. *Faulkner 1966*.
2. *Pantin 1962–3*; S. R. Jones, notes distributed to Vernacular Architecture Group members; *Faulkner 1969*.
3. *Pantin 1962–3*.
4. 38 King St., Sandwich described by E. W. Parkin to Vernacular Architecture Group members.
5. See contribution by W. J. Smith to *Chapman (ed.) 1971* for Lancashire/Yorkshire textile areas and *D. Smith 1965* for Midlands textile areas.
6. Examples illustrated in *Rasmussen 1960* and *Hall 1973*.

CHAPTER FOUR

Materials and Construction

In looking at a house one tends to see the building first and its plan second: the bricks or stone, tiles or thatch and then (if at all) the relative disposition of doors and windows, floor levels and chimney stacks. The architectural character of a village or town may appear to be set by the building materials and methods of construction rather than house planning: the soft mellow rubble walls and stone-tiled roof rather than the incidence of cross-passages and the use of dormers to light the loft. It is unlikely, to say the least, that the designers of houses, whether magnificent or humble, thought of it in this way. It is much more likely that they had a set of planning requirements to meet, practical and emotional, and that they met these requirements by arranging spaces in plan and section according to tradition and fashion, mixed as circumstances indicated, and then defined, enclosed, protected, served those spaces with a structure and set of building materials chosen primarily for economy but with tradition and fashion also as determinants.[1]

Taking England and Wales as a whole, a considerable variety of building materials has been available to house builders. The land provided stone of all sorts, clay and timber, and could be made to provide brick, tiles and thatch. Building materials being heavy and expensive to move it has until recently been customary to use the materials which were immediately to hand for all except the most important buildings (usually monumental buildings such as churches and castles). But often there is more than one material to hand: timber growing above stone, straw for thatch being reaped from clay lands suitable for tile-making; the choice of material was a matter of more than mere economy. The archaeological examination of houses involves the deduction of a sequence of construction, unravelling the layers of materials used as well as discovering the plan and section and deducing the way of life which such an arrangement of forms accommodated.

The structural methods used for house construction have been (as they continue to be) frame and mass. In frame construction the loads of roof and intermediate floors are conducted through the relatively small number of vertical elements of the frame safely to the foundations and the supporting ground. The wall serves as the enclosing element, keeping out rain and cold, keeping in heat, maintaining privacy. Except insofar as members of the frame may also be elements of the wall the enclosing envelope could be eliminated and the frame would subsist: indeed construction is usually a matter of frame first, walls last. In mass construction the loads of roof and intermediate floors are conducted through the wall to a foundation which carries both the load of the wall itself and the loads which are imposed on it. Without the wall, roof and floors could not be carried; the wall is built first, floor and roof construction follows. These points are obvious enough, but it is easy to be fascinated by constructional detail and less easy to concentrate on structural essentials.

Frame construction has been almost entirely timber-frame construction. In box-frame and post-and-truss construction the structural members also formed part of the wall; in cruck construction the structural members were concealed and the wall could be of any material – including timber frame. Mass wall construction has been of stone, including flint, cobble and pebbles, of brick or of clay or earth in various forms. Generally it seems that timber-frame construction was the normal method of building over virtually the whole country and has persisted in some parts right up to the present day; stone succeeded timber frame for quite humble buildings in certain parts of the country, remaining in use until the later nineteenth century; brick, while occasionally used for medieval Large Houses, was generally introduced for complete house construction during the early to mid-seventeenth century; clay and earth are of ancient use but continued in various forms to be used well into the nineteenth century.

Cruck construction

In cruck construction, pairs of stout inclined timber members spaced at intervals along the building collected roof loads by means of ridge purlins, side purlins and wall plates and transmitted them to the ground through padstones or by way of a continuous sill. Each cruck truss consisted of the two inclined cruck blades together with one or more horizontal members acting as tie beam, collar or yoke according to position between floor and ridge. The tie beam normally projected beyond the blades in order to carry wall plates; the collar sometimes projected to help carry the side purlins; the yoke in some cases helped to support the ridge purlin. The blades, often sawn from a single tree trunk to make a matching pair, might be straight or distinctly elbowed but usually were tapered and slightly curved from base to apex. Although the heavy purlins gave longitudinal restraint, straight or curved members were sometimes introduced between purlins and cruck blades as 'wind braces' or 'sway braces'. Cruck frames of this, the standard type, have been used for houses and farm buildings in the countryside (and sometimes in the towns) in all of England and Wales apart from a closely defined portion of eastern and south-eastern England from the early medieval period until quite late in the eighteenth century.[2]

One variation associated especially with late medieval Large Houses is the base cruck. This consists of stout, inclined, slightly curved timber members joined by a heavy collar above which there is a separate roof construction. Another variation associated particularly with part of west Wales and with the south-west peninsula of England, but found elsewhere in rather crude buildings, has the cruck blades in two parts either joined or scarfed together. Within a cruck-trussed structure there are variations in which the tie beam is omitted to make an open truss where headroom would otherwise be obstructed. There is another variation in which the truss at each end of a building is truncated at collar level in order to permit a thatched roof to be swept around half-hips. Upper crucks provided a sequence of development in which the blades did not run down to ground level but terminated in a horizontal beam which was carried by some type of mass wall; the curved feet of the inclined members acknowledged the cruck tradition but the structure was essentially that of the independent roof truss.

The walls, which in normal cruck construction carried no loads except their own weight, could be made of either mass or frame. Stone and clay were the usual mass walls but occasionally brick was used, probably as a substitute for some earlier material. In each case the walls were constructed quite conventionally and there need be no indication from outside the building that they do not carry the roof loads. Timber-frame walls comprised of vertical studs and horizontal rails with plastered panels between may also conceal the cruck trusses, except on the end walls where the inclined cruck blades show themselves clearly enough. Timber-frame walls usually included posts which were joined into the cruck feet where appropriate and steadied either by the ends of the tie beam or by spurs running out from the cruck blades. Often the timber-framed walls were rather more than one storey in height: then they carried a wall plate and through this some of the roof loads.

Cruck trusses were usually assembled on the site and then 'reared' vertically into position. Cruck-trussed buildings were quick and easy to erect and although sometimes cusped and moulded the trusses had very simple joints and made few demands on the carpenter's skill. They were inflexible, however, could not conveniently be used in multi-storey structures and were not easily extended laterally. Some trusses were of very considerable span, especially in barns – Leigh Court Barn in Worcestershire spans thirty-four feet – but such spans required immense trees selected or cultivated to the cruck shape.

Since cruck construction was distinguished as a structural form more than 2000 examples have been recorded, covering the major part of the country. The distribution shows an abrupt boundary omitting the eastern and south-eastern counties of England, and a less abrupt boundary so as to exclude practically all of Cornwall and south-west Wales. The structures are very difficult to date: the earliest (on documentary and carbon-14 dating criteria) appeared fully developed in the late thirteenth century, but no really satisfactory sequence of development has been confirmed which would add to the slight evidence from mouldings to date the rest.

Few cruck-framed buildings reveal themselves as such on external inspection; most crucks are concealed by contemporary or later walling and roofing materials. Even within a building crucks may not be easy to recognize. Sometimes the foot of the cruck or the end of a tie beam show in a stone or clay wall; sometimes elements of a cruck truss survive in the roof space or in the upper floor of a house when the lower portions have been cut away. Often a house will have portions of a central cruck truss preserved, though all the outer walls have been rebuilt in brick or stone. Often parts of cruck blades were re-used as lintels for barn doors or in a cartshed, indicating former use of the system of construction when all such buildings have been renewed.

Although the general distribution of cruck construction is now well established, many pockets of apparent scarcity remain to be investigated and much work still has to be done before dating can be entirely satisfactory.

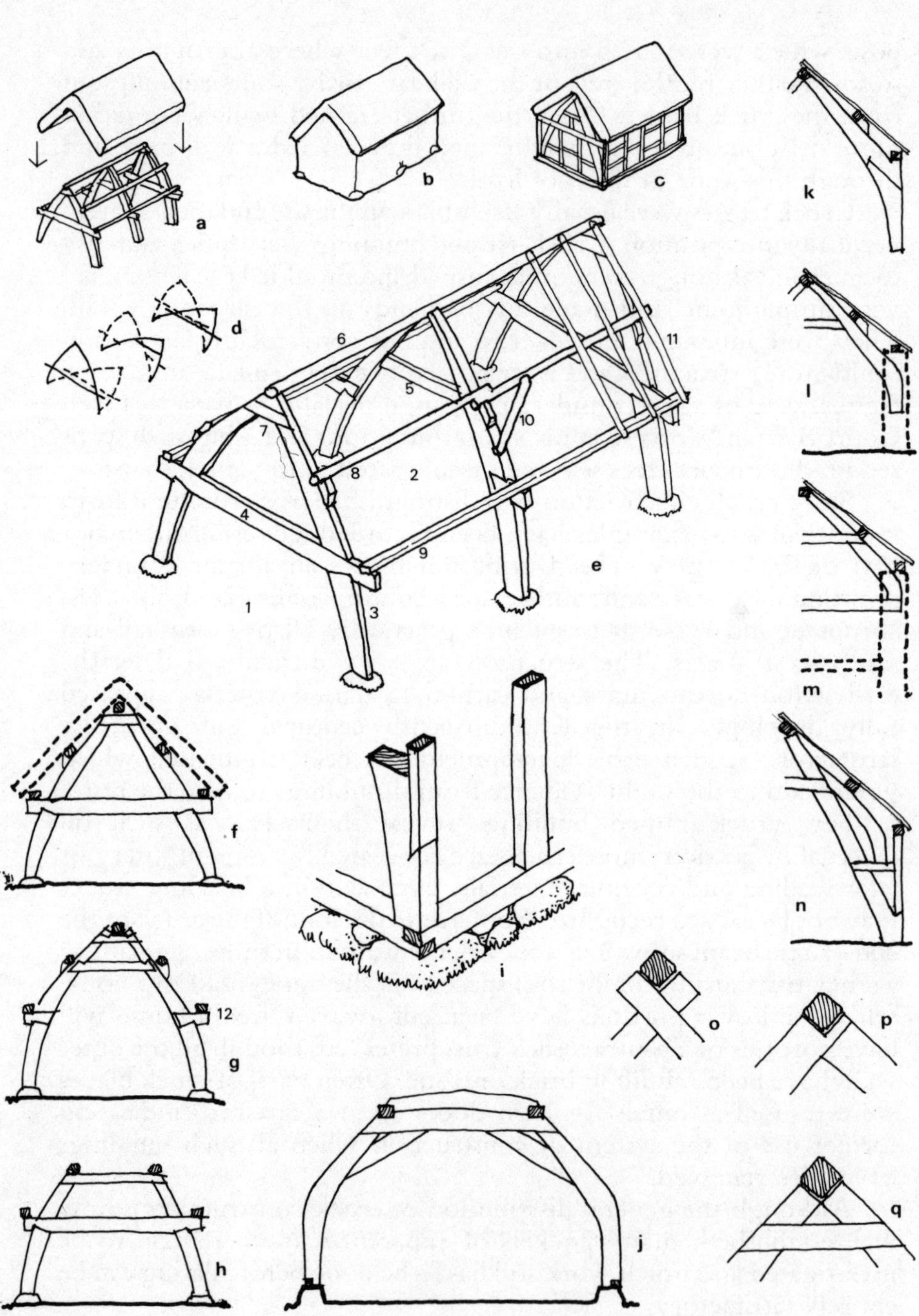
a
b
c
k
d
6
11
5
7
10
8
2
l
4
9
e
1
3
m
f
i
n
o
12
p
g
q
h
j

CRUCK CONSTRUCTION

a. Diagram showing how roof loads are carried through the frame to the ground.
b. Cruck frame concealed by mass walling.
c. Cruck frame revealed at the end of the building which has timber walling.
d. Diagram showing cruck trusses reared into position.
e. Two-bay cruck frame with closed cruck trusses (1), central open truss (2), cruck blade (3), tie beam (4), collar (5), ridge purlin (6), yoke (7), side purlin (8), wall plate (9), wind brace (10), rafters (11).
f. Full cruck with tie beam.
g. Open cruck truss with cruck spurs to carry wall plate (12).
h. Truncated cruck.
i. Timber wall post rising from the cruck blade which in turn rises from a timber sill.
j. Base cruck with purlins resting on a collar and locked by an upper collar.
k. Jointed cruck.
l. Raised cruck rising from part way up a solid wall.
m. Upper cruck tenoned into a floor beam.
n. Timber wall carrying wall plate; side purlin carried on blocking piece.
o. Cruck blades halved and crossed to carry ridge purlin.
p. Blades halved or tenoned at ridge.
q. Yoke joining blades near ridge.

Box-frame construction

The alternative way of assembling a timber-framed building is that in which the wall is considered as an entity which also carries any roof loads which may be imposed on it. The technique is sometimes called 'box frame', sometimes 'post and truss', though these two terms are more accurately used for certain aspects of the same timber-framing technique.[3]

In this form of construction, studs and rails are assembled together to form the frame of the wall whose panels are infilled or covered with some cladding material. The studs may be of uniform cross-section, as indeed they are in modern 'balloon-framed' or 'platform-framed' timber buildings, but in the past it was more customary to divide the walled box into a series of compartments or bays marked by stouter posts and with opposite walls held together by means of heavy timber beams which spanned from post to post. The so-called 'normal method of assembly' entailed the use of a special joint at the head of the post which was widened out in order to receive first the wall plate from one direction and then the tie-beam from the other direction. (Cruck construction makes use of the 'reversed assembly' in which the tie beam runs *under* the wall plate.) A timber-framed structural box of a series of bays was kept rigid by means of the wall plates running longitudinally at the head of each wall and the tie beams running laterally at bay intervals. There were also straight or slightly curved diagonal members which helped during the piece-by-piece erection process, bringing some of the loads back to the posts and also providing some triangulation.

Since the four walls of the building formed a rigid box the roofing was a separate item, the covering being carried on separate

---

BOX-FRAME CONSTRUCTION

a. Diagram showing a two-bay box-frame structure consisting of posts (1) with a rising brace (2) between post and sill (3) and a knee brace (4) between post and wall plate (5); the posts and wall plates are steadied by tie beams (6); the walls bay by bay are divided into panels by studs (7) and rails (8).
b. Roof and walls are separately considered in this type of construction.
c. Roofs may be made of coupled pairs of rafters.
d. Such roofs may be steadied by a collar purlin under each collar.
e. Alternatively, at each bay a heavy principal rafter may clasp a purlin.
f. The joint at the head of a post was carefully organized so as to keep members rigid in three directions: post thickened out in a jowl (9), wall plate (10) jointed into a rebate in the post (11), while finally the tie beam (12) locks both post and wall plate.
g. Square panels in half-timbered walls consist of staves, woven wattles, and a clay or plaster daub on each side.
h. Tall panels have the same components adapted to the tall shape.
i. Timber-frame walls may be clad with plain tiles hung on laths.
j. The mathematical tile (or brick tile) is a variation on the plain tile giving a brick effect.
k. Early weather boards were butted edge-to-edge, but most are now lapped.
l. Timber-frame walls may be entirely concealed by plaster on laths.
m. Jettied storeys consist of stud walls rising from a sole plate which is carried on cantilevered joists.
n. The mud and stud wall consists of rough posts, wall plates and tie beams without any of the conventional studs and rails which form panels; posts may be earth-fast rather than rising from a timber sill.

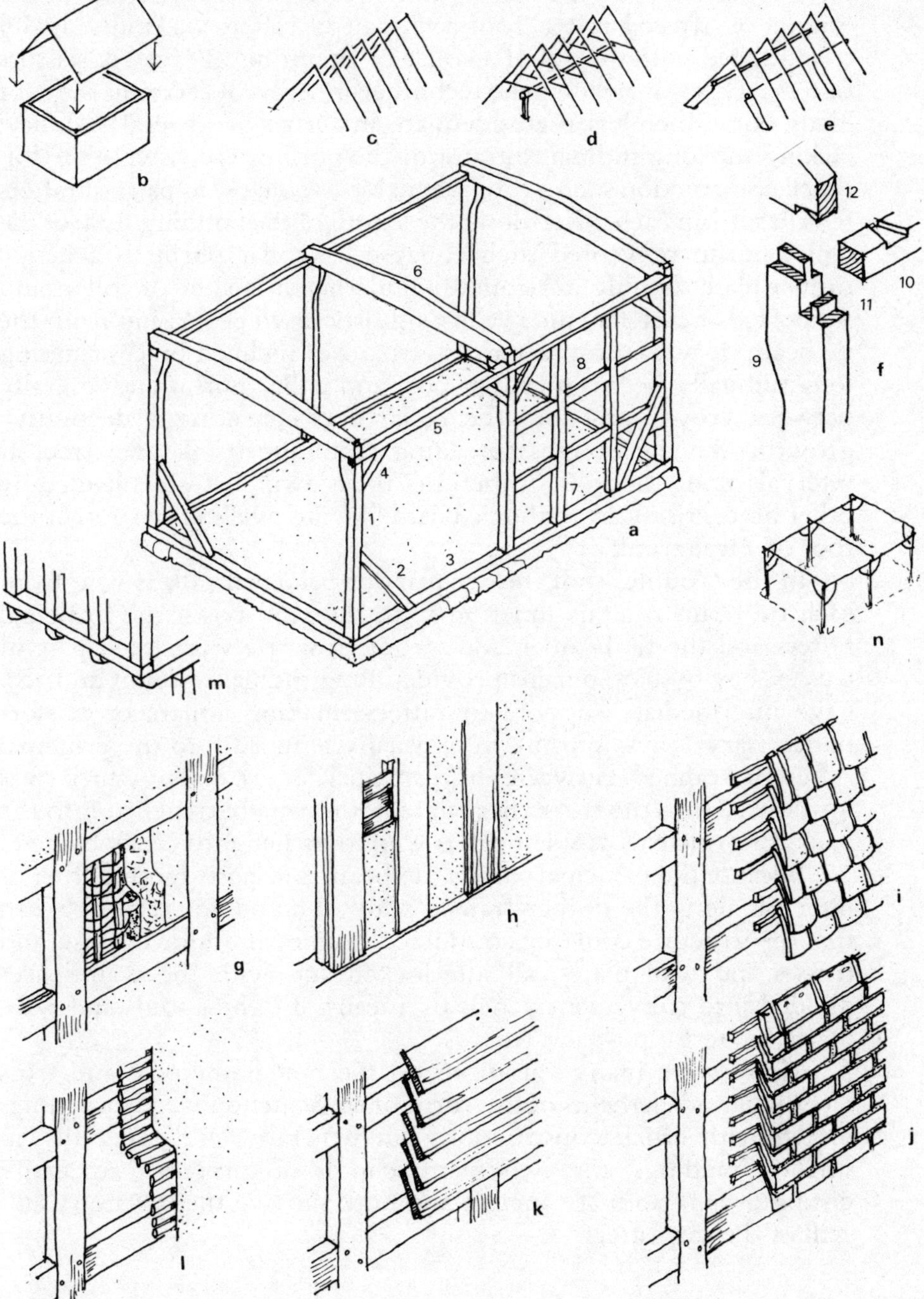
b
c
d
e
12
10
11
9
f
6
8
5
4
7
1
2
3
a
n
m
g
h
i
l
k
j

pairs of rafters or by a combination of rafters and roof truss. In the 'single' or 'trussed-rafter' roof each pair of rafters was individually triangulated with the aid of a collar or by means of crossed 'scissors rafters'. This was an adequate technique in terms of carrying the roof loads but rather less than adequate in terms of general stability; lacking the longitudinal restraint of the purlins which were used in cruck construction such a roof was liable to collapse as pairs of rafters fell apart from each other along the length of the building. Use of the collar purlin prevented such collapse. A collar purlin is a heavy timber plate running horizontally underneath the line of collars and supported at each bay interval by a short crown post rising from the tie beam. It was customary to have pairs of inclined braces running longitudinally between crown post and collar purlin and laterally between crown post and the collar above making a decorative growth, like the boughs spreading from the trunk of a tree, at intervals along the roof. Sometimes the crown post was steadied by other braces rising from the tie beam like the swelling of roots at the foot of a tree trunk.

In the 'double' roof, heavy pairs of principal rafters rose from each tie beam near its junction with the wall posts; the principal rafters and the tie beam made a roof truss. Between each pair of trusses, bay by bay, purlins provided longitudinal restraint and also gave intermediate support to rafters, making collars or scissors unnecessary. These purlins were usually tenoned into the principal rafter or trapped between the principal and a collar which was introduced into the truss; they were not normally trenched into the backs of principals as side purlins were trenched into cruck blades.

Because the principal rafters, tie beam and posts ran together at intervals along the timber-framed walls of a building it can be seen that the structure could be considered as an open frame of posts and trusses and wall plates, all interlocked and with the wall spaces divided into convenient panels by means of lighter studs and rails: hence the term 'post and truss'.

There were many variations on the box-frame/post and truss technique and elements of this form of construction were sometimes mixed with cruck construction; but generally, and especially in smaller buildings, the two main schools of carpentry are easily distinguished. Both are ancient and both showed the ingenuity and skill of the carpenters.

Infill and cladding

Infill is used when the timber members are exposed: so-called 'half-timber' buildings are those in which the timbering, both structural and decorative, makes a network around the light panels. There are two main varieties of half-timber work: that in which studs are placed close together to give narrow panels each a full storey in height; and that in which a combination of studs and rails makes square or wide rectangular panels, two or three in height to each storey. Tall panels predominate in the eastern half of the country and square panels in the western half, but there is considerable overlap, tall panels being used on western buildings or parts of buildings which had high status, and square panels being used in eastern buildings where economy of timber was important or where it was intended to cover the frame with a cladding. Tall panels might be made more decorative by the introduction of horizontal or inclined rails; square panels were quite often made more ornamental through the use of extra members to give herringbone or quatrefoil patterns. Tall panels were sometimes infilled with tiles or thin stone slabs, but were usually daubed on wattles and had a plaster finish; square panels were sometimes filled with thin wooden boards but usually had daub and plaster on a wattle base strengthened by staves. Nowadays, both types of panel generally display recent bricknogging as panels of brickwork replaced the wattle and daub.

Cladding occurs when the timber members are entirely concealed by a decorative or weather-protective skin. This usually consists of either plaster on laths, or plain roofing tiles, or slates, or horizontal weather boarding, though in the south of England there was an unusual technique called mathematical tiling or brick tiling in which tiles specially shaped to present a brick-like appearance were used. Cladding materials were applied to older buildings, especially in the towns, to make them more fire-resistant, more weather-resistant or more fashionable; but many of the later timber-framed buildings in the south-eastern counties were designed to be clad and their scrappy and inelegant timbers look particularly forlorn when the cladding is mistakenly removed in order to recreate an appearance which was never intended and which they never possessed.

Jettied construction

The technique of projecting or 'jettying' successive storeys in a timber-framed building was used both in town and country from the late Middle Ages, but was probably most popular during the sixteenth century. There may have been practical advantages in jettying: it provided extra floor area to upper rooms; it allowed short storey-height posts to be used in multi-storey buildings; it simplified jointing at each floor level; it made wall loads help to counterbalance floor loads; but it seems more than likely that jettying was a form of decoration giving a rich pattern of light and shade in receding surfaces which might well have appealed to the late medieval mind. Certainly every supposed practical advantage in jettied construction may be contradicted by the simultaneous use of conventional construction – often in the same building.

Mud and stud

The vast majority of timber-framed buildings conform to the cruck or box-framed constructional techniques but there is a further technique seen on some very humble buildings of late date. The mud and stud form of construction consists of an open framework of rough posts rising at bay intervals from padstones or as earth-fast posts and connected together with equally rough wall plates and tie beams. Spans were short, and simple rafter roofs were adequate. The walls, being storey-height bays, were not divided into panels but consisted of clay daubing about four inches thick and reinforced with staves. Such mud and stud buildings are known in Lincolnshire, Leicestershire, and the coastal plain of Lancashire.[4] They may represent the survival of a rather primitive form of construction appropriate for insubstantial and short-lived buildings and generally superseded by full timber framing when a more substantial and more durable building was required.

Roof construction: roofing solid walled houses

So far roof construction has been considered in terms of timber-frame building: cruck framed or box framed/post and truss. Many of the same constructional devices were used in roofing solid walled buildings. Single roofs of trussed rafters were carried on such walls with the addition of 'ashlaring' to help conceal the ugly gap at the top

19 *Manor House, High Street, Bewdley, Worcs.*
This house was built in 1607 but has been given an eighteenth-century facade. The two main storeys, boldly projecting wooden cornice and prominent pedimented dormer windows are characteristic of town houses of the early part of that century. (NMR)

20 *Castle Street, Farnham, Surrey.*
Apart from the later single-fronted house the cottage scale of the almshouses of 1619 is maintained in this street. (NMR)

21 *Cottages in Sun Street, Lewes, Sussex.*
Here we have a reflected pair of two-up and two-down cottages with extra accommodation in the roof space. Timber-framed walls are clad in weather boarding. (NMR)

22 *Almhouses at Brent Eleigh, Suffolk.*
Colman's Almhouses of 1731 consist of reflected pairs of single-fronted cottages. (NMR)

23 *Crown post roof truss, Little Stonham, Suffolk.*
The roof over this hall is carried on common rafters joined by collars and steadied by a collar purlin. This in turn is carried on a crown post which rises from the cambered tie beam. (NMR)

24 *Box frame and chimney hood, Carlton Husthwaite, Yorks. N.R.*
The illustration shows the upper part of one truss of a box frame or post and truss construction. There is a slightly cambered tie beam which rests on the flared tops of the posts and traps the wall plates at the head of the timber walls. Braces rise from post to tie beam – the brace at the right is missing. The rafters, some with collars, are independent of the truss and are connected by a light purlin on each side. Behind may be seen the studs and lath and plaster of a chimney hood over an inglenook. (NMR)

25 *Crucks in house at Poole, Dorset.*
Demolition has revealed part of a cruck truss. There are the remains of wattle and daub panelling between the members of the truss, but an external wall of stone and patching of brick may also be seen. At the elbow of the cruck are the remains of a spur which may have tied a timber-framed wall to the truss. (NMR)

of the wall. Trussed rafters steadied by collar plate and crown post were used since the tie beam which carried the crown post was just as useful in tying together the upper parts of solid walls as in tying the posts of timber-framed walls. Variations of cruck construction were used, especially raised crucks (consisting of conventional cruck trusses rising from part-way up a solid wall rather than directly from the ground) and upper crucks which had short curved cruck feet tenoned into a tie beam at the top of the building. Triangulated trusses of various sorts were carried on solid walls as the combination of principal rafters and tie beam served equally well in mass and framed construction.

Certain forms of roof construction, however, are more commonly to be seen with solid walls rather than as part of a timber frame. Pre-eminent is the king post roof truss. This consists of a heavy tie beam from which there rises a stout post carrying a heavy ridge purlin and receiving the tops of principal rafters which in turn carry the side purlins. Inclined struts were usually fitted between king post and principal rafters, and in early examples similar struts or braces ran longitudinally between king post and ridge purlin. The king post roof truss was in continuous use from medieval to modern times in domestic buildings. At first it was assumed that the post acted as a column taking ridge loads down to the tie beam, but during the nineteenth century it was realized that the opposite occurs and the king post served in fact as a tension member tying principals and tie beam together. Another roof truss, found more in solid-walled than timber-framed buildings, is the arch-braced collar beam truss. This is an 'open truss' i.e. there is no tie beam to block the room and so it was particularly suitable for use in an open hall or with a solar open to the roof at first-floor level. The truss consists of a pair of principal rafters rising from the top of the wall and tied by means of a collar but with braces running down from the collar to below the head of the wall and usually terminating in stout corbels or brackets. Such trusses were usually heavily moulded and might have cuspings or tracery above collar level.

Some of the more decorative trusses proudly displayed in churches and the more important public buildings – the hammer beam roof for instance – were rarely used in houses and all forms of decorative roof construction were abandoned when it became customary to provide timber or plaster ceilings. From the late sixteenth century onwards such ceilings concealed traditional forms of roof construction. The members were left plain with no mouldings or with only the simplest chamfer, but framing techniques continued to develop, and devices such as the upper cruck or the post and pad truss enabled the space within the roof and above the ceiling to be brought into use as garret bedrooms or for storage.

In southern and eastern counties the idea that the roof and wall are structurally quite separate items has dominated house construction until quite recently. Even now the gang-nailed lightweight roof trusses so popular for domestic roofing are simply a prefabricated version of the trussed rafter single roof of wide and early use. In northern and western counties the idea that roof and wall are part of the same structural whole has been the stronger influence and one can point to cruck construction as an early expression of this idea. As the open hall was abandoned, as ground and upper floors were divided by solid partition walls into separate rooms, and especially as the double-pile plan standardized a structurally convenient set of outer and inner walls, it was realized that partition walls could be carried up to support purlins and thus eliminate the need for roof trusses or self-supporting trussed rafter roofs of any kind.

ROOF CONSTRUCTION

Note: these types of roof construction are shown as if on solid walls though they could be used on timber walls equally well.

a. Simple couple rafter roof. Each pair of rafters is halved or tenoned at the apex; there is no ridge.

b. In the crown post and collar purlin roof each pair of rafters is joined by a collar (1); the collar purlin (2) runs underneath the row of collars, the crown post (3) rises from the tie beam to support the collar purlin and is braced to collar and collar purlin – and sometimes to tie beam also.

c. In the king post roof a stout member, the king post (6), rises from the tie beam to support the ridge purlin (4) which receives the common rafters. These are also given intermediate support by the side purlins (5), each one of which rests on the principal rafters (7) and rises from tie beam to be received by the king post; sometimes there are straight or curved angle struts (9) at the base.

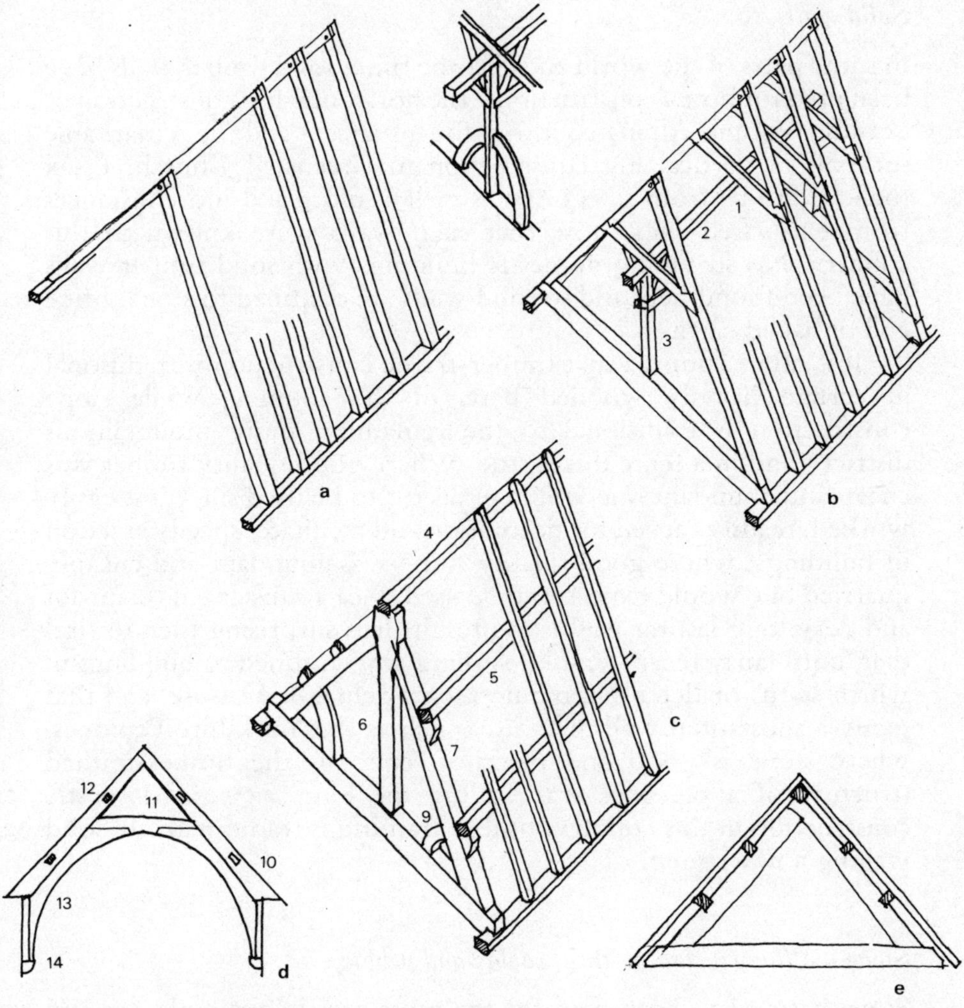

d. In the arch-braced collar beam truss principal rafters at bay intervals (10) are joined by a heavy collar (11), while between are butt purlins (12) which are joined into the principal rafters and do not rest upon them; the arch braces (13) help carry loads down to corbels or brackets in the walls (14) and also help to make all the other members of the truss into a rigid frame.

e. A simple triangular truss of two principals and a tie beam shown with side purlins of the 'through' or 'trenched' form which rest on the principals; common rafters are then carried on the side purlins.

Solid walls

In some parts of the world and at some times solid timber walls have been used for house construction – the horizontal log construction of Scandinavia and Alpine countries for instance – and the remarkable survival of vertical log construction in Greensted Church, Essex (believed to be from *c.* 845 AD) as well as more and more instances from excavated sites show that such walls were known in this country. No surviving domestic buildings with solid timber walls have been found here and so solid walls are confined to stone, brick and unbaked earth.

It is often assumed that timber-frame construction is traditional in certain heavily wooded parts of the country, while stone construction is traditional to the remaining more mountainous districts; and in a sense this is true. Where good quality timber was cheap and abundant one would expect it to be used since it is easily worked, readily carved for decoration and facilitates speedy erection of buildings; where good quality stone was abundant and cheaply quarried one would expect it to be used since a substantial rot-proof and very long lasting wall is the result. It is surprising then to find that, until fairly recently, solid walling was confined to buildings in which status or defensive requirements demanded its use, and that many a substantial wall in an area such as the Yorkshire Pennines, where stone is good and plentiful, conceals the timber-framed structure of a previous era. Taking the long view of domestic construction in this country, timber framing is traditional and solid walling a newcomer.

Stone walling (including flint, cobble and pebble)

Stone has always been used for the most prestigious buildings and good quality building stone was transported by water for some distance for such use. Where easily quarried, or found as outcrop, stone came into use for the construction of houses and, eventually, for farm buildings; it is fair to say that over more than half of England and Wales stone is the predominant building material to be seen in houses erected before the second half of the nineteenth century.

The technique of masonry construction was basically the same for lesser buildings as for the greater. The largest and best stones (including where available properly dressed stones) were placed by the mason at the corners and properly trued up. Between these

SOLID WALL CONSTRUCTION

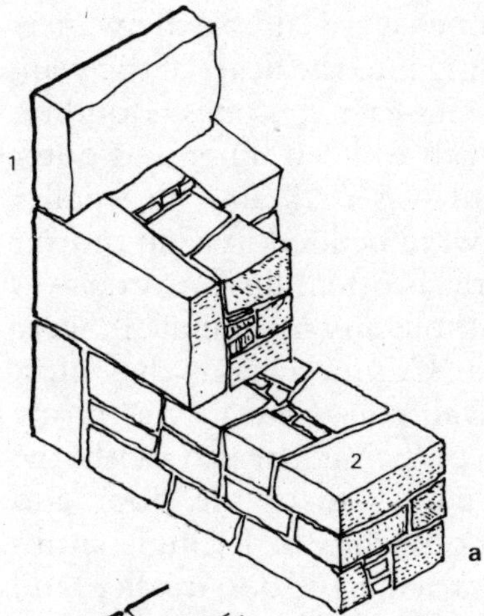

a. A stone wall of compact stones making use of quoins (1) to strengthen the corners and through stones (2) to keep together the inner and outer parts of the wall.

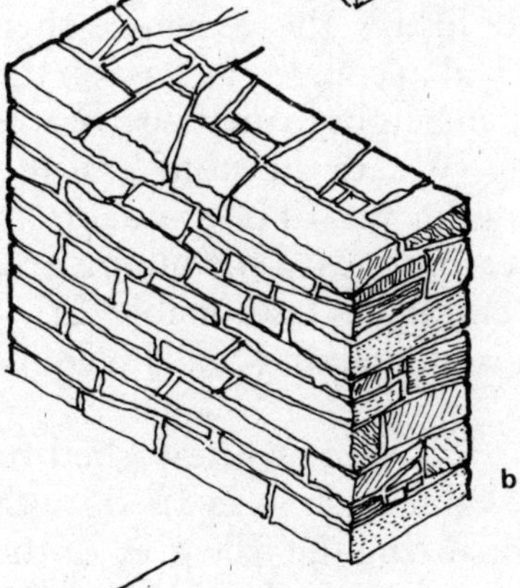

b. A stone wall of thin striated stones laid without the use of quoins.

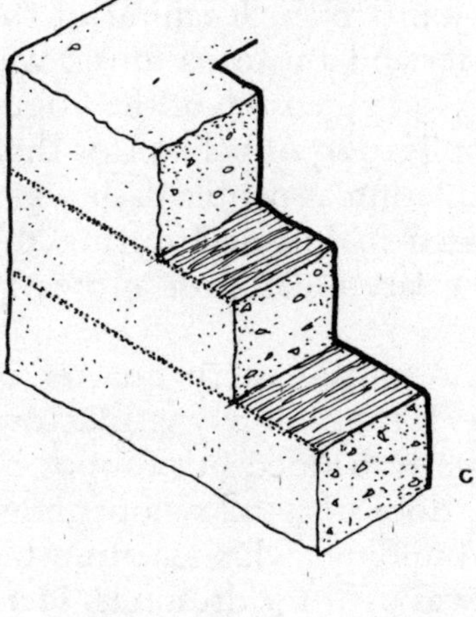

c. A cob wall showing the separate 'lifts' from each phase of construction.

alternate layers of quoins the inferior stones were laid by the wallers to show the best face outwards while tailing into the heart of the wall, interlocking where possible with the inner-facing stones. Bonding stones, or 'throughs', were laid at intervals to keep inner and outer skins together and the heart of the wall was packed with smaller stones or chips from the larger. Stones were bedded in lime mortar where this was available or in clay where, as often, lime mortar was not available. Stones laid 'dry', that is without any mortar at all, were certainly used for farm buildings in Cumbria and the most mountainous parts of Wales, but dry wall construction was rarely used in houses. Where stone capable of being dressed with the mason's chisel was available it was used to form the door and window openings, but elsewhere such openings had rough jambs and timber lintels. Where stone was of particularly good quality, and where the status of the houses would justify the expense, then partially or fully dressed stone would be laid in courses, at least on the main elevation, such courses diminishing in height from base to eaves to give a subtle liveliness to the building. Where the stone was too hard to dress, or too soft to retain dressing, or was of poor quality in some other respect, then brick was increasingly used for quoins and around openings. There are even instances of fashionable brick façades being included in buildings whose remaining walls were of stone.

At some times and in some places walls were whitewashed or rendered with plaster or roughcast. Whitewash was used with carboniferous limestone, for instance, enhancing the pale grey of the stone and helping to protect the wide joints from leaching of the bedding material. Rendering, with plaster and a painted finish, was popular in the early nineteenth century as an extension of the vogue for stucco in polite architecture. The application of pebbles or shell fragments to a wet cement or plaster rendering as pebble dash was a Scottish technique apparently popularized in England during the period of the Vernacular Revival in the late nineteenth and early twentieth centuries.

Flint is found in certain areas of the south-eastern quarter of England which lack good building stone. It is a perfectly satisfactory material for general walling when properly bedded but cannot be used for corners nor to make satisfactory door or window openings. For the older and more pretentious flint buildings which are humble in status and fairly recent in date brick was used for dressings. Here brick lacing courses were used at intervals in the wall to tie the flint together and it is sometimes difficult to decide whether the builder was aiming to produce a flint wall with brick reinforcement or a brick wall with flint as decoration. Naturally irregular flints were used in general walling, but split or knapped flints with the black interior facing outwards may be seen in walls of superior houses. Flint was also used decoratively with whatever other materials might be to hand; chequerboard pattern flint and limestone panels may be seen, for instance, in parts of Essex and Hampshire.

Cobble has similar virtues and defects to flint but is found in other parts of the country. Stones rounded by ice action may be found in areas of morainic deposit, and other cobbles may be gathered from river beds, having been rounded through the action of water. In the absence of any more suitable building material cobbles have been used, especially on the fringes of mountainous areas, for general walling purposes, with such finer stones as may be available sparingly used for quoins, dressings and as bonding stones. Cobbles may be split like flints, and a cobble wall with fieldstone admixture and bonding provides an economic wall for utilitarian buildings and quite a decorative wall for the humbler houses.

Seashore pebbles which are like small cobbles have been used for the walls of cottages and farm buildings, especially on the coast of East Anglia. It is even more difficult to use pebbles than flints as a walling material and one wonders if the neat rows of pebbles set in a network of bricks in early nineteenth-century cottages (and at least as often in pottery models of such cottages) were selected for their constructional economy or their ornamental qualities.

England and Wales are blessed with an intricate pattern of solid geology and surface drift; areas of some uniformity, as in parts of the Pennines, being more than balanced with other areas, as in Northamptonshire, where building stones seem to vary substantially within a few miles. Much of the attraction of domestic buildings in this country has come from the way in which many variations of stone walling material and technique have been played on a limited number of themes in planning and general organization.

Brick walling

While stone may cover the greatest area of house construction in this country, brick probably covers the greatest number – if only because of the vast spread of brick construction during the late eighteenth century and the nineteenth century.

Brick construction is relatively simple; the brick provided a material for general walling and for the formation of corners and openings; much of the mason's craft is exercised in the accurate reduction of the rude material into the desired shape, whereas the bricklayer's craft is exercised in the manipulation of more or less standardized units. Uniformity is limited and variety ensured through care in bonding (i.e. the way in which bricks are put together for strength and good appearance), through care in selection of the size and colour of the bricks, through the nature of the joints between bricks and through any patterning which is introduced into the brick surface. English Bond, which has alternate courses of headers and stretchers, was used comparatively little in domestic construction, though English Garden Wall Bond, with three or five stretcher courses between the header courses, was common enough. Flemish Bond, having alternate headers and stretchers in each course, was used in smaller houses quite extensively, especially on the main elevation; Flemish Stretcher Bond and Flemish Garden Wall Bond, which had extra stretchers in each course or extra courses of stretchers, were used for less important walls. Rat Trap Bond, in which bricks were laid on edge rather than on face, producing a wall with internal vertical cavities, was economical in bricks and labour and was used especially in the southern counties for cottages and other humble buildings. These bonds made use of bricks which at first were quite irregular in size between the various brickmakers and irregular in shape because of poor control of the firing process.

Gradually length and width became standardized, though depth

BRICK WALLING

a. English Bond with stretchers (1) and headers (2) in alternate courses.
b. English Garden Wall Bond.
c. English Cross Bond.
d. Flemish Bond with alternating headers and stretchers in each course.
e. Monk Bond.
f. Flemish Stretcher Bond.
g. Rat Trap Bond with brick laid on edge rather than on the flat.
h. Header Bond.
i. Dearne's Bond.

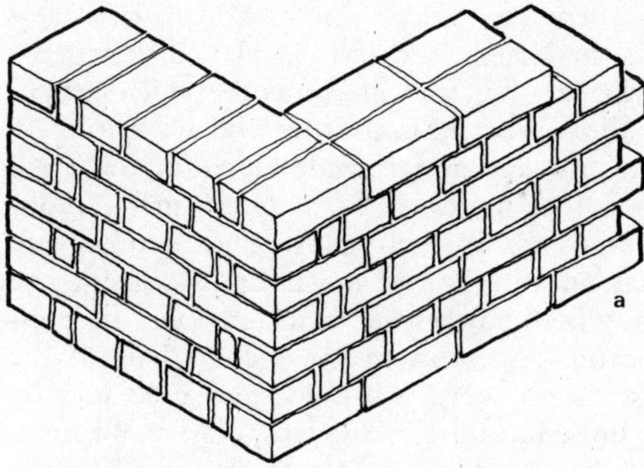

a

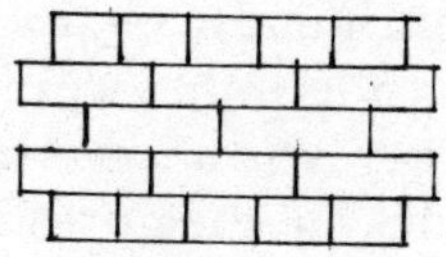

b

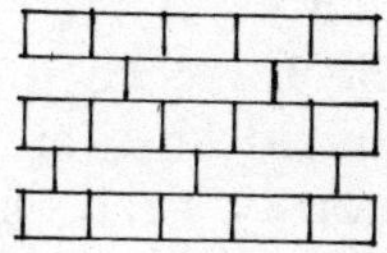

c

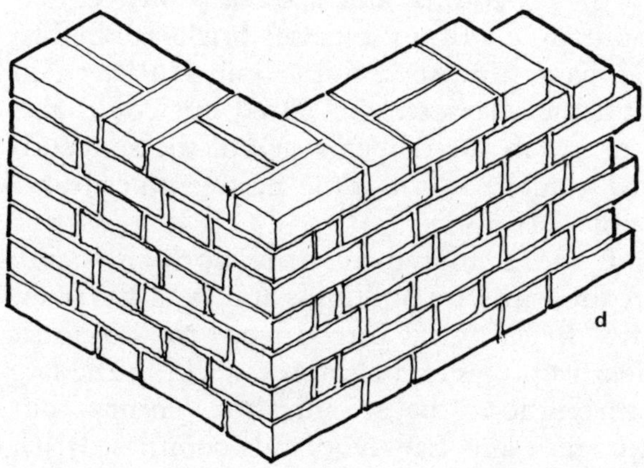

d

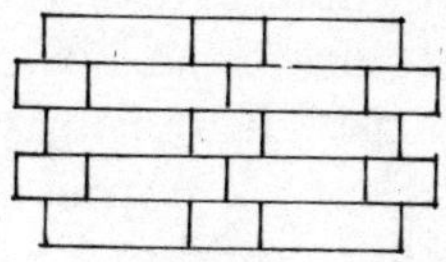

e

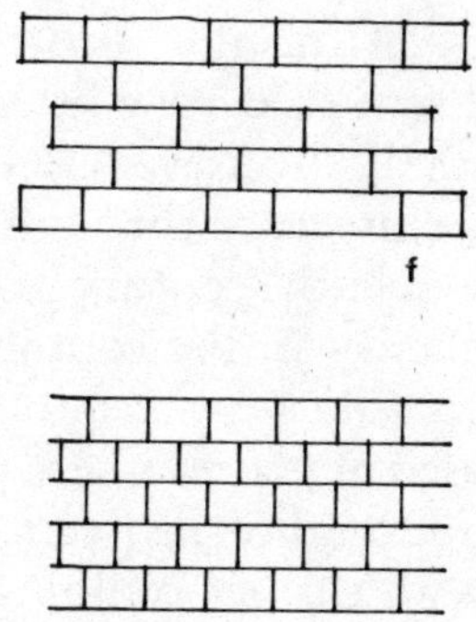

f

g

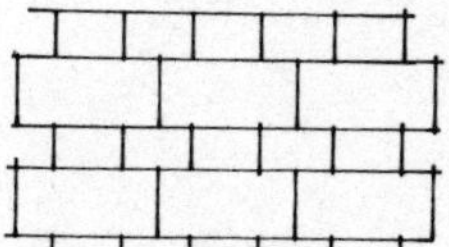

h

i

continued to vary from district to district and period to period as outside influences such as the Brick Tax of 1784 played their part. Only within the last few years has the difference between deeper bricks in the north and shallower bricks in the south been completely eliminated. Colour has never been standardized; depending on brick earth and firing methods, neither precisely to be determined, colour varied from site to site, especially in early days, when bricks were made for each individual building, fired in clamps alongside the intended site, and even when large-scale brick-making in continuously fired kilns became common in the second half of the nineteenth century, most bricks were still made and used locally. Jointing techniques were linked to the size and irregularity of bricks: irregular bricks required deep bedding and a thick joint, regular machine-made bricks could have a thin joint, soft bricks rubbed to precise dimensions could have almost invisible joints. Pattern in brickwork comes from all the characteristics listed but could also include deliberate selection, as in the diaper work of the sixteenth century, the chequerboard header pattern of the eighteenth century, and nineteenth-century polychromy.

Although more and more medieval brickwork is being discovered very little is from domestic buildings and even less from small houses. Generally brick was introduced to domestic architecture through brick fireplaces and chimney stacks in the late sixteenth century and throughout the seventeenth century, but mainly in the southern, eastern and East Midlands counties. Brick became very fashionable in the mid-seventeenth century and was used in places where perfectly adequate stone was available. With the mid-eighteenth century it had become competitive in price, both with timber building and stone construction, but brickwork made most headway in those counties in which structural timber was becoming scarce but timber for firing the abundant brick earth was still available.

Earth walling comprising clay, cob, mud and wychert

The cob buildings of Devon are well enough known and form the biggest concentration of earth-walled buildings in Britain; but the technique was widespread in use, was practised until fairly recently and has been discovered to be of ancient origin.

In earth construction the usual practice was to mix clay or chalky soil, dug from the house site, with dung and chopped straw and a little water to the consistency of stiff concrete, then to raise it roughly in a wall about three feet high, pare it down with a hay knife, allow it to set and then repeat the process until the required height was achieved. It was a slow process, but, if properly conducted, produced a strong solid wall which would last as long as a daub of plaster and a coat of whitewash kept the surface secure from attack by rain and rodents. There was an alternative quick process, used on both sides of the Solway Firth, in which three-inch layers of clay alternating with thin sprinklings of straw were laid in one operation and allowed to settle under self weight; this technique was suitable only for quite low walls. A completely different method of using earth in wall construction was to make sun-dried blocks out of the mixture and then build the wall as if with large bricks. This 'adobe' technique was used in East Anglia, though on surviving evidence it was a late eighteenth- and early-to-mid-nineteenth-century form of construction virtually confined to cottages and farm buildings.

Although many cob houses of Devon and adjacent counties are of sixteenth- and seventeenth-century date and some are medieval, and although the late seventeenth century is represented in clay and mud houses of Leicestershire, Northamptonshire and Cumberland, earth construction was most extensively used in the late eighteenth century and early nineteenth century, when there was a great demand for cottages but mass production of bricks and relatively cheap transport by railway had not yet become available.

Roofing materials

Of all the materials which could be used to cover house roofs, thatch was at one time the one most extensively used. Where available, stone tiles, stone flags, or natural slates were used for superior houses. Then plain tiles and, later, pantiles came into common use. From the mid-eighteenth century, first Westmorland Slates and then Welsh Slates, water-borne by coastal ship, river flat and canal barge, came into use, especially in the towns; finally, tiles carried on railways overwhelmed virtually all other materials.

Even the best roofing materials do not last more than two or three generations without needing attention, and most houses of any age have had one or two changes in roof covering. Since the roof pitch varies so much with the roofing material each change usually leaves some mark. Generally the larger the unit the lower the pitch or angle of slope at which it can satisfactorily be used; thus plain tiles require a steeper pitch than pantiles, stone tiles than stone flags, small natural slates than large mass-produced Welsh slates; thatch being of the smallest unit size does require a steep pitch but as a thatched roof absorbs rain rather than simply throwing it off the rule is confirmed but modified.

Special constructional features of urban houses

While the building materials and constructional methods used for houses in the towns were generally similar to those used in the countryside there were some differences. The most marked of these was the continued use of timber-framed construction long after it had passed out of use in the countryside, and its common use in towns in regions where its rural use was rare. Thus towns such as Totnes and Kendal have much timber framing – and that of some elaboration – though timber-framed construction, even of the rudest sort, is as scarce in the Devon countryside as it is in Westmorland. Paradoxically the affection for timber framing persisted even though most towns had regulations controlling the use of combustible materials, while country parishes rarely made any such provision.

One resolution of the conflict between the wish to use timber framing and the wish to avoid fires in towns lay in the use of stone or brick party walls and timber framing elsewhere. Timber-framed fronts and backs were popular: such a form of construction was economical, a non load-bearing front could be jettied and decorated and a back could be simply framed and panelled while the stone party walls could carry floor and roof loads, accommodate fireplaces and flues and provide fire stops. The 'three-quarter house' with all sides except the front built in solid walling was even more popular; here again the versatility and ease of ornament of the timber front seems to have been an important factor in its choice.

Stone was used in a town of timber-framed buildings for some houses of special importance or pretensions: in Salisbury for instance some houses had ashlar fronts and other walls of flint or stone rubble; for Exeter it has been suggested that the proportion of stone in a house indicated its importance. Partial or complete timber framing may be found in surviving urban houses of the fourteenth to late seventeenth century; in certain towns, such as Chester, in which half timbering remained fashionable, the frame is exposed though usually much restored; more generally the jettied upper storeys were underbuilt and the whole façade covered with plaster, tiles, or slate. Some towns, such as Lewes, built almost completely of timber frame, have hardly a piece of structural timber in view. Like stone, brick was used for important buildings in certain towns such as Hull and King's Lynn from the medieval period, but brick was not generally used until the late sixteenth century, and it did not supersede timber until the late seventeenth century. Even then in certain towns of south-eastern England, such as Dover and Hastings, walls of timber studs were built well into the nineteenth century.

In roofing, the almost universal use of thatch presented a far greater fire hazard than the use of timber for structure or decoratively in cornices. The enforcement of local building regulations must have been difficult, but plain tiles, pantiles, stone tiles and slate became more and more popular as roof coverings both in new construction and as replacement. The Royal Commission on Historic Monuments records that in Stamford, Lincolnshire, stone tiles were used as early as 1389 and became common in new construction during the eighteenth and early nineteenth century; plain tiles and pantiles came into use during the late seventeenth century and slate was used after 1850.[5] One further fire precaution adopted in Stamford and elsewhere was the use of a plaster floor immediately under the roof, and consisting of a layer of gypsum plaster about four inches thick, bedded on reeds and carried by laths on the floor joists. Such a floor helped to protect the rest of the building from a fire in the roof, but it also protected against the draughts which blew through ill-fitting tiles as well as providing a perfectly flat and rot-proof floor to the storage areas in the garret space.

One tends to assume that relatively cheap rail transport of bricks and slates from the mid-nineteenth century on gave a complete uniformity to domestic construction which has continued to the present day, but sight of towns such as Batley in Yorkshire or Bradford on Avon in Wiltshire confirms that other materials continued to be used in new construction long after that.

Roof shape, dormers, parapets and other details

As in so many other aspects of house design the choice of roof shape seems to have been affected by tradition and fashion operating through the resolution of conflicts between functions to be performed and available materials with which to meet those functions. Broadly speaking a roof may be hipped, i.e. with all four sides sloping, or gabled, i.e. with two sides sloping and two ends consisting of an extension of the walls; hipped roofs are suitable for box-framed construction, in which the roof is a lid placed on the box of the building, where gabled roofs are appropriate to cruck construction since roof and walls are one. Many box-frame and probably most post and truss buildings are gabled however, whereas some cruck-framed buildings have hipped roofs carried on half-trusses, and, whatever the form of wall and roof construction, hipped roofs of low pitch were used when the aim was to attempt to conceal the roof altogether. Thatch and plain tiles lend themselves to hipped-roof construction, whereas slate, stone flags and pantiles suggest gabled roofs: thus thatch conveniently swept round a hip to give a complete unitary roof, small plain tiles easily cut and covered with half-round hip tiles (or neat bonnet tiles) made satisfactory hips, whereas slate and stone flags are generally too large and heavy to be cut and mitred to give a weatherproof joint at the low pitch of a hip, while pantiles are too bold in their modelling.

All materials can be used for gabled roofs, though some are more suitable than others; it was probably to help in adapting thatch to gabled roof design that variations such as the half-hip were developed. In a half-hipped roof the end walls begin as gables, where they afford space for gable windows, and then continue as hips with thatch swept around; half-hipped tiled roofs often have a little extra gable termination to ease the roofing detail at the end of the ridge; half-hipped roofs in cruck-trussed buildings are quite easily constructed using truncated trusses.

A variation to gabled roofs which is occasionally found in hipped roofs is the double-pitch or gambrel roof, which is perhaps more accurately called the mansard roof in its hipped version. In such roofs a steep pitch is used at the eaves, changing to a shallow pitch to meet the ridge, and so giving headroom where it is most needed at the extremities of a garret or attic storey.

Apart from the flat roofs which were sometimes used to cover tower houses, house roofs were traditionally pitched, and at the angle appropriate to the material, and were exposed as pitched roofs meeting the wall at what was usually quite a boldly projecting eaves. The flat roof of a tower house would be hidden behind a parapet which was of military appearance if not always of much military value, but parapets were not generally used in house design until

Renaissance precedent suggested that the roof should as far as possible be hidden and that the plain walls should run up to meet the sky with the clear decisive line of a parapet coping. It was only with the introduction of such parapets that the collection and disposal of rainwater became a building problem. Thatched roofs tended to absorb rain which was then dripped clear of the walls with the aid of a deep eaves; tiled and slated roofs shed rain, but with the speed of a steeply pitched roof slope. Roofs draining to the back of a parapet necessitated gutters, rainwater heads and rain pipes, all introduced as decorated utilities in the late seventeenth and early eighteenth centuries and then adopted in a less decorative manner for nineteenth-century roofs.

Dormers are devices for adding light and increasing headroom in roof spaces. They were introduced, or at least multiplied, when floors were inserted in open halls and when a dormer was the only means of lighting the upper rooms so created, but they were used in terraced cottages when any other means of lighting was impracticable and in the garret floors of larger houses when the rooms to be lit were mainly contained within the roof space in any case. It is a testimony to the power of tradition that so many houses were built with cramped upper floors, awkwardly lit with the aid of dormer windows, when a few more courses of brickwork or masonry would have allowed full-height rooms and conventional windows. Dormers presented the problems of roof construction and covering in miniature, whether gabled or hipped, but with the additional problem of forming valleys, and, until lead became freely and cheaply available, valleys could only satisfactorily be formed by sweeping thatch or lacing tiles and stone tiles; dormer roofs of pantiles had to be treated as outshuts of the main roof with no valleys at all.

1. For building materials generally see *Clifton-Taylor 1972* and *R. W. Brunskill 1978*.
2. *Charles 1967*; *Alcock 1973*; *Gee 1977*.
3. *Harris 1978* gives an excellent expansion of the subject; much more detail appears in the many works by Hewett listed in the Bibliographies of Hall and Michelmore.
4. *Watson and McClintock 1979*.
5. *RCHM, Stamford 1977*.

CHAPTER FIVE

How Houses Develop

For the sake of clarity the type-plans illustrated in previous chapters have been prepared on the assumption that houses were built new and survived unaltered: in only a few cases have typical modifications been shown. Many houses do in fact remain fundamentally unaltered: maintained and repaired of course, modernized to some extent perhaps, but in plan, section and elevation largely as intended by their original designers and left by their original builders. Many others, however, represent the latest in a series of modifications.

While the process of detailed improvement may have been continuous, more radical changes were made at infrequent intervals. At one stage a plan has been transformed, at another there has been a change in section; sometimes plan and section have been changed together, sometimes the external cladding and architectural expression have been modified while plan and section remained largely unchanged. In some houses the modification has been strictly peculiar to the one building, but more often these changes appear as waves in a great swell of improvement. Just as in recent times a fashion for central heating, for double glazing or for bow windows seems to sweep through the country, so in the past fashions for deep plans, tall rooms, inserted floors, multiple chimney stacks and so on can be detected, responding to equally powerful demands.

The modifications testify to improvements in housing standards: small improvements slowly adopted at first but with rapid improvements in the late eighteenth century and the nineteenth century. But the process seems to have been more than simply improving standards, giving greater floor area or more efficient heating, rather a process of conforming to new models. The medieval hall house, when modified, might conform to the new model of an almost symmetrical plan and a multi-storey section. The

26 *Slatestone wall, Keswick, Cumberland.* This late nineteenth-century house has walls of the local slate-like stone. The main walling has joints apparently devoid of mortar. The quoins or cornerstones are carefully worked and laid to uniform heights. (RWB)

27 *Cob-walled house near Wantage, Berks.*
This lobby-entrance house has walls of clay or cob rising from a stone base and capped by a thatched roof. The easy lines of the thatch accommodate a half-hip at one end and the three dormer windows on the front. (PJME)

28 *House at Nether Alderley, Cheshire.*
This house was probably built originally as a small hall open to the roof with lofted wings on each side, one of the wings projecting slightly under a gable. Sometime probably in the late seventeenth century a floor was inserted in the hall and the chamber thus formed was lit by the delightfully decorated dormer window. The latticed lights between the wooden mullions of the dormer are probably original but other window frames have been replaced. (GW)

29 *Mud and stud cottage, Bratoft, Lincs.*
This single-storey cottage has walls of studs with thin mud or clay panels between. The roof is of pantiles, probably replacing thatch. (NMR)

30 *Brick porch on timber-framed house, Shere, Surrey.*
The main house is of lobby-entrance plan with two units rather than three, of timber-framed construction and with tiled gabled roof. The entrance has been marked later by a tall brick porch with Dutch gables and ornamental brickwork characteristic of the later seventeeth century. (RWB)

31 *House at Knutsford, Cheshire.*
At first glance this small house appears to be substantially as built to the two-unit plan, but a second glance shows that the doorway is modern and has been moved. The timber rail which formed the lintel of the original opening carries the initials IH EH and the date, 1715, which is presumably the date of construction. There was probably a loft to the right-hand side of the house, lit through the gable, but a modern dormer indicates that the remainder of the plan has been divided in section to provide an extra bedroom. (NMR)

32 *House at Holmes Chapel, Cheshire.*
Making use primarily of the evidence provided by the timber frame this house has been restored to its original form of a central hall open to the roof, heated by a hearth in an inglenook, and flanked by lofted service and retiring rooms. (Architect: J. Brotherhood). (JB)

two-unit farmhouse of one and a half storeys, when modified, might conform to the double-pile plan two storeys throughout. Very often, therefore, the idea seems to have been to change from what had been an up-to-date plan but was now old-fashioned to a new plan destined to become old-fashioned in its turn.

In some cases improved standards were achieved partly through increasing the ground area occupied by the building, throwing out a wing or an outshut, adding a couple of bays to the length and so on. In other cases, both in town and country locations, the available site area was virtually fixed and extension was confined to the vertical plane, adding storeys and attics to the original house.

In many cases the improvements led to change in use of certain of the rooms: the unheated parlour/bedroom became a heated dining-room at the same time as the unheated loft became the heated principal bedroom. Generally the greater and greater specialization of functions led to a multiplication of rooms: as, for instance, when a hall in which food preparation, cooking and dining were all undertaken became regarded as out of date, and in its place scullery, kitchen and dining-room were provided, leaving the hall as only a living-room. Such modifications to an existing house were following the examples set by other houses newly erected to the latest pattern.

Not all houses were improved, however. By the process of 'filtering down', which to some extent still persists, existing houses were modified to suit a new and inferior use. Thus the manor house in the village, becoming redundant for its original purpose, was used as the farmhouse for the tenant of the home farm and later was divided into cottages for farm labourers. Even here there was a tendency for the plan of the time to be adopted, so that the medieval manor house, perhaps already made into a multi-storey building for the tenant, was sliced into a series of cottages one and a half rooms deep and two storeys high according to the contemporary plans designed for cottagers.

Nor may all the houses which appear to combine fashionable and archaic features actually represent modification. The distinction in status between front and back, between attic and cellar and main port of an elevation, meant that archaic door and window styles, archaic details and even archaic materials were used in socially inferior parts of the building. Houses of the Vernacular Revival movement must also be distinguished. While archaeological correctness was no more a hallmark of the revival than of most other revivals, some architects and craftsmen of the late nineteenth and early twentieth centuries did in fact rate correctness of size, proportion, detail and craftsmanship rather highly. We must also acknowledge that a degree of 'built-in history' was often to be found, as in the mixture of materials for wall or roof or in the use of buttresses in imitation of those used to repair genuinely ancient structures.

In some cases the successive modifications to houses show themselves quite clearly. This is especially true of changes in section, where gable walls reveal successive alterations in roof pitch, or front walls reveal successive alterations in eaves line or even successive levels of window opening. It is always advisable to walk around the whole of the exterior of a house, if at all possible, so that surface indications of radical changes may be observed. In other cases the surface changes have been so complete that the various modifications can be seen only from inside. In many cases an inspection of roof timbers and assessment of such features as smoke blackening is required to assess the various phases of modification – remembering always that changes were so often from one typical plan to another. In these cases careful and complete archaeological examination is necessary for the story to be told.

In this chapter a few common sets of modifications have been selected and the various stages of development have been described and illustrated. Examples have been taken from houses of different social levels and from urban houses as well as those of the countryside. Approximate dates have been suggested for the various major changes; in some cases a long time span has been covered, in others a much shorter span with major changes at intervals of about fifty years. In all cases the most recent modifications have been ignored.

Development of a Large House

The development of a medieval manor house into a simple Georgian country gentleman's house.

Stage 1: c. *1300*

The building is of T-shaped plan and consists of an open hall with a two-storey wing placed at right angles. The hall contains an open hearth, the other rooms have no fixed means of heating. Walls may be of timber frame, clay, stone or even brick but have been taken as stone in this example; roof covering may be of stone-slates, tiles, shingles or slate but have been indicated here as thatch.

Stage 2: c. *1400*
At this stage the plan is substantially the same T-shape but the rooms are becoming more clearly distinguishable one from another and are taking specialized functions which are recognizable. The open hall is heated by an open hearth but is approached by the screens passage formed at the junction of the hall and cross-wing. The conventional arrangement of buttery, pantry, kitchen passage and winding staircase to the solar is maintained and the hall would be screened with the aid of spere truss partitions and a free-standing central screen.

Stage 3: c. *1500*
The main change at this stage is the addition of a cross-wing to transform the T-shaped plan into an H-shaped one. The two-storey additional cross-wing has private rooms on the ground floor and a great chamber above, all heated by fireplaces in the side wall of the wing. In the earlier portion of the house the only substantial change has been the replacement of the open hearth by a side-wall fireplace, improving conditions in the principal room but retaining the disadvantages as well as the fine proportions of an open hall. Externally, the new wing may usually be distinguished from the earlier building by a change of masonry as well as rather more generous dimensions, but the occasion might well be used to place a new roof covering over main block and new wing alike.

Stage 4: c. *1600*
The house has now been transformed from an H-shaped plan to that of a house multi-storey throughout. A floor has been inserted in the main hall, an improved staircase provided, all rooms have been given plaster ceilings, all main rooms are heated. The cross-passage, spere truss etc. have gone leaving only traces in the roof construction above the new ceilings; a new multi-storey porch and balancing bay window have been added and the eaves at the front of the hall has been raised to accommodate a new dormer window, though the low eaves at the rear might still indicate the shape of the former open hall. There are many windows, all fully glazed, and some with opening lights.

There is a tendency towards symmetry and a hint of the Renaissance in some of the details, inside and out, but the whole feel of the building remains medieval.

Stage 5: c. 1750
Little trace of any medieval origins may be seen in the house as it appears in the second half of the eighteenth century. Renaissance influence predominates and neither in planning, construction nor use of materials is the earlier history of the building obvious.

DEVELOPMENT OF A LARGE HOUSE

a. Plan *c.* 1300: hall open to the roof (1), open hearth (2), subsidiary rooms of indeterminate function (3 and 4) with a solar above reached by means of an outside staircase or ladder.

b. Plan *c.* 1400: hall open to the roof (1), heated by an open hearth (2), reached by a cross-passage (3) which also gives access to buttery (4), pantry (5), kitchen passage (6) and the winding staircase to the solar above (7).

c. Isometric sketch showing the T-shaped plan as it might have been about 1400. The walls are of stone but the roof might have been of thatch. The solar in the cross-wing has fine tall windows but other rooms are poorly lit.

d. Plan *c.* 1500: hall open to the roof (1) but heated by a fireplace on the rear wall (8); the cross-passage (3) still gives access to buttery, kitchen passage, pantry and staircase to the first-floor solar (7) as in the T-shaped plan, but the newly added parlours (9 and 10) with a great chamber above, have transformed the house into an H-shaped plan.

e. Isometric sketch of the house in the early sixteenth century showing the main hall and its two cross-wings of slightly different widths. The walls are of stone, the roofs of stone tile and there are several mullioned and transomed windows.

f. Plan *c.* 1600: hall now only one storey in height (1) with a side-wall fireplace (8); the cross-passage has gone and the entrance is marked by a multi-storey porch (11); the kitchen has come into the house (12) and has its own fireplace, but pantry (5) and kitchen passage (6) remain, as do the heated parlours (9 and 10).

g. The isometric sketch of the house at this period shows that there is a tendency to symmetry induced by the porch and the balancing bay windows. The two principal floors are now amply lit by many mullioned or mullioned and transomed windows. There is a suggestion of Renaissance detailing about the front doorway leading into the porch.

h. Plan *c.* 1750: the plan has been simplified as a result of modification and cladding in brick or a superior stone. The hall (1) is now a heated reception room and circulation space leading to kitchens (12 and 13), staircase (14) and reorganized dining-room and drawing-room (9 and 10).

i. The considerable alteration to the exterior is indicated on the sketch; a marked attempt at symmetry is foiled only by the different dimensions of the wings; similarly an attempt to give a flat-roofed appearance is unsuccessful only to the extent that the low-pitched slated roofs might appear over the parapet walls.

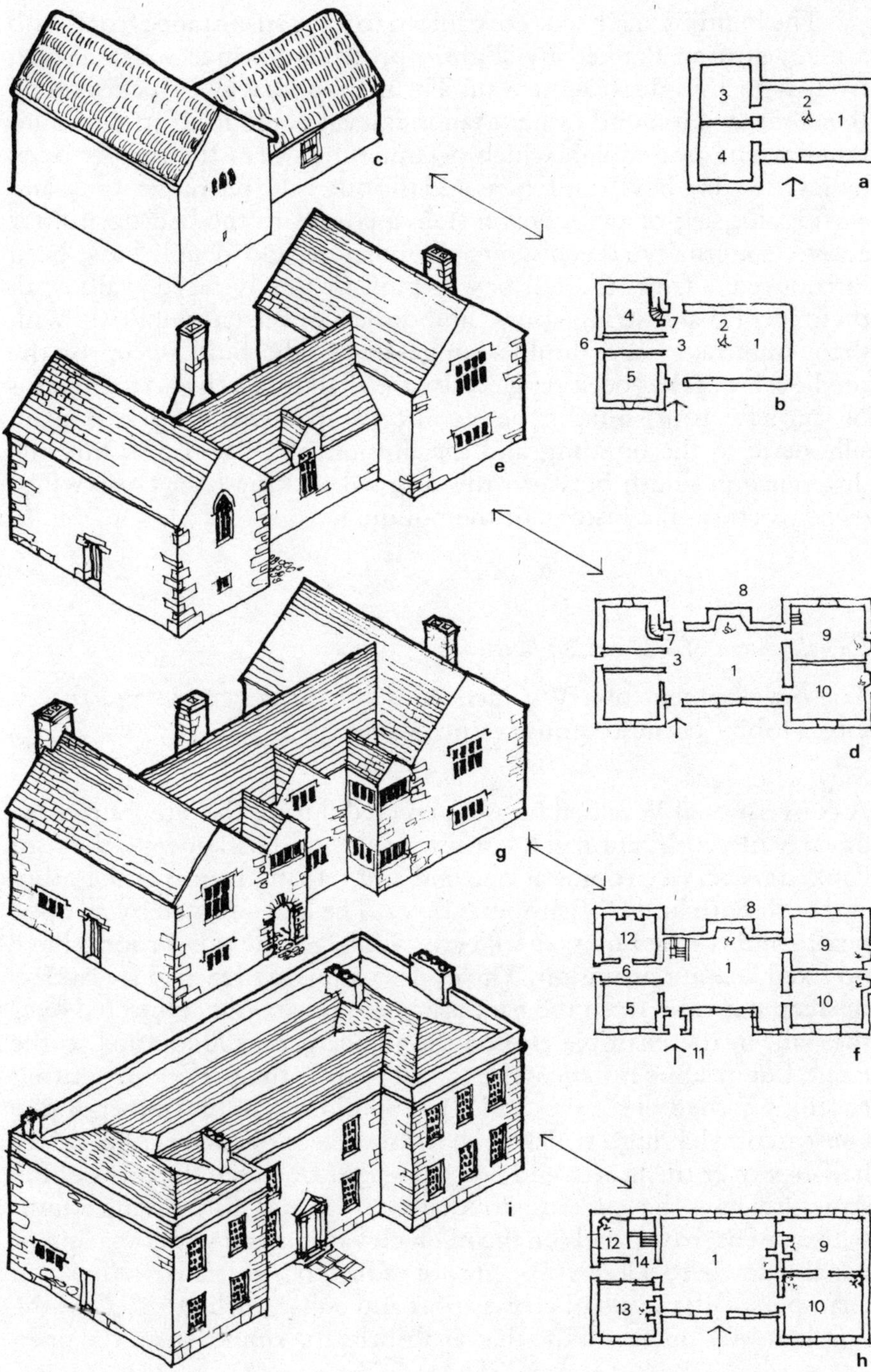
c
3
2
1
4
a
4
7
2
6
3
1
5
b
e
8
7
9
3
1
10
d
g
8
12
9
6
1
5
10
11
f
i
12
14
1
9
13
10
h

The building has been reorganized to have an entrance front with a main portion flanked by slightly projecting wings and a garden front with a single straight wall. The main doorway embellished by Renaissance surround rather than medieval porch leads straight into an imposing heated hall which occupies the site of the former open hall. One wing has the kitchens and the other the retiring rooms, and a wide dog-leg or open newel staircase leads to the bedroom floor above. Externally, Renaissance proportions and details have been introduced – from the tall newly built or newly faced walls with their cornice and string course and quoins to the tall windows with their architraves and double-hung sashes. The bold sweep of the medieval roofs has been replaced by the shallow pitch and many hips of the new roof, sinking below the parapet wall to give a plain silhouette to the building and the illusion of a flat roof. Only the difference in width between the original and the later cross-wings clearly betrays the history of the building.

Development of a Wealden house

The development of a Wealden house of timber frame and thatch into a lobby-entrance house of brick and tile.

Stage 1: c. *1400*
A conventional Wealden house is erected during the late fourteenth or early fifteenth century. It consists of a central hall open to the roof flanked by service rooms at one end and retiring rooms at the other end both with lofts or chambers above. The hall is heated by an open hearth and reached by way of a cross-passage, the other rooms have no fixed heating provision. The upper rooms are reached by ladders or steep staircases from the rooms below and are not connected over the hall. In the example chosen the upper rooms are jettied to the front, but in some instances the chamber over the parlour or retiring room is jettied into the hall. The building is of timber-frame construction having a structural bay for each of the main rooms and a half-bay over the hearth and cross-passage. Between the posts of the structural bays the walls are divided by studs and rails, giving a tight pattern of narrow panels on the main elevations and wider spacing of panels elsewhere. Here a hipped roof of thatch is carried over hall and chambers with the aid of crown-post and collar purlin trusses. As the whole roof is open and the thatch absorbs the smoke from the open

fire, all the roof timbers would be blackened though with a concentration of smoke blackening over the open hearth.

Stage 2: c. *1500*

The main change at this stage is the improved control of the open hearth. Its position is moved further away from the centre of the hall and towards the cross-passage, and the burning of the fire is made more effective through the use of a fireback of stone protected by a cast-iron plate. The smoke is guided upwards into a smoke bay formed out of the plastered partition wall of the service rooms and chamber and a newly plastered section of the truss which was previously visible from the hall floor. Smoke is allowed to leave through the gaps in the newly tiled roof or through louvres in the gablets or through a louvre specially formed over the smoke bay. Sometimes the smoke bay was carried downwards to enclose the hearth rather after the fashion of an inglenook. Blackening is now heavily concentrated within the smoke bay.

Stage 3: c. *1600*

The open hearth is now replaced by a wide brick fireplace inserted into the former cross-passage, blocking the rear entrance and making the front door open into a lobby against the fireplace jamb wall. An intermediate floor is inserted with beams and joists exposed to the room below, and with a boarded floor which might be at a slightly different level from that of the earlier floors alongside.

This new floor allows a great chamber to be formed, and this is lit by a dormer window proudly indicating on the front elevation what improvement has been made; it is heated by a small fireplace whose flue rises in front of that from the ground-floor room. The inconvenient access formerly provided to the chamber floor is now replaced by a winding timber staircase. All the first-floor rooms have plaster ceilings and now suffer from neither smoke nor draughts.

At this stage improvements were often made to the timber frame to produce both a more fashionable exterior and a more comfortable interior. Sometimes the frame was clad by weatherboard, more often it was covered in plain tile, most effectively it was clad in lath and plaster which eliminated draughts and allowed both a colourful and a smart external appearance. The two flues were combined into a tall brick chimney stack, often embellished with brick decoration or enlivened by a star shape on plan and emerging through a decorative capping to give a feature which dominated the whole house.

Stage 4: c. *1750*

There was no major change in planning at this stage. The Wealden house had already been transformed into a lobby entrance house but the change was reinforced through the provision of a kitchen fireplace, possibly incorporating an oven and placed back-to-back with the earlier fireplace of the living-room. The parlour no longer retained any function as even an occasional bedroom, but was given a fireplace, the better to establish its status, and the more efficiently to encourage its new use. At the same time the chamber above the

---

DEVELOPMENT OF A WEALDEN HOUSE

a. Plan *c.* 1400: hall open to the roof (1), open hearth (2), cross-passage (3), service rooms (4 and 5) with loft over, private room or rooms (6) with loft over.

b. Isometric sketch as built *c.* 1400 with simple rectangular ground floor and, in this example, both upper storeys jettied forward. The timber-framed walls are close-studded at the front and support a hipped roof of thatch.

c. Plan *c.* 1500: hall still open to the roof for one bay (1) but with open hearth set against a fireback adjacent to the cross-passage and served by a smoke bay above (7). Service room (4 and 5) with loft over and retiring room or rooms (6) with loft over flank the hall.

d. Isometric sketch as at *c.* 1500 showing the thatch replaced by tiles in gablet roof form but otherwise with no substantial alteration to the appearance.

e. Plan *c.* 1600: the hall (1) is now ceiled through the insertion of an intermediate floor, a massive brick fireplace (8) blocks the cross-passage giving a lobby entrance (9); there are service room (4) and parlour (6) at each end; the complete upper floor is reached by a staircase (10) rising alongside the fireplace.

f. Isometric sketch showing the tall brick chimney stack rising over a re-tiled gablet roof which is broken by the dormer window inserted to light the newly formed chamber over the earlier hall. The timber frame is now concealed by a lath and plaster cladding.

g. Plan *c.* 1750: the hall (1) has now become purely a living-room, served by the fireplace (8) and reached by the lobby entrance (9). The service room (4) has now become a kitchen with its own fireplace (11) backing on to the earlier chimney breast. The staircase (10) has become rather more spacious and convenient in use. The parlour (6) is now served by a brick fireplace.

h. Isometric sketch showing the house as in *c.* 1750 with its hipped roof of plain tile partly hidden by the parapet of the brick wall which forms a new facade. Other walls are tile-hung. The new chimney stacks serving many fireplaces are now prominent.

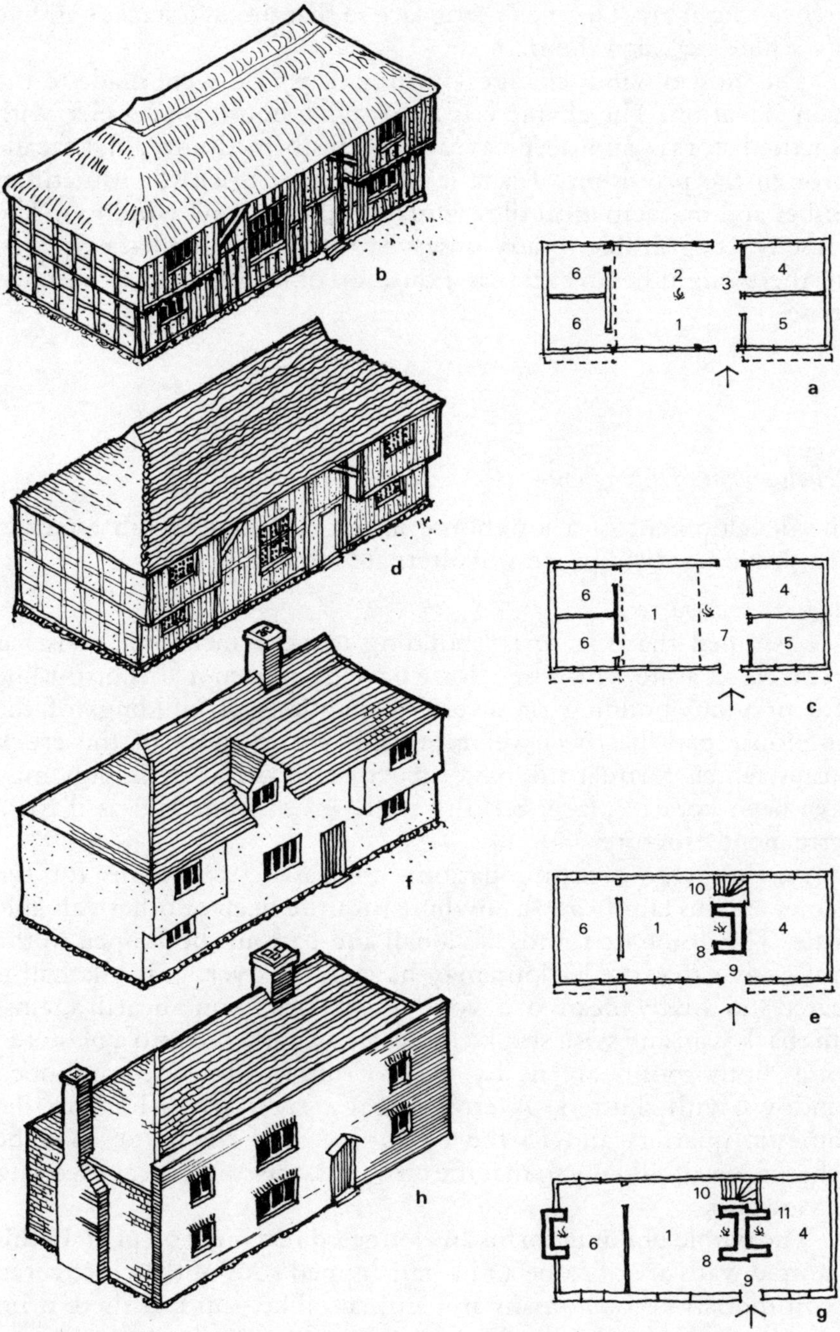

b
6
2
3
4
6
1
5
a
d
6
1
4
6
7
5
c
f
10
6
1
4
8
9
e
h
10
11
6
1
4
8
9
g

kitchen might also be given a fireplace so that the two stacks had five or six flues between them.

The most obvious changes during this period were made to the main elevation. The characteristic Wealden house appearance with its jettied storeys and deep eaves was transformed into a flat facade through the provision of a false elevation of brick (or sometimes timber and mathematical tiles) with completely new windows. The house is recognizable to any observer as having a baffle-entry plan but there might be no external indication of its origins as a Wealden house.

Development of a longhouse

The development of a longhouse into a farmhouse with attached farm buildings by a process of alternate rebuilding.

Stage 1: c. *1600*

It is assumed that the first rebuilding in permanent materials has occurred on a site which may long have been occupied. The outline of a previous building or several generations of buildings of the longhouse plan has been retained and one or more of the cruck trusses which formed the basic structure of earlier buildings may have been kept in place, but the walls are of stone laid as if for a permanent structure.

At this stage accommodation consists of two rooms for the farmer and his family and a cowhouse for the oxen or other valuable cattle. The domestic rooms are a hall and parlour, both open to the roof except that the parlour may have a loft over; only the hall is heated and this by means of a wood or peat fire set on a hearth against a fireback wall and with smoke imperfectly gathered into a plastered hood; both rooms are lit by way of unglazed wood-mullioned windows with shutters. A cross-passage gives access both to the domestic quarters and to the cowhouse, and the cattle may be tethered longitudinally so that the cross-passage could act as a feeding passage also.

The whole building forms an elongated rectangle on plan. In this example walls are of stone and a half-hipped roof of thatch covered accommodation for humans and animals alike – in fact there is no visual distinction between the two parts of the one building.

Stage 2: c. 1650

The process of alternate rebuilding has now begun. The cowhouse has been lengthened, allowing two rows of cattle to be tethered longitudinally so as to back on to a combined access and manure passage. Thus they need no longer use the common cross-passage though internal access between house and cowhouse is still available for the farmer. The eaves line of this part of the building has not been changed but the gable wall of the extended cowhouse would have a pitching hole serving a low hay loft.

The domestic part remains on the earlier plan but an intermediate floor has been inserted and a continuous loft has become available for storage use and for use by children or any resident servant. The domestic rooms would now be much more comfortable than before: the ceiling and newly glazed windows would reduce draughts, while the chimney hood would more efficiently take smoke away from the more completely enclosed inglenook. Externally a distinction is now to be detected between parts for humans and parts for animals; though the original cross-passage located within the *agricultural* part still gives access to the *domestic* part.

Stage 3: c. 1700

Fifty or sixty years later further changes have taken place, but in this instance the major improvement has been to the farm building. The whole of the cowhouse has been rebuilt, on much the same plan as before, but with better accommodation for the cattle and with a tall and capacious loft above. This would have been part of a general extension of farm buildings, for a new barn and stable might have been built at the same time. Rebuilding has been done in better quality masonry, and there is an odd contrast with the earlier stone walling of the domestic part which still survives. As part of the rebuilding a new stone flagged roof has replaced the former steeply pitched thatched roof. There have been fewer changes to the domestic part. Most improvement has taken place on the first floor: a new flagged roof has been laid on the same roof trusses as the old thatched roof, so as to give a raised eaves but the same ridge line as before; this has meant that the taller rooms at this level become bedrooms. They are reached by a new staircase projecting slightly from the rear of the building. On the ground floor the inner room no longer needs to double as a bedroom. The main room continues to serve as a kitchen/living-room, though a new fireplace may have been inserted into the earlier inglenook as coal becomes available as a fuel.

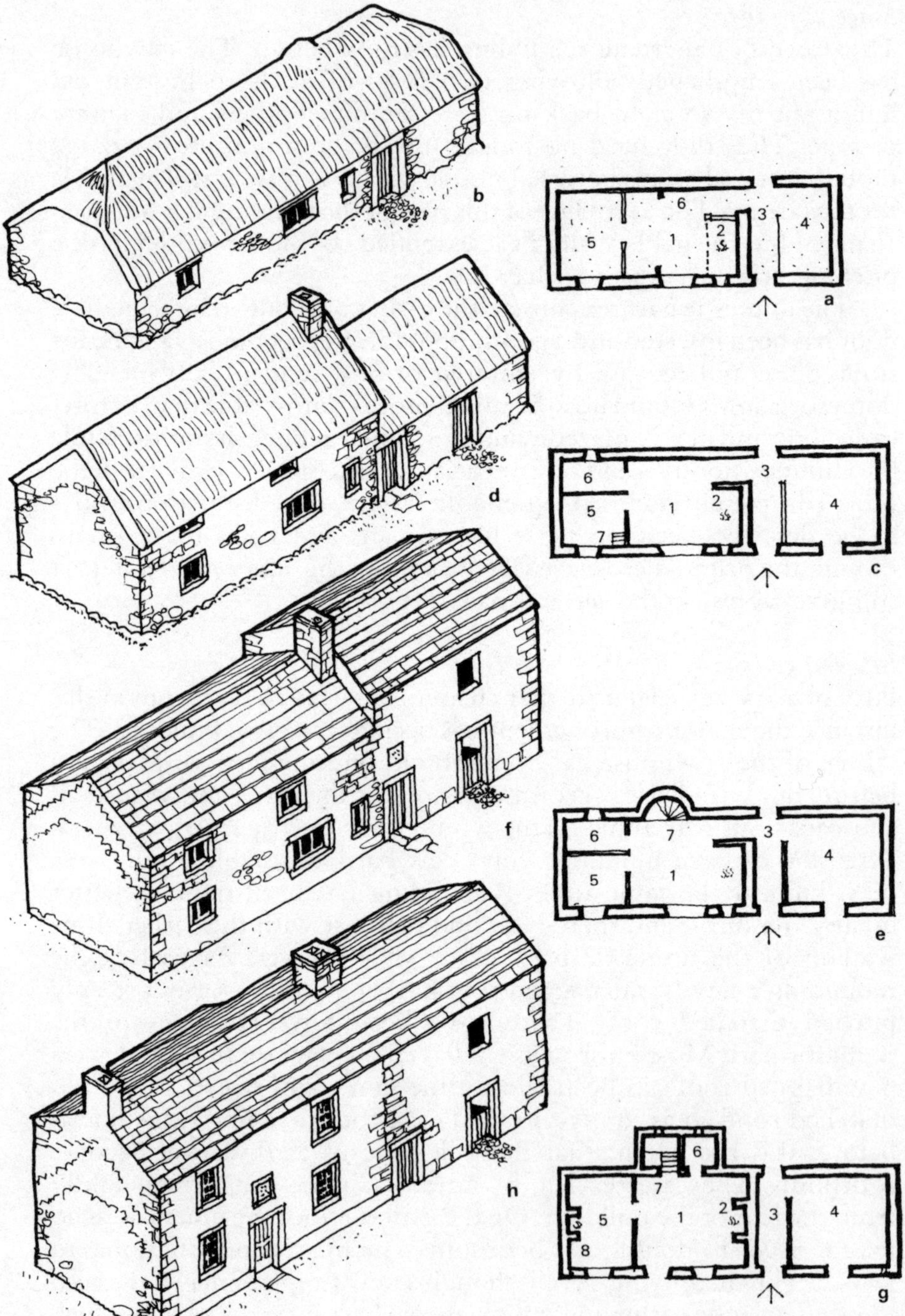

b
a
6
5
1
2
3
4
d
c
3
6
5
1
2
4
7
f
e
6
7
3
5
1
4
h
g
6
7
5
1
2
3
4
8

DEVELOPMENT OF A LONGHOUSE

a. Plan *c.* 1600: hall, open to the roof (1) and heated from a hearth in an inglenook (2); the cross-passage (3) gives access both to domestic quarters and to the cowhouse (4); the parlour bedroom (5) may be open to the roof or lofted over; a cruck truss (6) helps support the roof.

b. Isometric sketch as built at this time showing the whole accommodation contained within rectangular stone walls and covered by a half-hipped roof of thatch.

c. Plan *c.* 1650: kitchen/living-room (1) now ceiled by the intermediate floor but still heated by a hearth (2) in an inglenook and with smoke collected into a chimney hood; the cross-passage (3) remains but there is an alternative access to the cowhouse (4); the inner room is now split into a parlour/bedroom (5) and a pantry or dairy (6); a ladder-like staircase (7) rises to the low loft which extends over the whole of the domestic part.

d. Isometric sketch showing the house at about 1650: the cowhouse part remains unaltered except for the insertion of a door for the cattle, but the domestic part has been given new windows on the ground floor and has been heightened to allow for the formation of the loft. There is a new gabled roof of thatch over the whole building and a chimney stack forward of the ridge serves the chimney hood.

e. Plan *c.* 1700: the kitchen/living-room (1), the pantry (6) and the parlour (5) remain as before but a new staircase (7) rises to the improved first floor. The cross-passage (3) still allows an internal access to the cowhouse (4) which has been heightened.

f. The isometric sketch shows a further heightening of the roof to allow the loft over the domestic part to become a bedroom floor but shows a tall storage loft raised over a generally improved cowhouse. The thatch has been replaced by stone flags laid to a lower pitch.

g. Plan *c.* 1750: the kitchen/living-room (1) now has a fireplace (2) about to be further improved through provision of a cast-iron kitchen range; the parlour (5) now has a fireplace (8); a pantry (6) extends from the rear wall alongside the staircase (7) which rises to the further heightened first floor. The cowhouse (4) survives as does the redundant cross-passage (3).

h. As the sketch indicates, the whole building is once more under one roof, but a roof which has been raised to give taller rooms both on ground and first floors. The new position of the front door and the newly formal placing of windows now distinguishes domestic accommodation clearly from agricultural.

At this stage the various changes to the building may be seen in the exposed masonry. The cowhouse and loft have new stone of good quality, properly laid; the domestic parts have old stone, of indifferent quality and relatively crude construction at the lower levels, but with two layers of newer and better masonry above, and on the gable the various changes in eaves line and roof pitch may be seen.

Stage 4: c. *1750*

It is now the turn of the domestic part for considerable improvement. The whole of this part has been made taller: the ground-floor rooms (living-room and parlour) are taller and brighter as the intermediate floor has been raised and new windows of different proportions have been inserted; the first-floor rooms are also taller and have new windows. The domestic part has been made more spacious: the main room has taken in the site of the former inglenook and the inner room has taken over space formerly used for the pantry. A lean-to roof at the rear covers a gentle staircase rising to the first floor (and also perhaps falling to a small cellar) and with a pantry alongside. Both rooms are heated by coal-burning fireplaces. The cowhouse part remains unaltered but incorporates a cross-passage which is now quite redundant, for the access to domestic accommodation is now by way of a door at the front leading directly into the living-room.

Now the visual distinction between parts for humans and parts for animals is complete: the house has a formal arrangement of doors and windows and the front wall has been rendered to conceal the various levels of masonry; yet the continuous roof recalls that of the original longhouse.

Development of a two-unit house

Development of a small two-unit timber-framed house into a large lobby-entrance house of brick.

Stage 1: c. *1600*

At this stage the house consists of a hall open to the roof and two smaller rooms (parlour/bedroom and a buttery or storeroom) with a loft over. The hall is heated by a huge brick fireplace rising to a brick chimney stack. The house is timber framed, according to the box-frame constructional system, and is covered by a thatched roof; the front walls at least would have close studding and the roof thatch would finish at a peak on the gabled wall. The arrangement is that of the two-unit plan but the accommodation is rather mean and cramped.

Stage 2: c. *1650*

Now the house has practically doubled in size. The original two-unit plan survives, but the hall has been ceiled through the insertion of an intermediate floor and has become a kitchen/living-room. The balance of the plan has been completely altered through the addition of a new parlour and bedroom over; both rooms are heated and their fireplaces back-to-back with those serving the original house make for a massive heating block which rises through the roof as a prominent chimney stack. The upper floor of the extension has set the height for the newly-raised roof over the original building, for the cramped loft has now become two quite spacious chambers. In the example illustrated the entrance has been moved away from the fireplaces to a position near the partition wall between main room and inner rooms. The original timber frame has been modified by the alteration to the roof, as well as by the addition of the new parlour wing, and so the whole has been clad in lath and plaster, an operation which would also reduce draughts.

Stage 3: c. *1700*

The same basic outline is retained at this stage, but with quite considerable alterations in room uses, in construction and in architectural details. The plan has become that of the conventional lobby-entrance; fireplaces serving living-room and kitchen and the chambers above are placed back-to-back and their flues combine in the one great chimney stack. The entrance is against the jambs of the fireplaces but is protected by a porch open at ground-floor level and with a closet-like room above. Between entrance and fireplaces there is a framed newel staircase. The original parlour has now taken in the buttery, has gained a fireplace and now serves as heated parlour; the parlour of stage 2 has become a spacious kitchen. There are full-height heated bedrooms above and a garret storey now provides storage space. Brick and pantiles have replaced timber and thatch, though traces of the former timber frame may perhaps be seen internally or on the rear wall. Generally the newly fashionable brick details and door and window forms belie the humble origins of such a house.

b

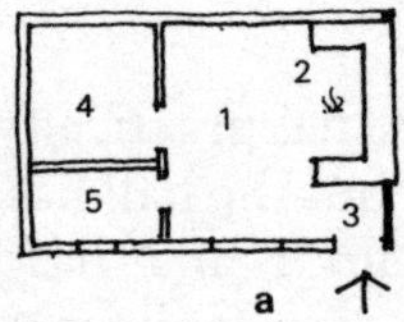

a

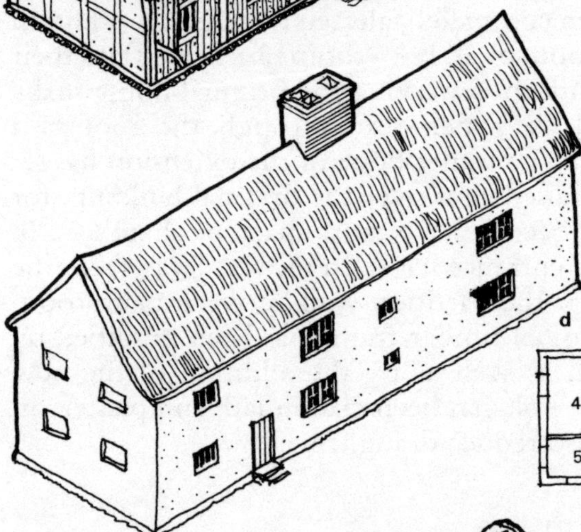

d

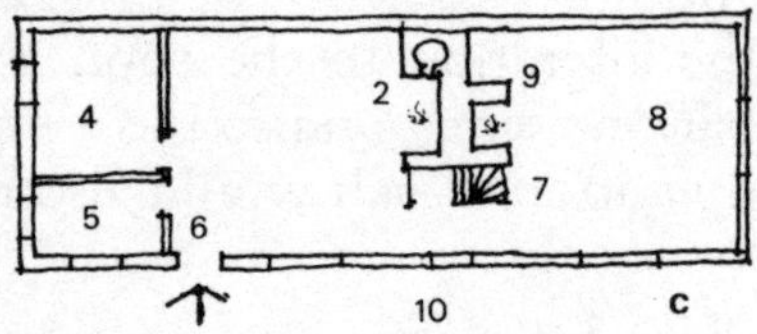

c

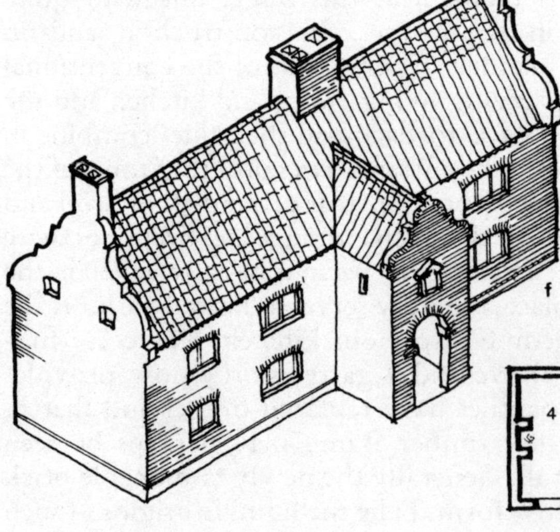

f

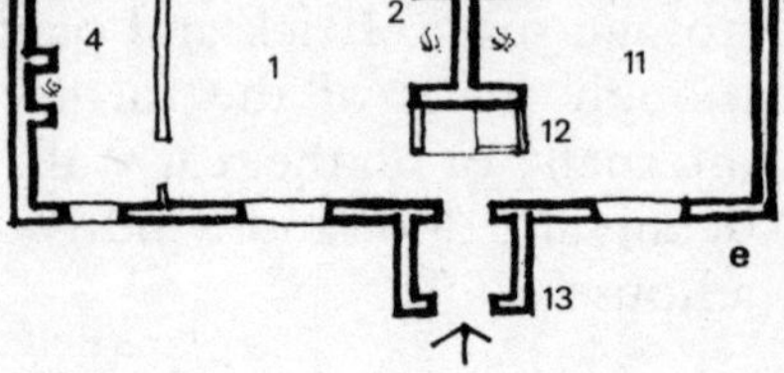

e

DEVELOPMENT OF A TWO-UNIT HOUSE

a. Plan *c.* 1600 with a small hall open to the roof (1) and heated by a massive brick or stone fireplace (2) and lobby entrance (3) against the jamb wall of the fireplace. The inner rooms: parlour (4) and buttery (5) have a loft over which is reached by ladder.

b. The sketch shows the house at this stage as of half-timbered construction with close-studding at the front and a gabled thatched roof above.

c. Plan *c.* 1650. The plan has now been considerably extended. The hall has become a living-room and kitchen combined and is served by a new fireplace (2) which incorporates an oven. There is a new entrance (6) but parlour (4) and buttery (5) remain. A new staircase (7) gives access to the upper floor which now extends over the whole of the plan. The main change, however, is the addition of a new parlour (8) heated by a fireplace (9) and with a chamber above. The alternative position for a door at (10) would have given the conventional lobby-entrance plan.

d. The isometric sketch shows the building extended, its timber-framed walls concealed by a plaster cladding, and the massive new chimney stack rising from a newly thatched roof.

e. Plan *c.* 1700. Now the plan has taken conventional lobby-entrance form. There is a living-room (1) heated from a fireplace (2) and giving access to a heated parlour (4); the site of the earlier heated parlour has now become the kitchen (11). There is a complete first floor of heated bedrooms and an unheated garret above, all reached by the framed staircase (12). The lobby entrance is both marked and protected by the porch (13).

f. The arrangement may be seen in the isometric sketch, which also shows that the timber-framed walls have been replaced by brick and the thatched roof by a roof of pantiles contained within Dutch gables.

Development of a cross-passage house

This sequence shows how an apparently homogeneous plan and section can conceal evidence of several stages of transformation.

Stage 1: c. *1550*

A mid-sixteenth-century date has been assumed for this stage, though it could be much earlier in some parts of the country and may be rather later in others. At this stage the house consists of three units: living, retiring and service in the arrangement of the conventional cross-passage plan. Heating was by means of a single open hearth. All the rooms were on the ground floor and separated by screens rather than by full-height partitions. There was a massive structural frame of cruck trusses but the walling and roofing materials were relatively insubstantial: perhaps turf or clay or mud-and-stud for the walls and thatch for the roofs.

Stage 2: c. *1600*

Here the main elements of the plan and structure are retained, but the detailed organization of the plan is beginning to take place. The main room is still open to the roof and heated by an open hearth, but one which has been fixed by a fireback wall and which is beginning to lead to the development of a canopy and louvre to channel the smoke above. At one end of the main room is the cross-passage running through a structural bay which also includes the service room; at the other end is the inner room divided into parlour and pantry. The inner room would normally be ceiled at tie-beam level both to improve the comfort of the parlour and the cleanliness of the pantry and to provide a loft above. At this stage the windows would be unglazed and control of draughts far from effective; smoke blackening could occur on any of the roof timbers apart from those above the inner room. While the basic cruck trusses remained in use to support the roof, the walls consist of studs and rails, forming wattle-and daub panels, related to the cruck framework but not necessarily loadbearing.

Stage 3: c. *1650*

The main change at this stage is the insertion of an intermediate floor in the central bay of the house. This is usually done by running a beam longitudinally between the tie beam of the truss which forms the partition to the inner room and the heavy beam or bressummer which forms part of the inglenook fireplace. The newly inserted floor is often at a slightly higher level than the older floor over the inner room, or that over the service room. At this stage the cross-passage has become a true passage, having been partitioned from the service room and running behind the fireback wall of the inglenook. Externally the main change in the appearance of the building comes from the addition of the dormer window which lights the newly-formed chamber: this window is often highly decorated with the aid of moulded beams and plastered coves as if the householder wanted to display his house improvements. A minor change come from the chimney stack rising from the top of the plastered chimney hood and emerging forward of the ridge.

Stage 4: c. 1750
The house is now substantially altered in plan and outward appearance. The three main elements of living-room, parlour and service room remain, but the cross-passage has been abandoned, and the entrance moved to a position between the two main rooms and into a lobby formed at the foot of a fairly convenient staircase. The service room has now become a kitchen with its own fireplace and indeed the former single source of heat has been multiplied to fireplaces in all the ground-floor rooms and some of those on the first floor. Externally the main change has been the replacement of timber frame and thatch by brick and slate. The cruck trusses survive, to a substantial extent, in the parlour partition wall and as truncated posts in the walls at each side of the fireplace. Other pieces of the former timber frame may be used as wall plates or as part of the low-pitch timber trusses which carry the roof slates. Generally the rooms have been made taller both at ground floor and first floor and as well as being properly heated they are adequately lit and ventilated from the tall sash windows. These changes were usually made during the second half of the eighteenth century, though sometimes rather later, and they give no external indication whatsoever of the phases of development of the plan, or the evidence of former structures which might be concealed within.

Development of a medieval town house

Although the pressures of commerce and increased population weigh heavily against the survival of early buildings in town and city centres, some do indeed remain – though heavily restored or considerably altered. Three stages in a typical progression are described.

Stage 1: c. 1350
In this instance the building complex comprises two parts on a fairly wide urban plot. Facing on to the street there is a two-storey timber-framed building raised over a stone vaulted half-basement. The timber-framed building consists of a series of shops with rooms over and reached by way of a gallery raised slightly from the level of the street or market place. The stone basement is a warehouse or workshop and it is reached by a set of steps dropping from the street level. At this stage the demarcation of communal street and private land is still rather imprecise and the space in front of the gallery and

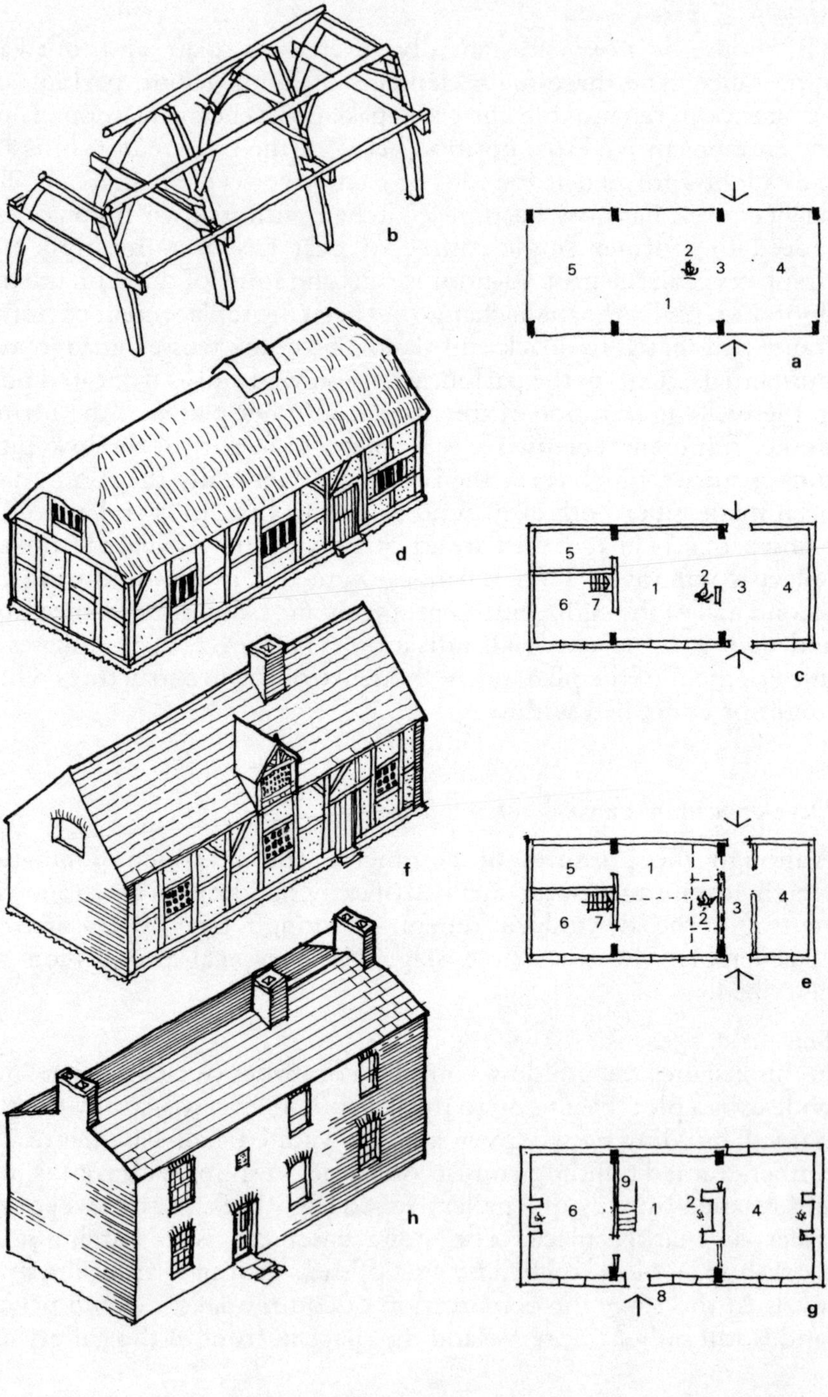
b
5
2
3
4
1
a
d
5
6
7
1
2
3
4
c
f
5
1
6
7
2
3
4
e
h
9
6
1
2
4
8
g

DEVELOPMENT OF A CROSS-PASSAGE HOUSE

a. Plan *c.* 1550: a hall (1) is heated by an open hearth (2) set near a cross-passage (3) and flanked by a service room (4) and a private or retiring room (5); all are open to the roof and contained within insubstantial walls.
b. The sketch simply shows the cruck framework for the three-unit cross-passage house; it is assumed that there would be a half-hipped roof of thatch, but in the absence of surviving examples it is difficult to be certain of the walling material.
c. Plan *c.* 1600: there is a hall (1) open to the roof and heated by an open hearth (2) set against a fireback; the cross-passage (3) leads to a service room (4) which is also open to the roof; the inner room has become dairy or pantry (5) and parlour/bedroom (6), a ladder or very steep staircase (7) rising to a loft over these two rooms.
d. The isometric sketch of the house as it might have been about 1600 shows the three units lit by unglazed windows, the timber-framed walls with wide panels are of box-frame type but set around the original crucks, and the half-hipped thatched roof with a saddle louvre over the hearth and a small window lighting the loft.
e. Plan *c.* 1650: the ground-floor plan remains substantially the same but an intermediate floor has been inserted in the hall to make it into a kitchen/living-room with chamber over. This room (1) is heated by a fire in an inglenook (2), still reached by a cross-passage (3) and flanked by service room (4), pantry (5) and parlour (6) with a staircase (7) leading to the now complete upper floor.
f. The isometric sketch shows that the only major changes have been the addition of a dormer window to light the new chamber and a brick chimney stack serving the chimney hood which rises from the inglenook. However houses of this stage which survive usually incorporate brick walls to the weather sides of the building and steeply pitched slated roofs replacing the thatch and the house has been so illustrated here.
g. Plan *c.* 1750: there is a living-room (1) with a fireplace (2); it is entered directly from the front (8); a kitchen (4) has its own fireplace, as does the parlour (6); a new staircase (9) rises to the improved first floor.
h. The sketch shows new brick walls and low-pitched slated roof; there is no external indication of the original plan or of the cruck trusses of which elements survive inside the house.

---

alongside the various steps might have been occupied by temporary booths on fair or market days. Facing on to the rear of the plot there is a stone-walled T-shaped hall, probably originally occupied in connection with the cellar workshops and the other shops, but later possibly in separate occupation. The T-shaped hall consists of hall

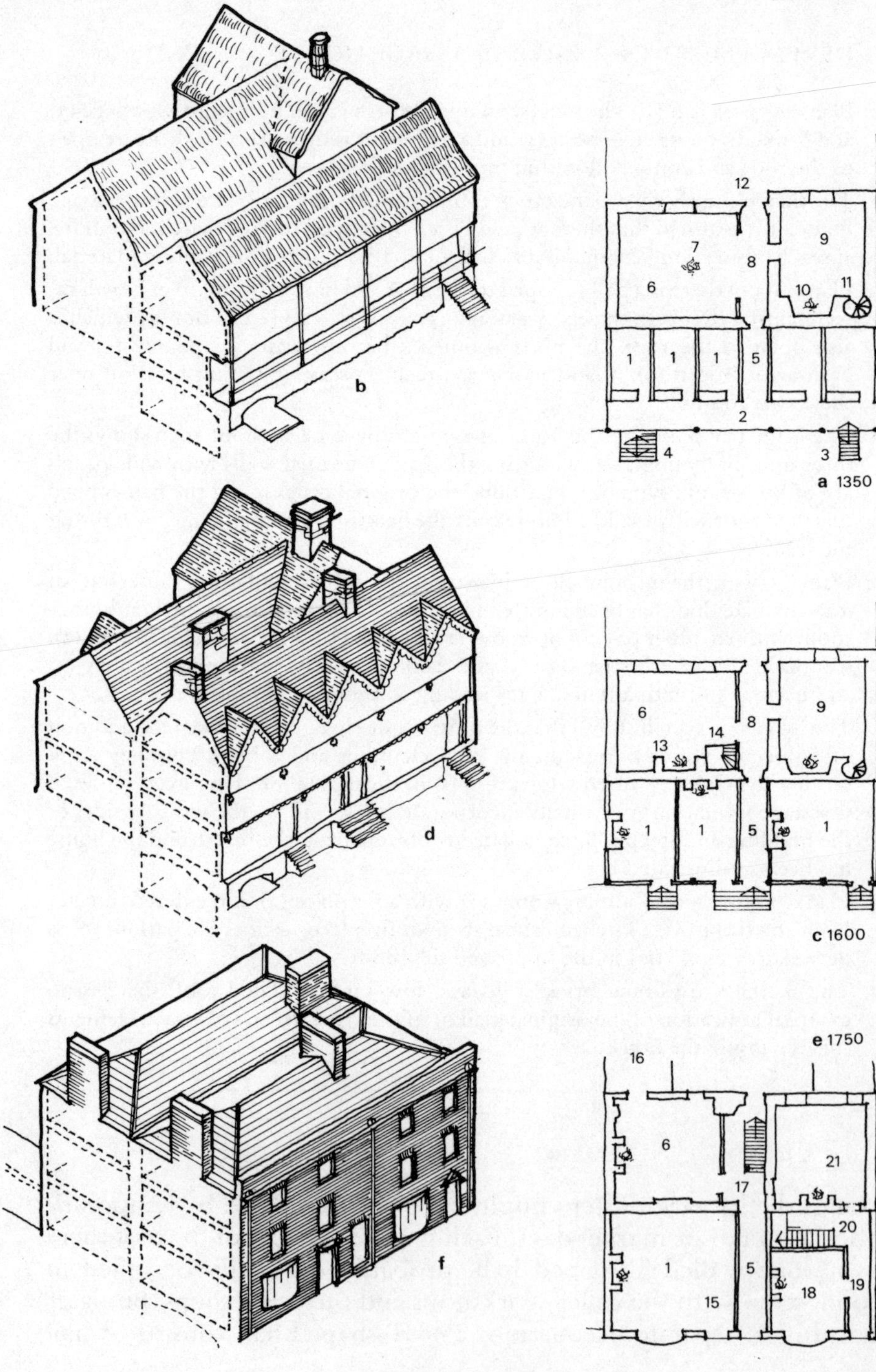

12
7
9
6
8
10
11
1
1
1
5
2
4
3
a 1350
b
6
9
8
14
13
1
1
5
1
c 1600
d
e 1750
16
6
21
17
20
1
5
18
19
15
f

DEVELOPMENT OF A MEDIEVAL TOWN HOUSE

a. Plan *c.* 1350: the building occupies a fairly wide plot facing on to a shopping street or market place. In the front portion there are shops (1) reached from a gallery (2) approached by a flight of steps (3). As the shop level is slightly raised a vaulted basement is sunk into the ground and approached by steps (4). The rear portion consists essentially of a T-shaped hall comprising the open hall itself (6) with its open hearth (7) and cross-passage (8) off which opens a private room (9) heated by an end-wall fireplace (10) and with a room above reached by a winding staircase (11). The passage (5) and cross-passage (8) give access from the street to the rear part of the plot (12).

b. The isometric sketch attempts to show the building complex as it might have been during the medieval period. It is assumed that the front portion was timber framed over a stone basement, that the rear portion was stone walled and the whole was covered by a thatched roof.

c. Plan *c.* 1550–1600: shops (1) each separately heated and reached by steps as necessary from the new road level. A passage (5) leads to the rear portion in which the hall (6) has had an inserted floor and a new fireplace (13) and a staircase (14) leading to the newly formed chamber. The passage (8), now enclosed, leads to the private room (9) as well as to the rear of the plot.

d. The sketch shows the front portion rebuilt to give two full storeys and a garret storey well lit by a line of dormer windows; access would be from the rear portion or by stairs within some of the shop units. The rear portion has gained a dormer and several chimney stacks and the whole roof has been given a fire-resistant roof of tiles.

e. Plan *c.* 1750: the building complex has now been reorganized to give two houses each two rooms deep and one room wide. A shop (1) has its own entrance (15) but another door and passage (5) lead to a rear room (6) with service rooms extending along the plot (16) and a staircase (17) leading to the upper floors. Another shop (18) is reached by way of a passage (19) which also leads to a staircase (20) and a rear room (21).

f. Just as the plan has been reorganized, the construction has been changed. Timber frame has been replaced by brick and steeply pitched tiled roofs by low-pitched slated roofs. The exuberance of timber decoration has also been replaced by the reticence of brick.

---

and cross-wing as in rural buildings of this type, but the cross-passage at the junction of hall and cross-wing serves also to give general access from the street to the rear part of the plot.

Stage 2: c. *1550–1600*

In any successful town, commercial pressures on the best frontages increased the accommodation on the plot and led to taller and taller buildings. In this instance it is assumed that the shops have been rebuilt to give three full storeys and fewer shop units of larger size. The overhanging storeys and the many gables of dormer windows help to give the well-known character to streets of some of our older towns. The building at the rear has also been altered. An intermediate floor in the hall and a garret floor in the cross-wing add to the available accommodation.

Stage 3: c. 1750

By now the distinction between public street and private building plot has been established, the front portion has taken over space formerly marked by the projection of steps or cellar steps, and a new brick structure has replaced the former jettied timber frame. At the same time the rear portion has been modified, some original stone walls retained and others added in brick. Generally the two sets of buildings have been reorganized to give two units at right angles to the earlier units, each one being one room wide and two rooms deep and both extending along the walls of the plot in a series of service rooms. All rooms have fireplaces so that stacks of multiple flues rise from the new low-pitched slated roofs.

CONCLUSION

The archaeological study of existing houses proceeds with ever-increasing momentum. It pushes back the limits of our knowledge of the oldest houses; but it also adds to our knowledge of comparatively recent and humble cottages such as are liable to be demolished so much more completely by the twentieth-century bulldozer than any villa or hut destroyed by Saxon or Scot. At the national level the Royal Commissions on Historic Monuments continue to set high standards for the study of an ever-broadening range of house types. At the regional level the County Archaeology Units supported by local and national government spread professional expertise and supplement the more intermittent work of some university departments. Amateurs, on which so much archaeological work has depended, add to the records of existing buildings while working through the county and local archaeological societies. More recently they have banded together in promoting the study of the smaller houses and farm buildings through the work of recording groups such as the Domestic Buildings Research Group (Surrey), affiliated to the national Vernacular Architecture Group.

Not only does the study quicken its rate and spread its limits but it continues to deepen. When houses are, sadly, demolished it is possible to make a record not only of the structure above ground but also of the layers of debris and foundations below ground through excavation. Thus for a few sites we are already able to see something of the predecessors of our standard house plans and to distinguish the various stages of modification or the sudden acts of innovation which produced the plans we recognize. Admittedly, few such total studies have yet been made but more are to be expected.

Through the expansion of the work of the National Monuments Records we now have the beginnings of a national archive wherein all the material may be deposited. This archive is essential since very little of the rapidly increasing amount of recorded information is ever likely to be published in the conventional way. But with the aid of this archive the study can proceed from the stage of collecting data and commentaries on individual houses.

Since recording and analysis are alternating processes (one needs to record to analyse, but one also records on the basis of previous analysis) the swiftly expanding collection of records will enable more analysis to be undertaken and to be better founded. One result will be new and more comprehensive classifications, another will be a better appreciation of the links between plan-types, of the process by which one type succeeds another, of the diffusion of plan-types from one region to another, and, eventually, a better understanding of such rules for proportioning of plan and section as were used by the house designers.

With better understanding of the houses as archaeological specimens one hopes will also come more appreciation of the effects of social, economic, historical and cultural factors on domestic planning. The widening and deepening horizons of the archaeologist have matched similar extensions of prospects by those working in other disciplines. It is to be hoped that broad classifications of house plans will be matched by even broader explanations of the interaction between domestic design and the many facets of domestic life in both the distant past and more recent years.

Finally it is worth mention that, to an architect, the archaeological study of houses may not be an end in itself but a means towards more distant ends. The more we can understand the characteristics of the houses of past centuries the better can we establish the criteria for their preservation, the better we can develop the administrative and technical processes for their conservation and the better can we understand how to design new houses to match in quality the houses of the past.

HOUSES OPEN TO THE PUBLIC

Examples of the houses described and classified here are numerous: every drive through the countryside, every walk through the town should reveal many recognizable examples of the various classes. Those accessible to the public are much smaller in number. Of the houses open to the public only a small proportion are of the traditional types discussed here and even of these a much smaller proportion still are of Small House or Cottage status. Only a relatively small number may be found in the towns and these are often arranged to show the mementoes of a famous individual rather than the planning and construction of the building. Of the houses open to the public few are in their original condition: most have been altered by generation after generation of their occupants, some have been reorganized according to various theories of exhibition design. It is therefore virtually impossible to set up a list of perfect examples, paradigms to represent each classification and match every description.

The following list is highly selective. It is based on houses believed to be open to the public at the moment but in every case it is essential to check accessibility, opening times etc. against a current issue of one of the lists published by the National Trust, the Automobile Association or the ABC Historic Publications for Houses and Museums. The list attempts a wide geographical spread and a wide range of the classification: many important and well-known examples of well-represented classes are omitted; some classes are represented imperfectly or not at all.

Museums of re-erected buildings are slowly developing in this country following the lead set by the Welsh Folk Museum at St Fagans, Cardiff. Others include the Avoncroft Museum of Buildings near Bromsgrove, Worcestershire, the Weald and Downland

Museum at Singleton in Sussex, the Museum of East Anglian Life at Stowmarket, Suffolk, the Ryedale Folk Museum at Hutton-le-Hole in North Yorkshire, and the North of England Open Air Museum at Beamish in Co. Durham. At all these and in the Ironbridge Gorge Museum at Telford in Shropshire examples of various types of houses may be seen together.

Examples of Large Houses in the countryside include the following: Edgar's Farmhouse, Stowmarket, re-erected in the Museum of East Anglian Life near that town illustrates an aisled ground-floor hall; Manor House, Donnington-le-Heath, Leicestershire incorporates a first-floor hall type of plan; the arrangement of a tower house may be seen at Dalton Castle, Dalton-in-Furness, Lancashire (now Cumbria). The house at Lower Brockhampton, Bromyard, Herefordshire and the Bishops House, Meerbrook Park, Sheffield, Yorkshire represent single-ended or T-shaped halls. There are many examples of H-shaped or double-ended halls and these include Great Chalfield Manor House, in Wiltshire, the much-visited Little Moreton Hall in Cheshire and Stokesay Castle in Shropshire and the less well-known Ordsall Hall in Salford, Manchester. A late example is Oakwell Hall at Birstall, West Yorkshire. Multi-storey houses are also well represented with examples as different as the timber-framed Churche's Mansion at Nantwich, Cheshire, the brick-clad Manor House at Alford, Lincolnshire and the stone Washington Old Hall in Co. Durham. This last has a boldly projecting porch to give something of the plan and appearance later developed among compact houses with projecting wings. Quebec House at Westerham in Kent will serve to represent the double-pile Large Houses.

Among the Small Houses of the countryside the Wealden and open-hall type is represented by Pattyndenne Manor, Goudhurst, Kent and the Old Clergy House at Alfriston in Sussex; but there are re-erected houses at the Weald and Downland Museum and the Avoncroft Museum which reproduce the original arrangement very well. The picturesque Old Post Office at Tintagel in Cornwall demonstrates the arrangement of Small Houses with chimney stack at the front. Longhouses and cross-passage houses are less well represented, though Sanders, Lettaford, Devon, a property of the Landmark Trust, is an excellent example of the former and the feel of the longhouse may be recaptured at the Welsh Folk Museum. For the common lobby-entrance plan it is very difficult to find an example open to the public, but some of the Wealden houses such as

Pattyndenne show conversion to this plan. The house at the Pennine Farm Museum at Ripponden, West Yorkshire, illustrates a late version of the two-unit plan while many of the smaller National Trust properties in the Lake District such as Hill Top, Near Sawrey and Townend, Troutbeck, Windermere show the plan but with various additions and extensions. T-shaped and L-shaped Small Houses are represented by the Kennixton Farmhouse re-erected at the Welsh Folk Museum and the house Whitehall at Cheam in Surrey has such a boldly projecting porch as to suggest such a plan. The famous Brontë Parsonage at Haworth, Keighley, West Yorkshire illustrates the development of the double-pile plan.

The rural Cottage plans are poorly represented among houses open to the public but the rise of museums on site such as the slate quarrying museums at Blaenau Ffestiniog in North Wales and those partly of original and partly of re-sited buildings such as those at St Fagans and Beamish mean that true rural single-storey cottages (e.g. that from Llainfadyn in Caernarfonshire re-erected at St Fagans), cottages one and a half rooms on plan and one and a half rooms in height (e.g. those re-erected at Beamish), and the universal double-pile single-fronted cottages may be inspected.

The essence of the Earlier Town Houses lies in the use of the open hall but no perfect example may be quoted. Something of the elements of these plans may be seen in vaulted undercrofts below the Rows of Chester, in Church House, Crane Street, Salisbury, Wiltshire and in Aberconwy House, Conwy in North Wales.

Later Town Houses are rather better represented. At 70 Fore Street, Totnes, for example, one may see the alternation of building and yard along a deep but narrow plot. The Ark at Tadcaster, near York, shows the narrow front gable of a timber-framed town house. Mompesson House in Salisbury and Peckover House in Wisbech, Cambridgeshire are good examples of wide frontage double-pile town houses. Two versions of the London Terrace House may be seen at Dickens House Museum at 48 Doughty Street, WC1 and Carlyle's House, 24 Cheyne Row, Chelsea, SW3.

For Urban Cottages one is now able to visit a few examples of workers' dwelling such as those at the Gladstone Pottery Museum, Stoke on Trent, including those designed for cottage industry such as that at the Colne Valley Museum, Golcar, Huddersfield in West Yorkshire, and the Framework Knitters' Museum at Ruddington, Nottinghamshire. One hopes that some representative examples of the back-to-back cottages of the Industrial Revolution will be preserved before all trace has been lost.

Study of farm buildings in relation to farmhouses as well as in their own right is now being aided through the development of farm museums. Three of the most important include the Acton Scott Working Farm Museum, near Church Stretton in Shropshire, the Manor Farm Museum at Cogges Hall, Witney, Oxfordshire, and the Home Farm museum part of the North of England Open Air Museum at Beamish, Co. Durham.

Among the individual buildings the best represented are the great barns but generally as monastic tithe barns rather than buildings for ordinary farming use. Among aisled barns those at Great Coxwell, Oxfordshire, Harmondsworth, Middlesex, and East Riddlesden Hall form a varied collection. Some idea of the ponderous mass of a cruck-framed barn may be seen at the altered Hall Barn at Rivington, near Chorley, Lancashire. On a slightly smaller scale is the Ashleworth Tithe Barn on the National Trust property near Gloucester.

Many country houses open to the public display the great stables – those at Peover Hall, Cheshire, are especially ornate – but these were for riding and carriage horses rather than for the horses working on the farm. More typical stables may be seen at Willington, Bedford and at the White House Museum at Aston Munslow, Shropshire.

Dovecots are interesting, ingenious and attractive and contrasting examples are found at Hawford, near Worcester, and Kinwarton near Alcester in Warwickshire.

TECHNICAL TERMS

Numbers refer to pages on which these terms are illustrated.

BIBLIOGRAPHY

Unless otherwise stated, all publications first appeared in London.

ADDY, S. O. 1975 (reissue of ed. of 1933). *Evolution of the English House.*

ALCOCK, N. W. 1971–3. Stoneleigh Houses. *Transactions of the Birmingham Archaeological Society*, Vol. 85.

ALCOCK, N. W. and LAITHWAITE, M. 1973. Medieval Houses in Devon and their Modernization. *Medieval Archaeology*, Vol. 17, 100–25.

ALCOCK, N. W. and others. Various issues from 1962 on. Devonshire Farmhouses. *Transactions of the Devonshire Association.*

ALCOCK, N. W. 1973. *A Catalogue of Cruck Buildings.* Chichester.

ARMSTRONG, J. R. 1979. *Traditional Buildings Accessible to the Public.* Wakefield.

BARKE, M. 1979. Weavers Cottages in the Huddersfield Area, *Folk Life*, Vol. 17, 49–59.

BARLEY, M. W. 1967. Rural Housing in England: contribution to J. Thirsk (Ed). *Agrarian History of England and Wales*, Vol. 4, 1500–1640 Cambridge.

BARLEY, M. W. 1961. *The English Farmhouse and Cottage.*

BERESFORD, G. 1978. Excavation of a Moated Site at Wintringham. *Archaeological Journal*, Vol. 134, 144–286.

BERESFORD, M. W. and HURST, J. G. (Eds). 1971. *Deserted Medieval Villages.*

BERESFORD, M. W. and ST JOSEPH, J. K. 1979. *Medieval England, An Aerial Survey.* (2nd ed.) Cambridge.

BORNE, P. and DIXON, P. 1979. *Hafoty, Llansadwrn, Anglesey.* Report, Department of Archaeology, University of Nottingham.

BRUNSKILL, E. 1960. *Some York Almshouses.* York.

BRUNSKILL, R. W. 1978. *Illustrated Handbook of Vernacular Architecture.* (2nd ed.).

BRUNSKILL, R. W. 1974. *Vernacular Architecture of the Lake Counties.*

BRUNSKILL, R. W. and CLIFTON-TAYLOR, A. 1977. *English Brickwork.*

CARSON, C. 1976. Segregation in Vernacular Buildings. *Vernacular Architecture*, Vol. 7, 24–9.

CHAPMAN, S. D. (Ed). 1971. *The History of Working-Class Housing.* Newton Abbot.

CHARLES, F. W. B. 1967. *Medieval Cruck-Building.*

CHESHER, V. M. and F. J. 1968. *The Cornishman's House.* Truro.

CLIFTON-TAYLOR, A. 1972 edition. *The Pattern of English Building.*

CORDINGLEY, R. A. and WOOD-JONES, R. B. 1959. Chorley Hall. *Transactions of the Ancient Monuments Society.* NS 7, 61–86.

COUNCIL FOR BRITISH ARCHAEOLOGY. 1980. *Recording Old Houses.*

CUMMINGS, A. L. 1979. *The Framed Houses of Massachusetts Bay 1625–1725.*

CURWEN, J. F. 1913 (reissued 1965). *Castles and Towers of Cumberland and Westmorland and Lancashire North of the Sands.* Kendal.

DEVONSHIRE COUNTY COUNCIL PLANNING DEPARTMENT. 1978. *Devon's Traditional Buildings.* (Especially contributions by P. Child, K. Coutin, M. Laithwaite.) Exeter.

EDEN, P. 1968. Smaller Post-Medieval Houses in Eastern England. *East Anglian Studies.* 71–93.

EDEN, P. 1969. *Small Houses in England, 1520–1820.*

FAULKNER, P. A. 1966. Medieval Undercrofts and Town Houses. *Archaeological Journal,* Vol. 123, 120–35.

FAULKNER, P. A. 1960. Domestic Planning from the Twelfth to the Fourteenth Centuries. *Archaeological Journal,* Vol. 95, 150–83.

FOX, SIR CYRIL and RAGLAN, LORD. 1951–54. *Monmouthshire Houses,* Vols. 1 to 3. Cardiff.

GAULDIE, E. 1974. *Cruel Habitations: A History of Working-Class Housing, 1780–1918.*

GEE, E. A. 1977. The Chronology of Crucks. *Transactions of the Ancient Monuments Society,* NS Vol. 22, 9–27.

GODFREY, W. H. 1955. *The English Almshouse.*

GRAY, P. 1978. *Charlwood Houses.* Guildford.

HALL, I. and E. 1973. *Historic Beverley.* York.

HARDING, J. M. 1976. *Four Centuries of Charlwood Housing.* Med. to 1840. Charlwood.

HARRIS, R. 1978. *Discovering Timber-Framed Buildings.*

HARTLEY, M. and INGILBY, J. 1968. *Life and Tradition in the Yorkshire Dales.*

HARVEY, N. 1970. *A History of Farm Buildings in England and Wales.* Newton Abbot.

INNOCENT, C. F. 1916 (reissued 1971). *The Development of English Building Construction.* Cambridge and Newton Abbot.

JONES, S. R. and SMITH, J. T. 1963–69. The Houses of Breconshire, Parts 1 to 5. *Brycheiniog.*

KELSALL, A. F. 1974. The London House Plan in the Later 17th Century. *Post-Medieval Archaeology,* Vol. 8.

LLOYD, D. and others. 1978 on. *Historic Ludlow*, Research Papers. Birmingham.
LOWE, J. B. 1977. *Welsh Industrial Workers Housing*. Cardiff.

MACHIN, R. 1977. The Great Rebuilding: A Reassessment. *Past and Present*, No. 77, 33–56.
MACHIN, R. 1978. *The Houses of Yetminster*. Bristol.
MARSDEN, T. L. 1962. The Manor House at Donington-le-Heath. *Transactions of the Ancient Monuments Society*, NS 10, 33–42.
MASON, R. T. 1964. *Framed Buildings of the Weald*. Handcross (Sussex).
MEIRION-JONES, G. I. 1971. The Domestic Buildings of Odiham, Hampshire. *Folk Life*, 9, 108–34.
MAJOR, KENNETH J. 1975. *Fieldwork in Industrial Archaeology*.
MERCER, E. 1975. *English Vernacular Houses*.
MICHELMORE, D. J. H. 1973. Yorkshire Aisled Houses. *Vernacular Architecture*, Vol. 4, 27–8.

NEAVE, V. 1971. Living-in in the East Riding. *Vernacular Architecture*, Vol. 2, 18–19.
NEWTON, G. D. 1976. Single-Storey Cottages in West Yorkshire. *Folk Life*, Vol. 14, 65–74.

PANTIN, W. A. 1947. The Development of Domestic Architecture in Oxford. *Antiquaries Journal*, Vol. 27, 120–50.
PANTIN, W. A. 1957. Medieval Priests' Houses in South-West England. *Medieval Archaeology*, Vol. 1, 118–46.
PANTIN, W. A. 1962–3. The Merchants Houses and Warehouses of King's Lynn. *Medieval Archaeology*, Vol. 6–7.
PANTIN, W. A. 1963. Some Medieval English Town Houses. A Study in Adaptation. In *Culture and Environment*, FOSTER and ALCOCK (Eds).
PANTIN, W. A. 1962–3. Medieval English Town-House Plans. *Medieval Archaeology*, Vol. 6–7, 202–39.
PARKER, V. 1971. *The Making of King's Lynn*. Chichester.
PEATE, I. C. 1946. *The Welsh House*. Liverpool.
PETERS, J. E. C. 1969. *Farm Buildings of Western Lowland Staffordshire*. Manchester.
PORTMAN, D. 1966. *Exeter Houses, 1400–1700*.

RAGLAN, LORD, 1964. *The Temple and the House*.
RAMM, H. G., MCDOWALL, R. W. and MERCER, E. 1970. *Shielings and Bastles*.
RASMUSSEN, S. E. 1960 (Ed). *London the Unique City*.
RIGOLD, S. E. 1963. The Distribution of the Wealden House. In *Culture and Environment*, FOSTER and ALCOCK (Eds).
ROBERTS, B. K. 1978. *Rural Settlement in Britain*. Folkestone.
ROYAL COMMISSION ON HISTORIC MONUMENTS, ENGLAND. *Inventories*. Especially 1968, *West Cambridgeshire*; 1972, *The City of York*, Vol. 3; 1977, *The Town of Stamford*.
RUBENSTEIN, D. 1974. *Victorian Homes*.

SMITH, P. 1975. *Houses of the Welsh Countryside.*

SMITH, D. 1965. *Industrial Archaeology of the East Midlands.* Newton Abbot.

SMITH, J. T. 1956. Medieval Aisled Halls. *Archaeological Journal*, Vol. 112, 76–94.

SMITH, J. T. 1970. The Evolution of the English Peasant House to the Late Seventeenth Century. *Journal of the British Archaeological Association*, 3rd series, 33, 122–47.

SMITH, J. T. and YATES, E. M. 1968. On the Dating of English Houses from External Evidence. *Field Studies*, Vol. 2, 537–77.

SMITH, P. 1963. The Longhouse and the Laithe House: contribution to FOSTER and ALCOCK (Eds). *Culture and Environment.*

STELL, C. F. 1965. Pennine Houses. *Folk Life*, Vol. 3, 5–24.

SUMMERS, N. 1975. A Place to Live. The Nottinghamshire Heritage.

SUMMERS, N. 1972. Old Hall Farm, Kneesall. *Transactions of the Thoroton Society*, Vol. 76, 17–25.

SUMMERSON, J. 1945. *Georgian London.*

SUMMERSON, J. 1969. *Architecture in Britain 1530–1830.* (5th ed).

TAYLOR, R. F. 1974. Town Houses in Taunton, 1500–1700. *Post-Medieval Archaeology*, Vol. 8.

WATSON, R. C. and MCCLINTOCK, M. 1979. *Traditional Houses of the Fylde.* Lancaster.

WOOD, M. 1965. *The English Medieval House.*

WOOD-JONES, R. B. 1963. *Traditional Domestic Architecture in the Banbury Region.* Manchester.

WOODFORDE, J. 1969. *The Truth about Cottages.*

Bibliographies

DE Z. HALL, SIR ROBERT (Ed). 1972. *A Bibliography on Vernacular Architecture.* Newton Abbot.

MICHELMORE, D. J. H. 1979. *A Current Bibliography of Vernacular Architecture, 1970–76.* York.

NOTE

This bibliography is limited to works which have been especially useful in the preparation of this book. Among other books and articles occasionally consulted mention must be made of the very many descriptions of individual houses which appear in the pages of national and local archaeological journals. The bibliographies by Hall and Michelmore are arranged regionally and references to most of the available descriptions may be found therein. The principal national archaeological journals which publish such descriptions are:

Antiquaries Journal (Society of Antiqua ries of London)
Archaeological Journal (Journal of the Royal Archaeological Institute)
Journal of the British Archaeological Association
Medieval Archaeology (Society for Medieval Archaeology)
Post-Medieval Archaeology (Journal of the Society for Post-Medieval Archaeology)
In addition articles on individual buildings sometimes appear in:
Folk Life (Journal of the Society for Folk Life Studies)
Transactions of the Ancient Monuments Society
Vernacular Architecture (Journal of the Vernacular Architecture Group)

Most such articles appear in the transactions of regional or local archaeological societies, ranging from *Archaeologia Aeliana* (Society of Antiquaries of Newcastle-on-Tyne) to *Transactions of the Woolhope Club* (Woolhope Naturalists Field Club, Herefordshire).

INDEX